First World War
and Army of Occupation
War Diary
France, Belgium and Germany

8 DIVISION
24 Infantry Brigade
Black Watch (Royal Highlanders) 5th Battalion
and East Lancashire Regiment 2nd Battalion
28 July 1914 - 30 June 1916

WO95/1719

The Naval & Military Press Ltd
www.nmarchive.com
Published in association with The National Archives

Published by

The Naval & Military Press Ltd

Unit 10 Ridgewood Industrial Park,

Uckfield, East Sussex,

TN22 5QE England

Tel: +44 (0) 1825 749494

www.naval-military-press.com

www.nmarchive.com

This diary has been reprinted in facsimile from the original. Any imperfections are inevitably reproduced and the quality may fall short of modern type and cartographic standards.

© **Crown Copyright**
Images reproduced by permission of The National Archives, London, England, 2015.

Contents

Document type	Place/Title	Date From	Date To
Heading	WO95/1719/1 1914 Aug & 1915 Dec 5 Btn Black Watch		
Heading	8th Division 24th Infy Bde 5th Bn Black Watch (Roy Hdrs) Aug 1914-Dec 1915		
Heading	24th Brigade 5th Battn T Q Royal Hrs Vol 1		
War Diary	War Diary Of 5th Battalion. The Royal Highlanders (The Black Watch) From 28th July 1914 To Volume 1	28/07/1914	30/12/1914
Heading	8th. Divison, 24th. Brigade. 1/5th. Black Watch. 1/1/15 To 28/2/15		
Heading	25th Brigade 5 Bn Royal Hrs (T) Vol II		
War Diary	War Diary of 1/5th Bn. The Black Watch From 1st Jany 1915 To 28th Feb 1915	01/01/1915	28/02/1915
Heading	8th. Divison, 24th. Brigade. 1/5th, Black Watch. March 1915		
Heading	25th Brigade 1/5 Royal Hrs Vol III		
Heading	1/5th Bn The Black Watch War Diary From 1st To 31st March 1915		
War Diary		01/03/1915	31/03/1915
Heading	1/5th, Black Watch. April. 1915		
Heading	1/5th Rl. Hrs Vol IV		
Heading	War Diary Of 1/5th The Black Watch For The Month Of April 1915		
War Diary		01/04/1915	30/04/1915
Miscellaneous	1/5th Bn The Black Watch Appendices To War Diary	24/04/1915	24/04/1915
Heading	1/5th Black Watch May. 1915		
Heading	1/5th Black Watch Vol V		
War Diary		01/05/1915	31/05/1915
Miscellaneous	Appendices To War Diary For May 1915		
Heading	1/5th Black Watch. June 1915		
Heading	1/5th R. Hrs Vol VI		
War Diary		01/06/1915	30/06/1915
Heading	1/5th Black Watch. July 1915		
Heading	1/5th Royal Hrs Vol VII		
War Diary		01/07/1915	31/07/1915
Heading	1/5th Black Watch August 1915		
Heading	1/5th Royal Hrs Vol VIII August 15		
War Diary		01/08/1915	31/08/1915
Heading	1/5th Black Watch September 1915		
Heading	1/5th Royal Hrs Vol IX Sept 15		
War Diary		01/09/1915	30/09/1915
Heading	1/5th Black Watch October 1915		
Heading	1/5th R. Highrs Oct 15		
War Diary	In The Field	01/10/1915	31/10/1915
Heading	5th Bn Roy. Hdrs (Blk Watch) Nov Dec 1915		
Heading	5th Battn The Black Watch (Royal Highlanders). November 1915		
War Diary	In The Field	01/11/1915	30/11/1915
Heading	5th Battn The Black Watch (Royal Highlanders) December 1915		
War Diary	In The Field	01/12/1915	31/12/1915

Heading	WO95/1719/2 8 Div 24 Bde 2 East Lancs Reg 1914 Nov-1916 Jan		
Heading	BEF 8 Div 24 Bde 2 East Lancs 1914 Nov 1916 June		
Heading	War Diary 2nd East Lancs November 1914		
War Diary	Southampton	30/10/1914	30/10/1914
War Diary	Hursley Park	31/10/1914	10/11/1914
War Diary	Neuf Berquin	11/11/1914	18/11/1914
War Diary	Point Du Hem	19/11/1914	29/11/1914
Heading	War Diary 2nd Bn Northamptonshire Rgt From Dec 1-1914 Dec 31 1914		
Heading	War Diary 2nd East Lancs December 1914		
War Diary		29/11/1914	31/12/1914
Miscellaneous	Appendix A B.N. 486		
Miscellaneous	OCommanding 2nd East Lancashire Regt 24th Brigade		
Miscellaneous	C Form (Original). Messages And Signals.	19/12/1914	19/12/1914
Miscellaneous	C Form (Original). Messages And Signals.		
Miscellaneous	A Form. Messages And Signals.		
Miscellaneous	C Form (Original). Messages And Signals.		
Miscellaneous	C Form (Original). Messages And Signals.	20/12/1914	20/12/1914
Miscellaneous			
Miscellaneous	Messages And Signals		
Miscellaneous			
Miscellaneous	C Form (Triplicate). Messages And Signals.	22/12/1914	22/12/1914
Miscellaneous	C Form (Quadruplicate). Messages And Signals.		
Miscellaneous	C Form (Original). Messages And Signals.		
Heading	2nd East Lancs January 1915 Oct 1915		
Heading	2nd East Lancs Vol II		
War Diary		01/01/1915	31/01/1915
Heading	2nd East Lancs February 1915		
Heading	2nd East Lancs Vol III		
War Diary		01/02/1915	28/02/1915
Heading	2nd East Lancs March 1915		
Heading	2nd East Lancs Vol IV		
War Diary		01/03/1915	31/03/1915
Miscellaneous	Appendix 1 H.Q 8th Div'n 164. K.	27/02/1915	27/02/1915
Miscellaneous	Appendix 2 O Commdg 2nd East Lancashire Rgt	13/03/1915	13/03/1915
Miscellaneous	Appendix 2 O.C. 2nd East Lancashire.	13/03/1915	13/03/1915
Miscellaneous		09/03/1915	09/03/1915
Miscellaneous	Summary Of events March 9th to 14th Inclusive	18/03/1915	18/03/1915
Miscellaneous	Appendix 1 O.C. 2nd Est Lancashire Regt.	28/02/1915	28/02/1915
Heading	2nd East Lancs April 1915		
Heading	2nd East Lancs Vol V		
War Diary		01/04/1915	30/04/1915
Heading	2nd East Lancs May 1915		
Heading	2nd East Lancs Vol VI		
War Diary		01/05/1915	31/05/1915
Heading	2nd East Lancs June 1915		
Heading	2nd East Lancs Vol VII		
War Diary		01/06/1915	30/06/1915
Heading	2nd East Lancs July. 1915		
Heading	2nd East Lancs Vol VIII		
War Diary		01/07/1915	31/07/1915
Heading	2nd East Lancs August 1915		
Heading	2nd East Lancs Vol IX		
War Diary		01/08/1915	31/08/1915
Heading	2nd East Lancs September 1915		

Heading	2nd East Lancs Vol X		
War Diary		01/09/1915	30/09/1915
Heading	2nd East Lancs October, 1915		
Heading	2nd East Lancs Vol XI		
War Diary		01/10/1915	31/10/1915
Miscellaneous	On the Field in France	17/10/1915	17/10/1915
Miscellaneous	Private Diary Lt Col Nicholson 2nd, East Lancs.		
Heading	Private Diary Lt Col Nicholson 2 E Lancs 1915		
Heading	Private Diary Lt Col Nicholson 2 E Lancs		
Miscellaneous	Lieut Colonel C.L Nicholson Commanding 2/East Lancs Regt. 24th Infantry Brigade, 8th Division, IV Corps.	18/11/1914	18/11/1914
Heading	2nd Bn East Lancs Regt Nov 1915 Jun 1916		
Heading	2/E Lancs Rgt Nov Vol XII		
War Diary		01/11/1915	30/11/1915
Heading	2/East Lancs Rgt Dec Vol XIII		
War Diary		01/12/1915	31/12/1915
Heading	2 E Lancs Regt Jan Vol XIV		
War Diary		01/01/1916	29/02/1916
Miscellaneous	O.C. East Lancashire Regt.	07/02/1916	07/02/1916
Miscellaneous	E.L.B. Head Quarters 24th Infantry Brigade	02/02/1916	02/02/1916
Heading	Headquarters 3rd Corps	04/02/1916	04/02/1916
War Diary	Billets	01/03/1916	21/03/1916
War Diary	Billets Map Sheet 36B SE 1/20,000 Sq R.19. C	22/03/1916	22/03/1916
War Diary	Billets	23/03/1916	25/03/1916
War Diary	Trenches	26/03/1916	29/03/1916
War Diary	Billets	30/03/1916	31/03/1916
War Diary		01/04/1916	30/06/1916
Miscellaneous	E.L. 606 Hd Qrs 24th Inf. Brigade		
Miscellaneous	Report On a Patrol		
Miscellaneous	19th Division No I 70	18/06/1916	18/06/1916
Miscellaneous	Bazentin Le Petit		
Miscellaneous	Martinpuich		
Map			
Miscellaneous			
Miscellaneous	Contalmaison		
Map			
Miscellaneous	Pozieres		

WO95/1719/1

1914 Aug → 1915 Dec.

5 Btn BLACK WATCH

8TH DIVISION
24TH INFY BDE

5TH BN BLACK WATCH (ROY HDRS)
AUG 1914 - ~~DEC~~ 1915

To 39 DN 118 BDE

74/8

Remembered
Home from
12? England 2/1/14
4044
Battn formed
Bte 13.11.14

1 & 2 Dec } After forming - Ammunition
4th "
+ Dec + Bayonet flying off rifles -

2 [?] Brigade

5th Battn. The Royal H.I.

Vol I.

28.4.14 — 30.11.14

CONFIDENTIAL.

WAR DIARY

of

5th BATTALION, THE ROYAL HIGHLANDERS, (THE BLACK WATCH),

from 28th July, 1914 to _____ .

Volume I.

28th July, 1914.	While the Battalion was in camp at MONZIE, near CRIEFF, undergoing annual training, the two Special Service Sections of the Battalion were called up for duty, and moved to DUNDEE to guard the TAY BRIDGE, part of the TAY DEFENCES, and to BROUGHTY FERRY.
4th August, 1914.	Mobilization of the Territorial Forces having been ordered, the embodiment notices were posted to-night.
5th August, 1914.	The Battalion today moved into its war station, the right half Battalion at BROUGHTY FERRY, the left half Battalion at DUNDEE. The major part of the right half Battalion was billetted in the vicinity of BROUGHTY CASTLE, with headquarters at FERRY HOUSE, one company - "D" - taking outpost duty to the north of the town on a line WEST BALGILLO-CASTLEROY-BARNHILL CONVALESCENT HOME. The left half Battalion was billetted at HAWKHILL SCHOOL, DUNDEE.
	The Battalion carried out various defensive works on the stations occupied, and after these had been completed, proceeded to undergo training, in addition to various guard duties. Part of the work undertaken by the Battalion included the erection of defensive works on SPIERS HILL, TAYPORT, where 50 men were encamped.

J.S. Wedderburn Lt.Col.

SEPTEMBER, 1915.

Sept., 1914.	Early in September, the Battalion was inspected by General Sir Spencer Ewart, G.O.C.-in-C., Scottish Command.
	Throughout this month, company training was proceeded with over the neighbouring farms to the north of BROUGHTY FERRY. No facilities forp proceeding with musketry were afforded.
26th Sept., 1914.	Today, about 300 men were transferred to FORFAR, under the temporary command of Capt. MALCOLM, to form the nucleus of our Reserve Battalion. These were chiefly composed of recruits, who had not qualified in musketry, of men under 19 years of age, and of men who could not pass medically as fit for foreign service.

OCTOBER, 1914. *J.S. Wedderburn Lt.Col.*

2.

OCTOBER, 1914.

24th Oct., 1914. Today the Battalion received a communication from the War office that it had been selected for service on the continent, and was ordered to be ready to entrain at BROUGHTY FERRY on 27th inst.

27th Oct., 1914. On this date, the order was countermanded, the date of the move being postponed to 29th inst.

Friday, 29th Oct., 1914. The right half Battalion entrained this morning at 7.10 at BROUGHTY FERRY and reached SOUTHAMPTON at 12.30 a.m. next morning; the left half Battalion entrained at 9.30 at TAY BRIDGE STATION, DUNDEE, and reached SOUTHAMPTON AT 2.30 a.m. The Battalion encamped at the CONCENTRATION CAMP, SOUTHAMPTON COMMON, under depressing conditions of rain and mud, and remained here all the 30th, being

Saturday, 30th Oct., 1914. fitted out with deficiencies in equipment,

NOVEMBER, 1914.

Sunday, 1st Nov., 1914. The Battalion embarked at 3 p.m. on S.S. Architect, and left SOUTHAMPTON at 7.30 p.m.
Monday, 2nd Nov., 1914. Good passage. Arrived at HAVRE at 8 a.m. Berthed at 11 a.m., when disembarkation commenced. Marched to No 1 Rest Camp, SANVIC, arriving at 2 p.m.

Tuesday, 3rd Nov., 1914. Battalion left Rest Camp at 6.30 p.m. on an hour's notice, leaving behind one man suffering from scarlet fever, and his tent mates, 6 in number, in quarantine. Battalion entrained at GARE MARITIME, and shortly after midnight, the journey commenced.

Wednesday, 4th Nov., 1914. The journey continued all today via ABBEVILLE (2 p.m.), BOULOGNE (7.15 p.m.), and CALAIS TO ST OMER, which was reached at 9 p.m. Detraining was completed at 11 p.m., and thereafter the Battalion marched for a distance of about 4 kilometres to the village of BLENDECQUES. Headquarters was situated in CHATEAU MONT SARAH, where the officers were also billetted, the men being billetted in two farms and a chateau close at hand.

Thursday, 5th Nov., 1914. Today was spent in completing details of billets, and in arrangements for completing the Battalion in arms, equipment etc, still deficient.

Friday, 6th Nov. 1914. The Battalion paraded for trench digging at LE HOCQUET, about 3 miles from billets. Two men were sent to Clearing Hospital, ST OMER.

Saturday, 7th Nov., 1914. Battalion paraded for field work. Orders for a move to be made the following day were countermanded to allow of typhoid inoculation being carried out.

Sunday/

3.

Date	
Sunday, 8th Nov., 1914.	11 men were sent to hospital, 4 at least serious for clearance home. In the afternoon the typhoid inoculation was begun, and this continued under regimental arrangements on 9th, 10th and 11th inst., 92% of the Battalion being inoculated.
Monday 9th Nov., 1914.	
Tuesday, 10th Nov., 1914.	On the 11th, orders were received for a move next day, and arrangements were made for those unable to march through inoculation remaining behing under Lieut. Dickie, till they were fit to rejoin.
Wedy., 11th Nov., 1914.	
Thursday, 12th Nov., 1915.	The Battalion moved off at 8.30 a.m., and marched by way of WITTE and BOESEGHEM, passing DORD ROBERTS on the road, and at 1.30 p.m. arrived at THIENNES, where headquarters were established in a brasserie, and the men billetted in barns and houses.
Friday, 13th Nov., 1914.	Moved off at 8 a.m. Raining hard, and a good many men dropped out on account of feet on the march. Passed through MERVILLE, reaching NOEUF BERQUIN at 1 p.m. Here the Battalion was attached to the 24th Infantry Brigade, 8th Division. Battalion headquarters were established in a cottage, the men being billetted in barns and houses.
Saturday, 14th Nov., 1914.	Left NOEUF BERQUIN at 10.30 a.m., arriving in ESTAIRES at 1 p.m., headquarters of the 8th Division, under GENERAL DAVIES. Battalion headquarters were established in a house at the corner of RUE DE LILLE and RUE DU PONT, and the men were billetted in a flax mill on south bank of river LYS, near the RUE DU PONT, also occupied by the 13th CITY OF LONDON regiment.
Sunday, 15th Nov., 1914.	Raining all day. Men were out doing field work.
Monday, 16th Nov., 1914.	Do do
Tuesday, 17th Nov., 1914.	Two companies were out last night digging reserve trenches, one at "A" lines, the other at the RUE DE BACQUEROT.
Wednesday, 18th Nov., 1914.	One company was out last night digging trenches 1 man was shot through the shoulder.
Thursday, 19th Nov., 1914.	Three companies were out digging last night at "A" lines at RICHEBOURG ST VAAST, and were sniped at on road from CROIX BARBEE. Each of these parties was usually out about 14 hours, setting out about 4 p.m. and returning at 6 a.m.
Friday, 20th Nov. 1914.	
Saturday, 21st Nov. 1914.	Parties out digging.
Sunday, 22nd Nov., 1914.	Last night town was shelled for 2 hours. The Battalion, having been granted facilities for getting clothes washed at the HOSPICE D'ESTAIRES, this was done under company arrangemnets. Very hard frost.
Monday, 23rd Nov., 1914.	Party of 200 out digging at CROIX BARBEE. 2 men/

men wounded. G.O.C. highly pleased with men's work. Hard frost continues.

Tuesday 24th Nov.
party out digging.

Friday 27th Nov.
Party out digging at "A" lines.

Saturday, 28th Nov.
No 1 Company left at 3 p.m. to occupy firing trench in "A" lines with WORCESTERS; No 2 company left at 4.30 p.m. to occupy firing trench in "B2 lines with NORTH HANTS. They are to be in for 3 days and 3 nights.

Sunday 29th Nov.
Cleaning, washing, Church parade at 2.15 p.m. for first time since leaving home.

Monday 30th Nov.
1 wounded in No 2 Company last night.

J.M. Wedderburn /Lt.

DECEMBER, 1914.

Tuesday, 1st Decr.
Captain Lyell, O.C. No 2 Coy. reported slightly wounded in the head. His Gracious Majesty, King George, passed through ESTAIRES today in the course of his visit to the troops at the front. The streets were lined by all the available troops, this Battalion being in position from The PARISH CHURCH to the GRANDE PLACE.

The left half Battalion set out in the afternoon for the trenches, No 3 Company going in with the SHERWOOD FORESTERS, No 4 with the EAST LANCS. Right half Battalion returned about 9.30 p.m. very tired, muddy, hungry and thirsty. The long march back to billets in their muddy condition after 3 days and 3 nights in the trenches, seemed to try the men considerably. O.C's. reported that the men had had a lot of trouble with rifles jamming and bayonets flying off.

Wednesday, 2nd Decr.
A report was rendered on the jamming of rifles, which was largely due to dirt getting into the action of the rifle, and largely to the rifles being unsuited to the MARK VII ammunition.

Thursday, 3rd Decr.
4 men reported wounded last night. 2 bathing parades for right half Battalion at 11 and 2 at Divisional Bathing Station. Men seemed to be very much invigorated by the hot baths. Clean shirts and socks were issued in place of the dirty ones.

Friday, 4th Decr.
Right half Battalion left in the afternoon for trench work. Left half Battalion came in at 10 p.m. No 3 Company's casualties were 2/Lieutenant Barrie slightly wounded in back of head, and 3 men wounded. O.C. Companies reported same trouble with rifles. One rifle burst but no one was injured.

Saturday, 5th Decr.
Causes of bayonets flying off were considered to be due to the bayonets not fitting the rifles properly, and to the ring of the bayonet protruding

5.

protruding beyond the muzzle of the rifle.

Sunday, 6th Decr.

Church parade at 9 a.m.

Monday, 7th Decr.

The right half Battalion returned last night and reported the following casualties. 2/Lieutenant Adam slightly wounded, 2 killed, 6 wounded, 1 N.C.O. died of his wounds at BOULOGNE.

Tuesday, 8th Decr.
Wednesday, 9th Decr.
Thursday, 10th Decr.

Right half Battalion went out this afternoon only about 150 strong on account of a great many men suffering from rheumatism, the draughty billet which they occupied being largely to blame for this. No 4 Company returned at 10 p.m. and reported 2 men wounded. No 3 Company returned at 11 p.m. and reported 1 killed and 3 wounded. A good many bombs had been thrown into their trench. One man going up with the ration cart last night was shot.

Friday, 11th Decr.

Heavy rain. Trenches in appalling condition. 3 wounded last night.

Saturday, 12th Decr.
Sunday, 13th Decr.

Church parade at 9 a.m. Brigadier General Carter inspected billets at 10 a.m. Condition of the billets, especially the surroundings, bad. A.D.M.S. inspected billets in the afternoon. Was of opinion that it was a very difficult billet to keep clean. Orders came in to move off tomorrow to other billets, the right half Battalion to remain for another night in the trenches.

Monday, 14th Decr.

Battalion moved out today at 1 p.m. to billets just west of REDBARN on NEUVE CHAPELLE road, headquarters being established in the house of MME. L'HERMITE.
Standing to arms from 5.45 a.m. to daybreak issued as a Standing Order. To provide guards for 23rd Brigade to which we are now attached.

Tuesday, 15th Decr.

Nos. 1 and 2 Companies came in last night very tired, their last night in the trenches having been spent under adverse conditions, rain falling all the time. The Adjutant, Captain Geoffrey Bowes-Lyon, was sent to hospital yesterday on account of a bad whitlow.

Wednesday, 16th Decr.

Fine day. Roads very dirty. Sick list small, only 15. Feet washing and inspection. General Davies inspected billets today. A/Adjutant, Major Blair-Imrie, attended Board of Enquiry to enquire into the amount of damage done to flax in previous billets.

Thursday, 17th Decr.

Brigadier General Pinney, 23rd Brigade, inspected Battalion in billets. Report on marksmanship of Battalion wanted.

Friday/

Friday, 18th Decr.	Orders to stand to arms in billets from 4.30 p.m., Battalion forming brigade reserve to 23rd Brigade in action. Heavy shell fire preceded infantry attack on German trenches by DEVONS and WEST YORKSHIRE REGIMENT. 50 men of No 3 company had to form escort for 26 prisoners into Divisional Headquarters at LA GORGUE. Heavy shell and rifle fire began in INDIAN lines about 3.30 a.m.
Saturday, 19th Decr.	parade dismissed at 7.30 a.m. Fatigue parties busy with dugouts. Orders received to form reserve to 24th Brigade.
Sunday, 20th Decr.	About 10 a.m. orders came to stand to arms on account of anticipated attack on "A" and "B" lines by 6 battalions of enemy massing behind these lines. Beautiful day. Left half battalion left at 10.30 a.m. for SHERWOOD'S headquarters, "A" lines.
Monday, 21st Decr.	1 man in No 3 Company wounded last night. Nos. 2, 3 and 4 companies all out in afternoon at "A" lines. No 1 at "B" lines. 2 men wounded.
Tuesday, 22nd Decr.	This afternoon, No 2 Company went to "B" lines; Nos. 3 and 4 to "A" lines. Improving trenches, doing fatigues, etc.
Wednesday, 23rd Decr.	No 4 company returned this morning. 2 men wounded whil repairing fire trench.
Thursday, 24th Decr.	Nos. 3 and 4 companies taking 24 hours about at "A" lines in billets, doing fatigues and repairing trenches. No 1 company away for 3 days to "C" lines, 23rd Brigade. Billetted in dugouts. No 2 company to provide half company each night at "B" lines.
Friday, 25th Decr.	2 men wounded last night. 1st reinforcement, numbering 2 officers and 191 men, arrived this afternoon at 4 under Captain Arbuthnott and Lieutenant Taylor. Came by steamer to ROUEN, disembarked there, and after a stay of days, entrained for MERVILLE, where they detrained. They brought with them 8 men discharged from hospital. Reinforcement rather on the young side, 58 being under 19. Battalion received Princess Mary's Gifts, which were much appreciated.
Sunday, 27th Decr.	Church parade at 2 p.m.
Monday, 28th Decr.	Last night in No 2 company, 3 wounded in "C" lines. In No 4 company 1 killed in "A" lines.
Tuesday, 29th Decr.	Inspection of billets by A.D.M.S.
Wednesday, 30th Decr.	Inspection of all men in Battalion under 19. Number is 228. 1 man wounded today.

Jan - Oct 1915

8th, Division,.

24th, Brigade.

1/5th, Black Watch.

1/1/15 to 28/2/15.

L.G.
8 sheets

2/8

121/4558

25th Brigade

5 Bn Royal Hrs: (T)

Vol II. 1.1 — 28.2.15

24 B.e.

Confidential

WAR DIARY
of
1/5th BN. THE BLACK WATCH.
From 1st Jany. 1915, to 28th Feb. 1915.

Jany.
- 1st No. II Coy. at C Lines. No. IV Coy. A Lines. Working Parties at B, and A Lines.
- 2nd No. II Coy. at C Lines. No. III Coy. A Lines. Working Parties at B Lines. 2 men were wounded
- 3rd No. I Coy. at C Lines. No. IV Coy. A Lines. Working Parties at B Lines.
- 4th No. I Coy. at C Lines. No. III Coy. A Lines. 3 Casualties-1 Killed 2 Wounded. Working Party at B Lines.
- 5th No. I Coy. at C Lines, No. IV Coy A Lines. B Lines Working party from No. II Coy.
- 6th No. II Coy at C Lines, No. III Coy. A Lines. 1 man wounded. B Lines Working Party
- 7th No. II Coy at C Lines, No. IV Coy. A Lines. B Lines Working Party
- 8th "   "   "   do "   No. III Coy. "   " 1 man wounded.
- 9th No. I Coy. do "   " No. IV Coy. "   " 1 " Killed.
- 10th "   "   "   do "   No. III Coy. "   " 2 men wounded.
- 11th "   "   "   do "   No. IV Coy. "   " 1 man "
- 12th No. II Coy. do "   " No. III Coy. "   " 1 " "
- 13th "   "   "   do "   No. IV Coy. "   " ~~1 " "~~
- 14th "   "   "   do "   No. III Coy. "   " 2 men wounded.
- 15th No. I Coy. do "   " No. IV Coy. "   " 1 man "
- 16th "   "   "   do "   No IV Coy.   "   " ~~1 man~~ "
- 17th "   "   "   do "   "   "   "
- 18th No II " do "   " No III " " "
- 19th "   "   do   "   "   "   "
- 20th "   "   do   "   "   "   "
- 21st No I   do   No IV " " 1 man wounded.
- 22nd "   do   "   3 men wounded, 1 man killed.
- 23rd "   do   "   2 men wounded
- 24th No II   do   No III "

Jany.,	25th	No II Coy. at "C" lines, No III Coy. at "A" Lines. "B" lines working party. Two men wounded.
	26th	No II Coy. relieved at "C" Lines, and proceeded with No IV. Remainder of battalion moved to RED BARN, at end of long ditch, "A" Lines at 8.30 pm. today to hold A1 redoubt in anticipation of an attack.
	27th	As yesterday. 2 men wounded.
	28th	Nos. I and III Companies and headquarters returned to Black Watch Lane early in morning. A new arrangement of companies was ordered. 2 companies were stationed permanently at "A" Lines, one in trenches and the other in "A" Lines reserve billets. Two companies were retained at Black Watch Lane - one extra brigade reserve, and one under orders from O.C. "B" Lines. Working party, "B" Lines.
	29th	The right half battalion was detailed for duties in "B" Lines, and were billetted in Black Watch Lane, the left half battalion in "A" Lines, one company being in the trenches, the other in reserve billets. Four men were wounded and one killed. Major Lord Glamis accidentally wounded himself in the foot with his revolver this morning.
	30th	Same arrangements as for 29th. "B" Lines working parties. Two men were wounded.
	31st	Two companies at "A" Lines, and two companies at Black Watch lane. "B" Lines working parties. Four men were wounded and one killed.
Febry.,	1st	Two companies at "A" Lines, two companies at Black Watch Lane. "B" Lines working parties. Two men wounded. Lieut. Col. Wedderburn proceeded on furlough, and Major H. Blair-Imrie assumed command of the battalion in his absence.
	2nd	Two companies at "A" Lines, two companies at Black Watch Lane. "B" Lines working parties.
	3rd	As yesterday. One man wounded.
	4th	As yesterday. One man wounded. "B" Lines working party.
	5th	As yesterday. Six men wounded. Three men killed.
	6th	As yesterday. Two men wounded, one killed.
	7th	As yesterday. Four men wounded, one killed.
	8th	As yesterday. One man wounded, one killed. [The Commanding Officer was unable to return from furlough owing to sickness.]
	9th	As yesterday.
	10th	As yesterday. Three men wounded.
	11th	As yesterday. Two men killed.
	12th	As yesterday.

Febry.,	13th	As yesterday. One man wounded.
	14th	As yesterday. Two men wounded. The two companies at Black Watch Lane moved down early in the morning to occupy B1 and 2 redoubts.
	15th	Two companies at "A" Lines, two companies at B1 and 2 redoubts.
	16th	As yesterday.
	17th	Two companies at "A" Lines. Two companies returned to Black Watch Lane.
	18th	Two companies at "A" Lines, two companies at Black Watch Lane. "B" Lines working party. One man wounded.
	19th	Two companies at "A" Lines, two companies at Black Watch Lane. Working party.
	20th	Two companies "A" Lines. One company at Black Watch Lane. Working parties. Yesterday one company moved to "B" Lines - one platoon in B1 and another in B2. Rest of Company in billets at corner of Black Watch Lane and LA BASSEE Road.
	21st	Two companies at "A" Lines, one company at Black Watch Lane, one company at "B" Lines. Two men wounded, one killed.
	22nd	Two companies at "A" Lines, one company at Black Watch Lane, one company at "B" Lines. Working party at "B" Lines. Lieut. J.W.N. Gordon and one man killed.
	23rd	Two companies at "A" Lines, one company at Black Watch Lane, one company at "B" Lines. Working party at "B" Lines. Two men wounded, one killed.
	24th	Two companies at "A" Lines, one company at Black Watch Lane, one company at "B" Lines. Working party at "B" Lines.
	25th	Two companies at "A" Lines. One company at Black Watch Lane. One company at "B" Lines. Two men wounded.
	26th	The battalion was relieved by the 4th Cameron Highlanders and marched to LA GORGUE, and was billetted round the square. Billets very comfortable and roomy for men.
	27th	The battalion started training and refitting, with physical drill, and squad and section drill, in mornings and company drill and route marching in afternoons.
	28th	As yesterday. In addition to the above training, the Battalion had to supply a working party of one hundred men in "B" Lines.

8th, Division.

24th, Brigade.

1/5th, Black Watch.

March, 1915.

3.G.
10 sheet

1 M
2 A / 25th Brigade   121/4871
1/6 Royal H⁴
Vol III 1–31.3.15

Confidential.

1/5th Bn. The Black Watch.
War Diary
from 1st to 31st March 1915.

Mar. 1.] The Battalion in billets at LA GORGUE. Physical exercises, squad and company training for the men who were not on working parties [the previous evening] Working party of 100 men at B Lines. One man was killed and two were wounded. [Nos. 2 & 3 Coys.]

2.] As yesterday. [Deficiencies in clothing and equipment were gone into with a view to completion. Working party of 150 men at B Lines, from Nos. 1 & 4 Coys.

3.] As yesterday. Working party at B Lines. 3 men were wounded, 1 of them dangerously. Nos. 2 & 3 Coys.

4.] As yesterday. Working party at B Lines. One man dangerously wounded on night of the 3rd inst. died today.

5.] As yesterday. Working party at B Lines. One man wounded. [Nos. 2 & 3 Coys.]

6.] As yesterday. [Working party at B Lines.

7.] As yesterday. [Working party B Lines.

8.] As yesterday. Working party B Lines. The Machine Gun section with 2 guns, took up

position in S1, the remaining 2 guns in
S1 Redoubt by B Lines H.Q.

9th The Battalion, less Machine Gun detach-
ment and Grenadiers – who were attached
to 1/4th CAMERONS manning C Lines –
marched from LA GORGUE at 5.30 this
evening into advanced billets. [Battalion
Headquarters were established in farm in
B A LANE (Ref. Map BELGIUM 36 M 27d
4/3), where one Company was also billeted,
the remainder of the Battalion being
billeted in houses and farms close at hand
on the ESTAIRES – LA BASSEE Road, and the
Regimental Aid Post being established in
one of the latter houses. (Ref Map BELGIUM
36 M 27d 7/6).]

10th At 7.30 a.m. the operations of the day
began by artillery bombardment. Captain
McNAB with No 1 Coy. moved to PINK FARM
opposite LIME KILN for the purpose of guarding
and escorting German prisoners. Headquarters
were moved up to orchard in SIGN POST LANE
where at 9.30 a.m. they were joined by
the remainder of the Battalion. No 4
Coy. was furnished as a digging party on
a communicating trench to join up
British and German front lines, and 50 men
of No 3 Coy. also formed a party for the same

3.

purpose. One platoon of No 2 Coy. occupied B.1 redoubt and one platoon of that Company was employed escorting German prisoners to No 1 Coy. the remaining two platoons of the Company being employed as a working party digging trenches and fortifying at Point 6 in extreme left. Captain A.L. WATT, in charge of this party, was killed there. No 3 Coy. furnished another party fortifying buildings in NEUVE CHAPELLE, and this party suffered heavily, Captain H.R.C. ARBUTHNOTT being wounded. While escorting prisoners, Lieut. J.M.S. DUKE, No 1 Coy, was wounded by shrapnel, along with 4 others of that Company.

The 24th Brigade moved forward to attack at 5 p.m., and the Battalion was ordered to remain as divisional troops at SIGN POST LANE, with instructions to collect and bury all dead, and collect all arms and equipment. Our stretcher bearers behaved nobly all day, and were carrying for everyone.

11th. Heavy bombardment all day. Nos 3 and 4 Coys. endeavoured to collect and bury dead, but had to desist owing to shell fire. The Battalion was ordered to count German dead within our lines in neighbourhood of NEUVE CHAPELLE, but fire was too heavy

4.

to permit of this being done. Two platoons of No 3 Coy. brought R.E Stores and rations forward from B Lines near train head. No 2 Coy. moved to C Lines in rear of train head, and brought forward all rations from R.E Stores for them. They remained there in billets, working all night. No 4 Coy. were assisting & acting as stretcher bearers in carrying wounded from Dressing Station to Collecting Station on LA BASSEE Road. No 1 Coy. remained at PINK FARM & furnish guards and escorts for German prisoners. Our trenches in SIGN POST LANE, as well as the billets in BA LANE and ESTAIRES – LA BASSEE Road, were under extremely heavy shell fire all day, but luckily our casualties were not heavy.

12th. The trenches occupied by us at SIGN POST CORNER were heavily shelled. [Captain J.A. WILSON was severely wounded in the head by shrapnel fire.] The bombardment continued all day. In the evening, No 4 Coy collected dead in the vicinity, and buried them in second orchard SOUTH of SIGN POST LANE. No 2 Coy. was engaged in taking forward rations & R.E Stores from rear train head. No 1 Coy continued escorting prisoners to ESTAIRES, & brought up rations and water. No 3 Coy. dug graves and collected dead in the evening. 2/Lieutenant F.M.E. KITSON was slightly

5.

wounded at the advanced billet in
B.A. LANE while bringing up supplies on
cook's waggon.
2/Lieut. N. AIRTH GRANT joined Battalion, &
was posted to No 1 Coy.

13th No 4 Coy. was engaged collecting & burying
dead on both sides of SIGN POST LANE &
between the British and German trenches in
that vicinity. No 2 Coy. continued at TRAM
HEAD, C Lines, taking forward rations and
R.E. Stores by tram to the front lines They
suffered considerably from shell fire. No 1
Coy at PINK FARM were engaged in bringing
up rations and water. No 3 Coy. took R.E
stores forward to front trenches assisting
13TH LONDON REGIMENT. Heavy bombardments
and attack on our left flank in the morning,
and on our right flank in the afternoon.
Received orders at night that the Division
was to dig itself in on the position gained.
The Battalion was notified that it would be
attached to the 23rd Brigade for the night of
the 14th - 15th inst. for administrative purposes.

14th Nos. 3 & 4 Coys. were out this morning
collecting and burying German dead. Two
platoons of No 1 Coy. were collecting arms and
equipment, and stacking them at PONT
LOGY.

15th Nos. 3 & 4 Coys. were again out today collecting and burying dead, and clearing the field of arms and equipment. Two platoons of No 1 Coy. were carrying arms to PONT LOGY. No 2 Coy. was at RUE de BACQUEROT. 3 of No 1 Coy. were wounded by shrapnel.

16th Nos. 3 and 4 Coys. were again out today, collecting and burying dead, and collecting arms and equipment &c. two platoons of No 1 Coy. conveying same to PONT LOGY. The Battalion was relieved this evening and marched to billets at LA GORGUE, arriving at 8.30 p.m. Rejoined 24th Infantry Brigade. The casualties suffered by the Battalion during the operations of the past few days were:-

	O.	O.R.
Killed	1	13

	O.	O.R.		O.	O.R.
Wounded	4	67		4	67
Missing	-	-			
				5	80

These figures include the casualties suffered by the Grenadiers who were, throughout the operations attached to 1/4th CAMERONS, operating from C Lines.

17th The Battalion in billets at LA GORGUE. [Squad and Company training was started and deficiencies were made up.]

7.

18th Battalion still in LA GORGUE. Two parties were sent to PONT LOGY to load transport waggons with rifles, equipment &c taken from the field. The remainder of the Battalion continued training as on the previous day.

19th The Battalion still in LA GORGUE. Training as before. Intimation was received of the deaths of two men, wounded during the operations at NEUVE CHAPELLE.

20th As yesterday.

21st This afternoon at 1 the Battalion moved into billets at LA FLINQUE, [with the exception of No 1 Coy, two platoons of which occupied Redoubts C1 and C2.]

22nd As yesterday. Today the Battalion was joined by a 3rd Reinforcement consisting of 2/Lieuts. R.S.L. McPHERSON and IAN M. BAIN and 62 other ranks. The officers were posted to nos. 1 and 2 Coys. respectively.

23rd Billets were shelled more or less intermittently during the day, and in the afternoon, the Regimental Aid Post was destroyed by a shell, most of the medical equipment being destroyed, and several of the Orderlies having extremely narrow escapes. The Battalion moved into billets at LA GORGUE this afternoon.

24th In accordance with 24th Infantry Brigade

8.

Operation Order No. 13 of yesterday's date, the Battalion [as part of the Brigade] started from PONT de la LYS, LA GORGUE, and marched] to NEUF BERQUIN Road, where it occupied billets for the night. Headquarters were established in an estaminet. The weather which, from the time the Battalion moved to LA FLINQUE, had been excellent, broke down this evening and resulted in depressing conditions of rain and mud.

25th Weather conditions today continued bad. At 4 o'clock in the afternoon, the Battalion, as part of the 24th Brigade, [started from NEUF BERQUIN Road, and marched by way of ESTAIRES and SAILLY sur la LYS] to billets on RUE de la LYS beyond BAC ST MAUR. Battalion Headquarters were established in a new chateau on the RUE de la LYS. Ref. Map BELGIUM 36 H 3 b 8/4.

26th The Battalion moved at 2.30 p.m. today. Nos. 3 and 4 Coys. occupied the trenches by Convent CHARTREUX S.W. of LA BOUTILLERIE, which were handed over by the 7th Canadian Battalion

9

1st British Columbian Regiment. Trench Headquarters were established at a point Ref. Map BELGIUM 36 N ~~3 4~~ Sc 1/6 Nos 1 & 2 Coys. occupied billets on a crossroad, connecting RUE BIACHE and RUE DU QUESNES at points Ref. Map BELGIUM 36 H 26 a 3/7 and 36 H 26 b ~~& 9/4~~ respectively. The roads and fields continued soft and muddy, but the weather was hard and fairly clear.

27th — The disposition of the battalion continued the same as yesterday. 1 man of No 4 Coy was killed. Weather conditions also continued. Lieut. F.W. MILNE R.A.M.C. joined the battalion today as Medical Officer in place of Major WHYTE sick.

28th — The disposition of the battalion continued as yesterday, and the weather conditions also continued. Headquarters were shifted to DEAD DOG FARM, also the headquarters of the EAST LANCS REGIMENT.

29th — Nos 3 & 4 Coys were relieved from the trenches this evening, and returned to billets. Nos 1 and 2 Coys went into the trenches, occupying however a different section from that vacated by the other companies. Weather still continued hard and clear.

30th — Matters continued as yesterday. Weather still hard and clear.

31st — As yesterday, both regarding dispositions and weather. Today Lieut. R.F.D. BRUCE rejoined the Battalion, and 2/Lieutenant

R.M. RITCHIE joined.   10.

Major,
Comdg. 1/5th Bn. The Black Watch.

8th, Division.

24th, Brigade.

1/5th, Black Watch.

April. 1915.

121/5256

1/5 Rl: Hd. Highlanders
Vol IV 1 – 30.4.15

H.G
15 sheet

Confidential.

War Diary
of
1/5th The Black Watch
for the month of
April, 1915.

APRIL 1915.

WAR DIARY
or
INTELLIGENCE SUMMARY.
(Erase heading not required.)

Army Form C.-2118.

Hour, Date, Place	Summary of Events and Information	Remarks and references to Appendices
1st	[In accordance with 24th Infantry Brigade Operation Order No 16 of yesterday] the Battalion [as part of the Brigade was] relieved. The reserve companies [Nos 3 and 4] were relieved [by 1st LONDON REGIMENT and accordingly marched to BAC ST MAUR, where they took over that regiment's billets in a factory.] The trench companies [Nos 1 and 2, were relieved] by the 13th KENSINGTON REGIMENT [and also marched to the] billets in BAC ST MAUR. Battalion head-quarters were established in the ESTAMINET de la CLOCHE opposite the billets. The transport lines remained in their position on RUE BIACHE. The weather has had and clear, and the roads and fields dry.	Appendix No 1.
2nd	The Battalion continued in the six billets. At night the weather broke somewhat, a heavy shower [rain] falling. The Battalion received company training with	

APRIL, 1915.
WAR DIARY
INTELLIGENCE SUMMARY.
(Erase heading not required.)

Army Form C. 2118.

Instructions regarding War Diaries and Intelligence Summaries are contained in F. S. Regs., Part II. and the Staff Manual respectively. Title pages will be prepared in manuscript.

Hour, Date, Place	Summary of Events and Information	Remarks and references to Appendices
2nd	Physical drill, and made good officers cadres during its tour of trench duty	
3rd	The Battalion continued in the rest billets. The Battalion took part in a Brigade route march, starting at 8 a.m. The weather was dull and showery	
4th	The Battalion continued as yesterday. The weather appeared to have thoroughly broken again	
5th	As yesterday. In the forenoon the Battalion paraded for physical drill and company training and in the afternoon, for route marching. Two working parties were found for to-night, of 50 and 100 men, rendezvous at Bn. H.Q. (2) R1 BERKS REGT, block 2, N.3. b.10. and ELBOW FARM, H.28.D.5.3 respectively, working under 2nd field by. R.E. and 1st home counties field any. R.E.	

APRIL, 1915.
WAR DIARY
INTELLIGENCE SUMMARY.
(Erase heading not required.)

Army Form C. 2118.

Hour, Date, Place	Summary of Events and Information	Remarks and references to Appendices
6th	Today Captain [T.D. DUNCAN] and 2/Lieutenant [G.M.] ADAM [in accordance with instructions] left before luncheon to A.D.M.S. BOULOGNE] on their being appointed to commissions in the Royal Army Medical Corps. The 24th Infantry Brigade today relieved the 23rd Infantry Brigade in the left Brigade trenches and billets in accordance with 24th Infantry Brigade Operation Order No 17. The billets which the Battalion were ordered to take over having been heavily shelled in the earlier part of the day, other billets were ordered to be occupied. Vide route shewn in Appendix No 2 (viz. accordingly annexed) after ROAD JUNCTION H26A, 6 ROAD JUNCTIONS H23A and ROAD JUNCTIONS H21D. billets being occupied in and N.W. of FLEURBAIX in squares H21D, H22C and H22A, headquarters being established at point H22A 5/3. In 4 Coy. quarter Captain AUBERTIN, succeeded to the advanced billets at CROIX MARÉCHAL. The weather was finer than yesterday though still rather broken.	Appendix No 2.

APRIL 1915.
WAR DIARY
INTELLIGENCE SUMMARY.
(Erase heading not required.)

Army Form C. 2118.

Hour, Date, Place	Summary of Events and Information	Remarks and references to Appendices
7th	The Battalion continued in billets. Physical drill and company training were engaged in during the morning. A observation from hostile aircraft this way carried out as much as possible under cover in the orchards. The weather was still broken.	
8th	The Battalion still in billets. Continued training as yesterday. In the morning, the commanding officer and officers commanding companies by arrangement with O.C. No 4 section of trenches visited that section in order to gain some acquaintance with it, it being allotted to the Battalion's use during next tour of duty. Weather conditions similar to yesterday's. Tambs today.	
9th	In the morning and forenoon the Battalion engaged in Physical drill and Company training, which was several times interrupted by extremely heavy showers of sleet and hail. At 6.30 pm, the Battalion paraded and marched off to relieve the NORTH HANTS REGIMENT	2nd edition of BELGIUM & FRANCE ("B" series) sheets 3rd edition of 36 N.W. + 36 S.W. came into use at 12 midnight 8/9th April and should be used for future reference therein

APRIL 1915
WAR DIARY
INTELLIGENCE SUMMARY.
(Erase heading not required.)

Army Form C. 2118.

Hour, Date, Place	Summary of Events and Information	Remarks and references to Appendices

9th: No 4 Section of trenches. Headquarters were established on RUE DAVID at point where road intersects H34d and 35c. Two platoons of No 4 Coy. occupies the posts 4H and I respectively, the remainder of the Company being with the Battalion in the trenches. 1 man (armourer staff sergeant) slightly wounded.

Water is these extreme

10th: Dispositions continued as usual last night. The weather was bright. One man belonging to No 3 Coy. was seriously wounded in the head.

11th: Dispositions as before. The Brigade Commander this morning inspected the lines. The man wounded last night, died today in 24th Field Ambulance. One other man was slightly wounded. Weather excellent.

12th:

APRIL 1915.
WAR DIARY
INTELLIGENCE SUMMARY.
(Erase heading not required.)

Army Form C. 2118.

Hour, Date, Place	Summary of Events and Information	Remarks and references to Appendices
12th	Weather still excellent. The war wounded in week. The battalion was relieved this evening by the 2nd NORTHAMPTONSHIRE REGIMENT. Nos. 3 & 4 Coys occupied advanced billets at CROIX MARECHAL and ELBOW FARM respectively, the remaining Companies with headquarters returning to FLEURBAIX. Headquarters were established at H.21.d.4.6. Good weather continued.	
13th	The battalion in FLEURBAIX. Physical drill and Company training.	
14th	As yesterday.	
15th	The battalion this evening relieves 2/NORTHAMPTON: SHIRE REGIMENT in the 4 section of trenches. The dispositions were as during previous tour of duty:- two platoons of No 4 Coy. occupies the posts 4 H	

APRIL 1915
WAR DIARY
INTELLIGENCE SUMMARY

Army Form C. 2118.

Hour, Date, Place	Summary of Events and Information	Remarks and references to Appendices
15th	Nos 4 & 1 respectively the remainder of M/Gd Company being with the battalion in the trenches. Headquarters were as formerly Capt. G.S. RAE (Army) joined the Battalion.	
16th	(Hony 2/Lt) stock listed. Dispositions as yesterday.	
17th	Dispositions as yesterday.	
18th	One man wounded today. In accordance with 24th Infantry Brigade Operation Order No 18 dated 17th inst (not 14th inst) the Battalion (exclusive of the Brigade fire) relieved by 13/KENSINGTON Bn. belonging to 25th Infantry Brigade, and returned to BAC ST. MAUR where the billets previously occupied were taken over. Headquarters again were in ESTAMINET de la CLOCHE. During the Battalion's tour of duty, the weather continued excellent.	Appendix No 3
19th	Battalion in rest billets. Companies were inspected and	

APRIL 1915.
WAR DIARY
INTELLIGENCE SUMMARY.
(Erase heading not required.)

Army Form C. 2118.

Hour, Date, Place	Summary of Events and Information	Remarks and references to Appendices
19th	deficiencies made good. Three working parties to the night. Officer Sic 164. 19/20 were found by the Battalion. Each consisted of 100 men and were employed making assembly trenches and straightening our present line of trenches in Sections 5 & 6	
20th	Battalion still in rest billets. Physical drill and bayonet fighting and company training. Intimation having been received that No 1302 Pte J. Nicoll, No 3 Coy. had been awarded the Distinguished Conduct Medal for gallantry during the operations at NEUVE CHAPELLE the following battalion order was published:— "The C.O. on behalf of the Officers, N.C.O.'s and men of the Battalion heartily congratulates Pte. Nicoll on the honour that has been bestowed on him, which reflects credit to the regiment	
21st	The Field Marshal Commanding in Chief today inspected	

Army Form C. 2118.

APRIL, 1915
WAR DIARY
or
INTELLIGENCE SUMMARY.
(Erase heading not required.)

Hour, Date, Place	Summary of Events and Information	Remarks and references to Appendices
21st	inspected the 24th Infantry Brigade. In addressing the Battalion, he said that in words his could adequately express his admiration for the true patriotic spirit that had been shown by some territorial units in the way they had volunteered their services to their country for duty over the seas. He also admired their courage and soldierly training, which compared most favorably with the majority of the regular units of the British Army. He thanked them also for their invaluable services during the recent operations at NEUVE CHAPELLE	
22nd	The Battalion today engaged in the morning in physical drill and bayonet fighting, wire cutting and bomb and working parties, and in the afternoon in route marching and artillery formations. 3 digging parties of 100 men each were supplied for Working	

APRIL 1915
WAR DIARY
INTELLIGENCE SUMMARY.
(Erase heading not required.)

Army Form C. 2118.

Hour, Date, Place	Summary of Events and Information	Remarks and references to Appendices
22nd	Working under the Engineers at night.	
23rd	As yesterday.	
24th	In accordance with 24th Infantry Brigade Operation Order No 19, dated 23rd inst, the Brigade relieved the 23rd Infantry Brigade in the Right Brigade Trenches and billets this evening. The Battalion accordingly went into billets on RUE DU QUESNES [in H.32.a and H.31.b.c. Headquarters being established at farm on RUE DU QUESNES. Two working parties were found by the Battalion each numbering 100 men.	Appendix No 5
	2/Lieut T. KENNEDY 2nd Bn. The Black Watch having been posted to the Battalion for a tour of duty as Ad-jutant, assumes that duty today.	Appendix No 6.
25th	A working party of 50 men was found by the Battalion this morning.	Appendix No 7.

APRIL, 1915.

WAR DIARY

INTELLIGENCE SUMMARY.

(Erase heading not required.)

Army Form C. 2118.

Hour, Date, Place	Summary of Events and Information	Remarks and references to Appendices
26th	The Battalion paraded in the morning for Physical training and Bayonet fighting in the forenoon, for instruction in bombing and blocking, and in the afternoon for Company training.	
27th	The Battalion paraded in the morning for physical training and in the forenoon for Company training. At 7.30 p.m. the Battalion marched out to relieve the 2/EAST LANCASHIRE REGT, and Nos. 1, 2 and 4 Companies took over No. 1 Section of trenches, our Company relieving the 1/WORCESTER REGT, making up the complement by manning the extreme left of the section. No 3 Company occupied the posts 1A, 1B and 1C. French Headquarters were established in "RUE PETILLON" at N.8.b.6.6.	
28th	Dispositions as made last night. The excellent weather continued; the heat experienced in the trenches being unbearable.	

Army Form C. 2118.

APRIL 1915.
WAR DIARY
INTELLIGENCE SUMMARY.
(Erase heading not required.)

Instructions regarding War Diaries and Intelligence Summaries are contained in F. S. Regs., Part II. and the Staff Manual respectively. Title pages will be prepared in manuscript.

Hour, Date, Place	Summary of Events and Information	Remarks and references to Appendices
28th Contd.	2/Lieut. K.G.F. AIRTH GRANT joined today from 2/5 BLACK WATCH, and was posted to No 2 Coy.	
29th	No yesterday. The Enemy engaged in a certain amount of shelling during the afternoon, but only slight damage was done.	
30th	As yesterday. The battalion was this evening relieved by 2/EAST LANCASHIRE REGT. and returned to the billets to previously occupied in RUE DU QUESNES, having been lucky enough to suffer no casualties during its tour of trench duty.	

2-5-15.

Major
Comdg. 1/5th The Black Watch

1/5th Bn. Black Watch.

Appendices to War Diary (?)

1. Excerpts from 24th Infantry Brigade Operation Order No. 16, dated 31.3.15.

    The Brigade will be relieved tomorrow evening by the 25th Infantry Brigade, and move into divisional reserve billets as follows:-

Unit	Relieved by	Starting Point	Time	Route	Take over billets from
Hd. Coy. 1/5 B. Watch	London Regt.	Cross roads at H.26A	3.30 p.m.	Road junction H.26A – H.20C – H.13A	London Regt. in Factory BAC ST MAUR
Trench Coys. 1/5 B. Watch	13/Kensington Regt.	"	"	CROIX BLANCHE	London Regt. in Factory BAC ST MAUR

2. Excerpt from 24th Infantry Brigade Operation Order No. 17, dated 4.4.15.

    (1) The Brigade will relieve the 23rd Infantry Brigade in the Left Brigade trenches and billets on the evening of the 6th instant.
    (2) Battalions will march as follows:-

Unit	Relieved by	Starting Point	Time	Route	Take over billets or trenches from
1/5th Black Watch	2/Devons	Road Junction G.18.C	2.15	Cross roads G.29.D – ROUGE de BOUT – Junction H.26.A – CROIX BLANCHE	W. Yorks on road S.S. of FLEURBAIX Sq. H.27. 1 Coy. to proceed to advanced billets at CROIX MARECHAL

3. Excerpt from 24th Infantry Brigade Operation Order No. 18, dated 17.4.15.

    The Brigade will be relieved in the Left Brigade Area by the 25th Infantry Brigade tomorrow, and march to Divisional Reserve billets as follows:-

Unit	Starting Point	Time	Route	Take over billets from	Relieved by
1/5 Black Watch	"	"	Bn. NOT to use the roads WEST of the road CROIX BLANCHE to Road Junction H.26.A (inclusive)	London Regt. in Western Factory	13/Kensington Bn.

P.T.O.

4. Excerpts from message B.M. 614 of 24th Infantry Brigade, dated 19-4-15.

To be detailed by	No. of men	Rendezvous	Tools to be taken	Time	To work under
24th Inf. B.	100	Tool depot Cross Rds. RUE du BOIS, N 2 c 6.2.	nil	8.0 p.m.	2nd Field Coy. R.E.
do	100	do	nil	8.30 p.m.	do
do	100	ELBOW FARM, H 28 d. 10.4	100 Shovels	8.0 p.m.	1st Home Counties F. Coy. R.E.

* * * *

Please detail above parties.

5. Excerpts from 24th Infantry Brigade Operation Order No. 19, dated 23rd April 1915.

(1) The Brigade will relieve the 23rd Inf. Brigade in the Right Brigade trenches and billets on the evening of the 24th inst.

(2) Battalions will march as follows:—

Unit	Starting Pt.	Time to leave St. Pt.	Route	To take over billets or trenches from
1/5 B. Watch	Rd. Jn. H 13 c. 4/9	2.45 p.m.	Rd. Jn. H 19 A 9/8 — " — H 19 c. 4/9 — " — H 26 a. 1/4 La Croix Lescornez	1/7 Middle. Regt. on RUE du QUESNES in H 32 A and H 31 B & C.

* * * *

6. Excerpts from message B.M. 657 of 24th Infantry Brigade, dated 23-4-15.

Detail of working parties for night 24th & 25th April 1915.

To be detailed by	No. of men	Rendezvous	Tools to be taken	Time	To work under
24th Inf. B.	100	Tool Depot RUE du BOIS N 2 C. 8.1	NIL	8.30 p.m.	2nd Field Coy. R.E.
do	100	do	NIL	9.0 p.m.	do

* * * *

7. O.C. 1/5 B. Watch
Please detail the above parties. Acknowledge.
(Sgd) F. Tyrwhitt Captain
Staff C. for Bde. Major.

2. Excerpt from 24th Infantry Brigade message B.M.665. dated 24-4-15.

Detail of working parties for morning 25-4-15.

To be detailed by	No. of men	Rendezvous	Tools to be taken	Time	To work under
24th Inf. Bde.	50	R.E. Tool depot, RUE du BOIS N.2.d.2.3.	nil	8.30 a.m.	2nd Field Coy. R.E.

*   *   *   *

Officer Commanding
1/5 B. Watch.

Please detail the above party. Acknowledge.

(Sgd) R.M. Luckock Captain,
Brigade Major

24-4-15

8th, Division.

24th, Brigade.

I/5th, Black Watch.

May, 1915.

5G
15 sheet

2/8

121/55/14

5th Division

1/5th Black Watch

Vol V 1 — 31.5.15.

Army Form C. 2118.

MAY 1915.
WAR DIARY
INTELLIGENCE SUMMARY.
(Erase heading not required.)

Hour, Date, Place	Summary of Events and Information	Remarks and references to Appendices
1st	The Battalion remained in the billets occupied last night on RUE du QUESNES, and engaged in company training.	
2nd	The Battalion paraded for divine service, Church of England at 9 a.m. and Presbyterians at 12 noon. Nos. 18 and 20 men remained tonight in one platoon of No. 1 Coy. and one platoon of No. 2 Coy. respectively.	
3rd	Companies paraded at 9 a.m, 9.30 a.m. and 2 p.m. for training under Company officers. In accordance with B.M. 807 and 4th Infantry Brigade dated 2nd inst., a fatigue working party of 50 from No 3 Coy., under the command of Lieut L.A. ELGOOD, was detailed to work under 2nd Field Coy. R.E. commencing from tonight. One platoon of No 3 Coy and one platoon of No 1 Coy	App. 101

Army Form C. 2118.

MAY 1915.
WAR DIARY
INTELLIGENCE SUMMARY.
(Erase heading not required.)

Instructions regarding War Diaries and Intelligence Summaries are contained in F.S. Regs., Part II. and the Staff Manual respectively. Title pages will be prepared in manuscript.

Hour, Date, Place	Summary of Events and Information	Remarks and references to Appendices
3rd	Relieved the garrisons furnished last night for into 18 and 20. Relief took place at 11pm. Working parties of 200 men under Capt McNAB and 100 men under Lieut TAYLOR, were provided tonight. Work under 2nd Field Coy. RE	
4th	In accordance with Operation Order No 20 of 24th Infantry Brigade the Battalion as part of the Brigade who relieves this afternoon and moved to billets in G.10.X, G.4.C. and G.3.d. [the billets vacated being taken over by 2/MIDDLESEX REGT. Headquarters were established in farm at G.10.X.7.8. The garrisons of posts 18 and 20 were relieved after dark and the permanent working party under Lieut ELGOOD remained.	App. No 2.
5th	The Battalion today engaged in company training	

MAY 1915.
WAR DIARY
INTELLIGENCE SUMMARY.
(Erase heading not required.)

Army Form C. 2118.

Hour, Date, Place	Summary of Events and Information	Remarks and references to Appendices
6th	No spectacle. Various preparations were made in view of impending offensive operations.	
7th	Parades for running drill and for fitting equipment. The orders which had been issued for the battalion to move out tonight to take part in offensive operations were cancelled late in the afternoon. The operations being postponed for 24 hours. The Machine Gun Detachment had however, previously left and taken up machine gun emplacements in No. 1 R. Section of trenches, posting 2 guns in cap: in orchard in front of 1.R. and the other 2 guns in emplacements between that and the SALLY- ROUGES BANCS Road.	
8th	Company parade. Inspection by C.O. in forenoon of Battalion in full fighting order.	

Army Form C. 2118.

WAR DIARY
INTELLIGENCE SUMMARY.
(Erase heading not required.)

MAY, 1915.

Hour, Date, Place	Summary of Events and Information	Remarks and references to Appendices
8th (contd)	This evening in accordance with 24th Infantry Brigade Operation Order No 21, the Battalion left Divisional Reserve billets at 9 p.m. and marched to starting point at G.16.a. Entraining departure was unevent[ful]. the Battalion following 2/EAST LANCASHIRE REGT. The Battalion arrived at G.Assembly trenches at 12 midnight opposite Brigade Headquarters in RUE PETILLON.	
9th	Artillery bombardment started at 5 hrs. a.m. on time HQ bombardment. Immediately on its cessation the battalion left the assembly trenches to gain the fire trench to advance in close touch with 1/WORCESTERSHIRE REGT. The movement was unfortunately checked by reason of the SHERWOOD FORESTERS not being able to exit the fire trenches, and from RUE PETILLON forward the Battalion suffered badly from very heavy machine gun and artillery fire. On attaining the objective, the	

Forms/C. 2118/10

WAR DIARY
INTELLIGENCE SUMMARY
(Erase heading not required.)

Army Form C. 2118.

MAY 1915

Hour, Date, Place	Summary of Events and Information	Remarks and references to Appendices
9th (cont'd)	Battalion occupied the assembly and communication trenches in rear of 15 Redan in the proximity of where the RIVIÈRE des LAYES crosses the trenches. Here the Machine Gun Detachment rejoined, having closed in on the right. At 9 a.m., a fresh bombardment was begun by our artillery. During the whole forenoon the Battalion remained in the assembly trenches and suffered considerably from heavy shell fire. At 1 p.m. our artillery began a further bombardment as a result of which many casualties occurred in the Battalion through shells dropping short. Throughout the afternoon, the trajection in the trenches continued, and towards nightfall the enemy's bombardment of our trenches increased, especially in the neighbourhood of the RIVIÈRE des LAYES and the SALLY Road.	

WAR DIARY
INTELLIGENCE SUMMARY

Army Form C. 2118.

MAY, 1915

Hour, Date, Place	Summary of Events and Information	Remarks and references to Appendices
9th (cont)	At 10 p.m. Brigade message (B.M. 50) was received ordering the Battalion to proceed to Divisional Reserve and bivouac in locality towards S. of ROUGE De BOUT, in consequence of which the Battalion was collected in communicating trench by SALLY RD and in Section I.R., and orders were issued to O.Cs. Companies to proceed independently to the crossroads RUE de QUESNES, where the Battalion would reassemble. At about 1.30 a.m. on 10th inst., the Battalion arrived at Road Junction at ROUGE de BOUT, and bivouaced in field north of the junction. During the day, all ranks of the Battalion (history illegible) excellent conduct and the C.O. accordingly forwarded, in course, a number of recommendations for favourable consideration of the conduct of various officers and N.C.Os. (Appx No 3)	

MAY, 1915

WAR DIARY
INTELLIGENCE SUMMARY.
(Erase heading not required.)

Army Form C. 2118.

Instructions regarding War Diaries and Intelligence Summaries are contained in F.S. Regs., Part II. and the Staff Manual respectively. Title pages will be prepared in manuscript.

Hour, Date, Place	Summary of Events and Information	Remarks and references to Appendices
10th	The Battalion remained all day in bivouac and casualty lists were prepared. The details of these lists were:— Officers Wounded 8 viz:— Lieut. R.F.D. BRUCE. 2/Lieut. Hon. T. BOWES LYON. 2/Lieut. A.S. QUEKETT. 2/Lieut. R.M. RITCHIE. Lieut. A.P. DICKIE Capt. T. AUBERTIN. Lieut. H.R. McCABE. Lieut. A.W. DUKE. Other ranks:— Killed 32 Wounded 108 Missing 8, of whom 2 reported later in the morning.	

MAY 1915.

Army Form C. 2118.

WAR DIARY
INTELLIGENCE SUMMARY.
(Erase heading not required.)

Instructions regarding War Diaries and Intelligence Summaries are contained in F. S. Regs., Part II. and the Staff Manual respectively. Title pages will be prepared in manuscript.

Hour, Date, Place	Summary of Events and Information	Remarks and references to Appendices
10th	In accordance with Brigade message B.M. 114 the Battalion (less part of the Brigade moved) into billets nr LA BASSEE and starting at 2 a.m. on 10/11th inst. en route being by LAVENTIE hereunder M.G.d. — Batt In HEM. Billets were occupied in M14C. rd. Headquarters being established in estaminet crossroads at PONT du HEM.	
11th	The Battalion continued in billets resting. In the evening the Brigade moved to other billets, and accordingly the Battalion moved to ESTAIRES where they occupied billets in LE FRANC Factory.	
12th	The Battalion continued in billets resting. Parades were under Company Officers.	
13th	Do. yesterday	
14th	Do. yesterday	

MAY 1915.

WAR DIARY

INTELLIGENCE SUMMARY.

(Erase heading not required.)

Army Form C. 2118.

Hour, Date, Place	Summary of Events and Information	Remarks and references to Appendices
15th	In accordance with 2/8th Infantry Brigade Operation Order No 25 dated 14th inst. the Battalion (exclusive of the Brigade stock of ammunition) Pots 11,12 +13 in rear of the 8th Infantry Brigade. The distribution was — Posts 11, one platoon, Post 12, two platoons and machine guns, Post 13, one platoon. No 1 Coy. came under orders of C.O. 2/Lincolnshire Regt. and reinforced Post Headquarters were established at Mangerie.	
16.	Dispositions continued as made yesterday.	
17th	The weather, which for a long time had been excellent, broke down today. The Battalion was relieved this evening and marched back to billets along road ═══ LA FLINQUE — LAVENTIE, headquarters being in house opposite Hospice Toulouse	

WAR DIARY
INTELLIGENCE SUMMARY.
(Erase heading not required.)

Army Form C. 2118.

MAY. 1915.

Hour, Date, Place	Summary of Events and Information	Remarks and references to Appendices
15th	The Battalion continued in billets occupied last night	
19th	As yesterday.	
20th	This evening, the Battalion organised as two Companies occupied Section 3rd C. Lines, as mine to tunnelling. The Command of A.C. of NORTHAMPTONSHIRE REGT., that battalion being similarly organised as the two Acting as one Battalion. The O.C. NORTHAMPTONSHIRE REGT. having however, seniority, took over as C.O. Later in the day, the command was taken over by O.C. 1/5 BLACK WATCH. A.C. adquarters were in RUE TILLELOY. 1 man wounded	
21st	Dispositions as made yesterday. 1 man accidentally wounded.	
22nd	As yesterday. 1 man wounded.	

Army Form C. 2118.

MAY 1915
WAR DIARY
or
INTELLIGENCE SUMMARY.
(Erase heading not required.)

Hour, Date, Place	Summary of Events and Information	Remarks and references to Appendices
23rd	As yesterday. 1 man wounded.	
24th	As yesterday. 1 man wounded accidentally. This evening, in accordance with 25th Infantry Brigade Operation Order No 24, dated 23rd inst. the Brigade was relieved by the 25th Brigade. The Battalion was relieved in the trenches by 2/ROYAL BERKSHIRE Regt. and marches back to ESTAIRES where billets in RUE de LILLE were taken over from 2/RIFLE BRIGADE. Headquarters were established in house at Sheet 36a. L.30.d.7.8.	
25th	The Battalion continued in billets occupied last night.	
26th	Parades were held at 6.30 am at 9.30 am, the later parade being for route marching.	

Army Form C. 2118.

MAY 1915

WAR DIARY
INTELLIGENCE SUMMARY.
(Erase heading not required.)

Hour, Date, Place	Summary of Events and Information	Remarks and references to Appendices
27th	Parade for Physical training and Company training.	
28th	Parade for Physical training and enroute marching.	
29th	LA GORGUE Batts having today been allotted to Battalion Companies paraded each hour from 7 to 10 am. for "batting".	
30th	Parades for divine service.	
31st	Nos. 2 & 3 Companies made up by the 1st Company, went out for duty with 2/NORTHAMPTON-SHIRE REGT. & 1/WORCESTERSHIRE REGT. and occupied HILL'S REDOUBT and CHURCH REDOUBT, and also reserve trenches in rear of NEUVE CHAPELLE. Battalion headquarters were established on	

13.

Army Form C. 2118.

MAY, 1915
WAR DIARY
or
INTELLIGENCE SUMMARY.
(Erase heading not required.)

Instructions regarding War Diaries and Intelligence Summaries are contained in F. S. Regs., Part II. and the Staff Manual respectively. Title pages will be prepared in manuscript.

Hour, Date, Place	Summary of Events and Information	Remarks and references to Appendices
ESTAIRES – LA BASSEE Road in farm at M.8.6.3.1.		
31st	As yesterday. The revised figures of casualties incurred in the operations reported above on 9th & 10th inst. (other ranks) to date are:— Killed & died of wounds 31 Wounded 106 Missing — 137 (Sd) 1/5th The Black Watch. Major	

APPENDICES to WAR DIARY
for
MAY 1915

1. To O.C. BM 80 of 24th Infantry Brigade dated 1st May 1915
"Will you please detail a permanent working party of 50 men under an officer to work under the 2nd Field Coy R.E. commencing tomorrow night.

(1) There is no objection to changing the men, but the officer will not be changed oftener than every three days and then only after reference to this office.

(2) Please instruct the officer so detailed to report his name and the position of his billet to the O.C. 2/Field Coy. This he can do through the Signal Service.

(3) The O.C. 2/Fd. Coy. will then send him orders direct through you."   (sgd). R.M. Luckock Capt.
Bde. Major 24 I.B.

Please acknowledge.
2/5/15

2. Excerpts from Operation Order No 20 of 24th Infantry Brigade dated 4th May 1915.

The Bde. will be relieved by the 23rd I.B. in the 1+2 sections of Reserve billets tonight.
(1) Bn. will march in accordance with attached march table.
(2) Transport will move to new lines in BN areas and be clear of present lines by 2 P.M.
(3) Garrisons of Posts 18 and 20 will not move until relieved by 23rd I.B. after which they will move to new BN. billets by shortest route.

Unit	Starting Pt.	Route	Line	Billets to	Present Billets taken over by
1/5 Blackwatch	CROIX L'ESCORNEX	P.M. Rd. in BRIGES into G16A3	H19c 419 Rue du Sailly	to G16A, G16c, G3D	7/Middx R.

3. Excerpt from Report by Officer Commanding 1/5th. The Black Watch to 24th. Infantry Brigade on operations of 9th May 1915.

"It is with great pleasure that I would report the excellent conduct displayed by all ranks under my command in particularly trying circumstances and I wish to bring to your notice for favorable consideration the gallantry displayed by the following Officer and NCO's and men of this battalion in receiving and attending to the wounded under heavy machine gun and shell fire. Personally noticed 2/Lieut. G. ARTH GRANT and No. 2009 Sgt. S.S.B. MILNE perform many acts of gallantry and exceptional coolness under heavy fire. The latter N.C.O. would recommend be granted a commission in the battalion under my command, which I know he would accept, and I personally would be glad to have him as a commissioned officer.

2/Lieut. G. ARTH GRANT.
No 2009 Sgt. S.S.B. MILNE.
655 Sgt. M.G. BEVERLY.
1628 Pte. G. GUILD   Stretcher bearer.
2025 " J. DAVIDSON   "   "
1286 " C. PETRIE   "   "
2095 " A. FERRIER   "   "
2667 " D. SMART   "   "
2406 L/Cpl. W. KEEN.

I would also commend the excellent control and calmness and initiative displayed by Captains T. McNAB & T. LYELL & T. AUBERTIN in the handling of the units under their command, and also in work prior to recent operations the following N.C.O. rendered great assistance to 2/Lieut. L.A. ELGOOD - - - - - viz: No. 2309 Sergt. G.E. MILLAR."

8th, Division.

24th, Brigade.

1/5th, Black Watch.

June, 1915.

L.B. 6.G.
gahus

121/5992

8th Division

1/5th R. Hd.

Vol VI 1 — 30.6.15

Army Form C. 2118.

JUNE 1915
WAR DIARY
or
INTELLIGENCE SUMMARY.
(Erase heading not required.)

Hour, Date, Place	Summary of Events and Information	Remarks and references to Appendices
1st	As yesterday.	
2nd	Today Headquarters and No 1 Coy moved to finish shell C.B. Headquarters were established in house opposite ESTAMINET de la BELLE CROIX at G.31.c.2.2. No 1 Coy. met detachment of billets along RUE de GENDARMERIE.	
3rd	As yesterday. No 1 Coy. occupies CHATEAU REDOUBT in the vicinity of NEUVE CHAPELLE, under direct command of the O.C. NORTHAMPTONSHIRE REGT.	
4th	As yesterday.	
5th	In accordance with Brigade Message BM 373, dated 3rd inst. the relief which was due to take place on 2/3rd inst. took place tonight. the tour of	

Army Form C. 2118.

JUNE, 1915

WAR DIARY
INTELLIGENCE SUMMARY.
(Erase heading not required.)

Instructions regarding War Diaries and Intelligence Summaries are contained in F.S. Regs., Part II. and the Staff Manual respectively. Title pages will be prepared in manuscript.

Hour, Date, Place	Summary of Events and Information	Remarks and references to Appendices

5th. Tout all threw h duty having been attended to & ay the battalion returned to billets in RUE de GENDARMERIE and in LE FRANC factory.
Lieut. W.C.O. BARRE was wounded severely in the knee during this relief.

6th. Parade for divine service, much for inspecting of equipment, ammunition &c.

7th. Parade for physical training and for company training.

8th. As yesterday.

9th. As yesterday. Lieut. J.F. DICKSON having been transferred to England on 30th ult, was today struck off the strength as from that date.

10th.

JUNE 1915

WAR DIARY
INTELLIGENCE SUMMARY.
(Erase heading not required.)

Army Form C. 2118.

Hour, Date, Place	Summary of Events and Information	Remarks and references to Appendices
10th LA GORGUE	Baths having been allotted for the use of the Battalion today, Companies paraded (each hour) from 7 to 11.30 a.m. for bathing. Parades for physical training and Company training. The man, belonging to No. 1 Coy. was drowned in the L/S near LE FRANC factory yesterday, and a Board of Enquiry were this morning held to investigate the circumstances. Wiring parties were found tonight for working on the support line trenches.	
11th	Tonight the 1/5th SHERWOOD FORESTERS and 2/EAST LANCS were relieved by the 3/NORTHANTS, /WORCEST-ERS and 1/5th BLACK WATCH. The battalion marched to CHATEAU church and till relieved to Battalion Headquarters were established at EUSTON POST, M.29.d.9.1. No 3 Coy. manned the latter, the remain...	

HWV

4.

JUNE 1915

Army Form C. 2118.

WAR DIARY
INTELLIGENCE SUMMARY.
(Erase heading not required.)

Hour, Date, Place	Summary of Events and Information	Remarks and references to Appendices
12th	As yesterday.	
13th	As yesterday.	
14th	As yesterday.	
15th	As yesterday. Two men wounded	
16th	As yesterday.	
17th	Tonight the Battalion was relieved and returned to LE FRANC factory, ESTAIRES, Battalion Headquarters being established at G.25.c.8.6.	
18th	The Battalion was Engd. cleaning up and completing deficiencies. No. 1 Coy. provided a working party of 50 & guard.	
19th	Battalion paraded for running, drill and physical training at 6.30 a.m. under P.C. Coy. instructors	

JUNE 1915

WAR DIARY
INTELLIGENCE SUMMARY.
(Erase heading not required.)

Army Form C. 2118.

Hour, Date, Place	Summary of Events and Information	Remarks and references to Appendices
19th (cont)	Situation hasn't been received. Mnd the following warrant officers and non-commissioned officers has been awarded the Distinguished Conduct Medal for gallantry and devotion to duty, the following of Today are included:— The officers thoroughly understand sympathy and appreciate with & hearty concurrence of the Battalion, wish to congratulate these W.O's and N.C.O's on obtaining to the honour, which he knows are so well merited; and be at the same time wishes to thank them for the honour they have rendered the regiment by gaining these awards. We have & M.c. Maj. med. N.C.O's aned.— No 310 C.S. Major J. MARNE 11819 C.J. Lt/Sgt. J. PATTISON Sgt. A. CHRISTIE 12114 L/Sgt. F. WEBSTER 543 F/Cpl. J. ANDERSON 655 Sgt. M.G. BEVERLEY 2009 C.S.M. S.S.B. MILNE	

JUNE 1915

WAR DIARY
INTELLIGENCE SUMMARY.
(Erase heading not required.)

Army Form C. 2118.

Hour, Date, Place	Summary of Events and Information	Remarks and references to Appendices
19th (contd)	The G.O.C. 8th Division today presented the medal ribbons to those men (excepting C. Major MARNE wounded on 17th, 7. WEBSTER killed, and Lt. Bn 2. Lt. T. HICOX who has previously been awarded (vide War Diary 24th April 1915). On conclusion the presentation the G.O.C. thanked the Battalion for their good work during the past seven months, and especially at NEUVE CHAPELLE. He also mentioned that the number of D.C.M.s awarded to these NC., NCOs and men reflected great credit on the Honour and good service of the Battalion. The medal ribbons by men to review the gallant services and devotion to duty that had been shown by the absolute heroes of the Battalion.	
20th	Battalion paraded for Divine Service at 2:30 p.m.	
21st	LA GORGUE baths having been allotted for the use of the Battalion to-day from 7 a.m. to 1 p.m. Companies paraded in parties of 100 for bathing. No. 4 Company supplied a Working Party of 50 men at night under the command of 2nd Lieut. Wainscot, No. 3 Company for work under Lieut. Hawthorne R.E., at C Lines.	
22nd		

JUNE 1915.

WAR DIARY
INTELLIGENCE SUMMARY.
(Erase heading not required.)

Army Form C. 2118.

Hour, Date, Place	Summary of Events and Information	Remarks and references to Appendices
22nd	Parades for Physical training and Company training as yesterday.	
23rd	As yesterday. Orders for the next tour of trench duty, which should have commenced to-night, were cancelled, and the Battalion was ordered to remain in billets.	
24th	Parades for Battalion drill and Company training.	
25th	Battalion was engaged cleaning up billets. This evening, in accordance with 24th Infantry Brigade Operation Order No. 26, dated 25th inst., the Battalion marched from ESTAIRES and took over No. 3 Section trenches along with one Company of 2nd EAST LANCS, from 1/6th Battalion WEST RIDING REGIMENT. Trench Headquarters were established at N.4.a.2.3. No. 4 Company occupied the Posts at DEAD DOG FARM and Post 3F. The	

Army Form C. 2118.

JUNE 1915.
WAR DIARY
OF
INTELLIGENCE SUMMARY.
(Erase heading not required.)

Instructions regarding War Diaries and Intelligence Summaries are contained in F.S. Regs., Part II. and the Staff Manual respectively. Title pages will be prepared in manuscript.

Hour, Date, Place	Summary of Events and Information	Remarks and references to Appendices
25th Cite	The Front Line being held as follows:— Sub-Section 3 Q by A Company 2nd EAST LANCS; Sub-Section 3 R by No 1 Company and 2 platoons of No 3 Company; Sub-Section 3 S, by No 2 Company and 2 platoons of No 3 Company, with 3 Machine Guns in position in 3 R, and 1 in 3 Q.	
26th	As yesterday. In the evening 2 platoons of A Company 2nd EAST LANCS were withdrawn and received instruction to proceed to billets at CROIX BLANC, the line being readjusted to meet the deficiency in numbers caused by this with-drawal.	
27th	As yesterday. 1 man wounded. This evening the remaining two platoons of A Company 2nd EAST LANCS were relieved by 1st LONDON REGT, 25th INFANTRY BRIGADE, who took over Sub-Section 3 R, and —	

Army Form C. 2118.

9.

JUNE 1915.
WAR DIARY
or
INTELLIGENCE SUMMARY.
(Erase heading not required.)

Instructions regarding War Diaries and Intelligence Summaries are contained in F.S. Regs., Part II. and the Staff Manual respectively. Title pages will be prepared in manuscript.

Hour, Date, Place	Summary of Events and Information	Remarks and references to Appendices

27th Contd and 3 S, the Battalion then holding Sub-Sections 3 P and 3 S, 3 P being taken over from 2nd NORTHANTS. No. 4 Company holding the posts as beforementioned, with the addition of one machine gun and team withdrawn from the Front Line to Post 3 F.

28th As yesterday.

29th As yesterday. 1 Sergeant of No. 2 Company killed, and 1 man wounded.

30th As yesterday.

Wauchope
Lieut- Colonel
Commanding 1/5th Bn. The Black Watch

4th July 1915.

8th, Division.

24th, Brigade.

I/5th, Black Watch.

July, 1915.

7.G
21 sheets

121/6357

8th/15 wrocin

1/5th Royal H^d
Vol VII
1-31.7.15

Army Form C. 2118.

WAR DIARY

INTELLIGENCE SUMMARY.

(Erase heading not required.)

July 1915

Hour, Date, Place	Summary of Events and Information	Remarks and references to Appendices
1st July 1915.	As yesterday. One of the sentries on duty at French Headquarters wounded in the early morning. To-night, in accordance with Brigade Operation Order No. 27 dated 30th June 1915, the Battalion was relieved by the 2nd Bn. DEVON REGT., 23rd INFANTRY BRIGADE, and went into the billets evacuated by this Battalion round the Cross Roads G.29.d. with Battalion Head-Quarters G.30.A. 2/1. RUE du QUESNOY. 1 man wounded while marching to billets. The Battalion while resting, form the Rear Battalion of the Brigade Reserve.	
2nd.	The Battalion was at the disposal of O.C. Companies, for Coy. training and inspection of Arms & Equipment.	
3rd.	As Yesterday. A party of 4 N.C.O's' and 40 men, detailed in equal	

WAR DIARY

INTELLIGENCE SUMMARY

July 1915.

Army Form C. 2118.

Hour, Date, Place	Summary of Events and Information	Remarks and references to Appendices
3rd (continued)	Equal numbers from each Company, paraded at 9.30 a.m., under 2nd Lieut. IAN M. BAIN, No 2 Coy, for instruction in bomb-throwing. This evening two working parties, consisting of 150 men detailed from No. 1 and No. 2 Companies & under the Command of Lieut. MURRAY, Machine Gun Officer; and 100 men detailed from No. 3 and 4 Companies under the command of Lieut. TAYLOR, No. 4 Company, paraded at 9.45 p.m. and 9.15 p.m. respectively, for work under 1st HOME COUNTIES F.D. Coy. R.E.. Both parties had, in addition to number of men stated, the required number of N.C.O's to take charge. The work was done on support & shelter trenches behind present front line trench.	
4th	Party for instruction in bomb-throwing paraded as yesterday. The battalion paraded for Divine Service at/-	

July 1915.

WAR DIARY

INTELLIGENCE SUMMARY.

(Erase heading not required.)

Army Form C. 2118.

Hour, Date, Place	Summary of Events and Information	Remarks and references to Appendices
4th (continued)	at 11 a.m. Information was received in the evening that one man of No. 4 Coy employed at Transport Lines, had been drowned in River Lys while bathing this afternoon.	
5th	The bombing class paraded at 9 a.m. and 9 a.m. under 2nd Lieut. BAIN. The Company were at the disposal of Company Commanders today for training. Special attention being given to the practice of passing verbal messages. No. 1 and 2 Companies provided a Working Party of 150 men and 4 N.C.Os. under the Command of 2nd Lieut. R.M. LESLIE No. 4 Company fought for work under 1st HOME COUNTIES FIELD Coy. R.E.	

H/

July 1915.

WAR DIARY
INTELLIGENCE SUMMARY.
(Erase heading not required.)

Army Form C. 2118.

Hour, Date, Place	Summary of Events and Information	Remarks and references to Appendices
6th	As Yesterday. In accordance with orders received from Brigade Headquarters, two Companies and Battalion Headquarters remain in present billets, the other two Companies namely No.3 and 4, being attached to 2nd. NORTHANTS and 1st WORCESTERS respectively, for a tour of trench duty. No.4 Company not being required to man part of the section of trenches taken over by the 1st WORCESTERS remain in reserve to this unit, occupying the advanced billet at RUE-DU-BOIS. One Machine Gun and team, according to instructions, took up a position in the front line along with No.3 Company. A Working Party of 150 men was detailed for	

July 1915.

WAR DIARY

INTELLIGENCE SUMMARY.

Army Form C. 2118.

Hour, Date, Place	Summary of Events and Information	Remarks and references to Appendices
6th (continued).	for work under R.E's. tonight but orders were received later to cancel same, as another Unit had furnished the party required. The body of No. 943 Pte. D. CRAWFORD, No. 4 Company, drowned on 4th inst. was recovered from the River LYS today and buried near Cemetery Post on Estaires–Sailly Road.	
7th.	This morning No. 1 Company removed to billets vacated by No. 3 and 4 Companies. Companies at the disposal of O.C., Companies for training as yesterday. A Court of Enquiry was held this morning at the Transport lines at 11 a.m. to investigate the circumstances connected with the death by drowning of No. 943 Pte. D. CRAWFORD aforementioned. From the evidence forthcoming it appears that No. 1475 Pte. D. ARCHER made a gallant	

Army Form C. 2118.

6/
July 1915.
WAR DIARY
INTELLIGENCE SUMMARY.
(Erase heading not required.)

Instructions regarding War Diaries and Intelligence Summaries are contained in F. S. Regs., Part II. and the Staff Manual respectively. Title pages will be prepared in manuscript.

Hour, Date, Place	Summary of Events and Information	Remarks and references to Appendices
7th (continued).	attempt to rescue CRAWFORD but got into difficulties himself and might have been a second victim had not N°. 13449 PTE H. FRANKS, 1st WORCESTERS, come to the rescue and got him out of the water. On it was, PTE. ARCHER was in a very exhausted state when taken out, and artificial respiration had to be resorted to, to bring him round. Great credit is due PTE. FRANKS for his gallant conduct, as he was handicapped with having all his clothes on at the time of rescue. In order that his gallantry may be recognised, his Commanding Officer was notified of what had occurred. Working Party, as detailed for evening of 6th inst. was supplied tonight.	

Army Form C. 2118.

WAR DIARY

INTELLIGENCE SUMMARY

(Erase heading not required.)

July 1915.

Hour, Date, Place	Summary of Events and Information	Remarks and references to Appendices
5th	No. 1 and 2 Companies paraded at 11 a.m. for drill under Adjutant. Other parades under Coy. arrangements. Intimation of further honours to the Battalion was received today as follows:— (EXTRACT FROM LONDON GAZETTE SUPPLEMENT dated 22.6.15). "Recommended for Gallant and Distinguished Conduct in the Field:— (TEMP). MAJOR H.F. BLAIR-IMRIE. LIEUT. I.M. BRUCE-GARDYNE 2ND. LIEUT. L.A. ELGOOD. 1941 L/CPL. TAYLOR. J. No. 4 Coy. 2025 PTE. DAVIDSON. J. No. 2 " 2095 PTE. FERRIER. A. No. 3 " 2004 PTE. HIGH W. No. 1 " 1568 PTE. HOWIE A. No. 2 " 1629 PTE. REDFORD A. No. 4 " The 1st last mentioned being Stretcher Bearers whose good work has already been referred to. (EXTRACT)/-	Killed.

Army Form C. 2118.

July 1915.

WAR DIARY
INTELLIGENCE SUMMARY
(Erase heading not required.)

Hour, Date, Place	Summary of Events and Information	Remarks and references to Appendices
8th (continued)	(Extract from London Gazette Supplement dd 23-6-15). "Major Hew Francis Blair-Imrie:- To be Companion of the Most Distinguished Order of St. Michael and St. George, to date from 3rd inst." "Lieut. I. M. Bruce-Gardyne." Awarded the Military Cross." A working party of 150 men was furnished tonight by the two Companies and Machine Gun Section.	
9th	Parades as yesterday. In view of the threatened hostile attack on the British lines Special Orders were issued today to the battalion so as to be in readiness when required.	
10th	Parades as yesterday. Nos: /-	

July 1915.

WAR DIARY

INTELLIGENCE SUMMARY.

(Erase heading not required.)

Army Form C. 2118.

Hour, Date, Place	Summary of Events and Information	Remarks and references to Appendices
10th (continued)	Nos. 1 and 2 Companies and Machine Gun Section furnished a working party of 150 men tonight.	
11th	Nos. 1 and 2 Companies and Machine Gun Section paraded at 10.15 a.m. for Divine Service which was held in Orchard adjoining Headquarters.	
12th	Nos. 1 and 2 Companies paraded at 10.30 a.m. for Drill under Adjutant. Other parades under Company arrangements. Tonight Nos. 3 and 4 Companies returned to billets, No. 4 Company occupying the billets vacated by No. 1 Company and No. 3 Company occupying new billets next to No. 1 Company. 1 man of No. 4 Company was wounded just before relief took place.	

Army Form C. 2118.

WAR DIARY
of
INTELLIGENCE SUMMARY.
(Erase heading not required.)

July 1915.

Hour, Date, Place	Summary of Events and Information	Remarks and references to Appendices
13th	Battalion paraded at 10.30 a.m. for drill under Adjutant. Other parades under Company arrangement. Officer Commanding No. 3 Company today reported that, during the last six days of trench duty, his company had discovered the bodies of three men of the Battalion killed in action on 9th May last. Two of them were identified as 1631 Pte W. Coutts No 1. Coy. and 987 Pte. J. Hutchison No. 4. Coy. No proper identification of the third man could be established. The bodies were interred 200 yards behind front line trenches at N.9.C.9.10. Reference Map FRANCE and BELGIUM 3rd Edition Sheet 36 1/40,000. Tonight the Battalion supplied two working parties of 150 men each. 4 Officers found the Battalion this evening and	

Army Form C. 2118.

July 1915.

WAR DIARY
INTELLIGENCE SUMMARY.
(Erase heading not required.)

Hour, Date, Place	Summary of Events and Information	Remarks and references to Appendices
13th (continued).	and were taken on the strength and posted to Companies as follows:- Lieut. R.F.D. Bruce } to No. 1. Company. 2nd Lieut. I.S. Paterson } " " D.S. Guthrie - To No. 2. Company. " " G.S.M. Wilkie } To No. 3. Company. " " K.G. Yarrow } " " W.D. McBeth } To No. 4. Company. " " W. McIntyre }	
14th.	Parque an Yesterday. The gallantry of L/Cpl. H. Franks and Pte. D. Archer on 4th inst. was again referred to in Divisional Routine Orders for 12th July 1915, The G.O.C., 8th Division wishing it brought to the notice of the whole Division. Instructions were also received to have a special entry put in their Conduct Sheets K.R. 1919 (XIV) in commendation of their gallant efforts. Accordingly an extract from the Routine Orders/-	

WAR DIARY

July 1915.

Army Form C. 2118.

Hour, Date, Place	Summary of Events and Information	Remarks and references to Appendices
14th (continued).	Orders was published in to-day's Battalion Orders, issued yesterday evening. The weather which had been favorable for some time back, broke down this afternoon. A heavy fall of rain all afternoon and evening, rendering the roads in soft condition again.	
15th	The weather conditions were better today, the rain having stopped during the night. The Battalion paraded at 10 a.m. for a Route March. Other parades as yesterday. Captain T. LYELL having been transferred to England on 7th inst. was today struck off the strength of the Battalion from that date.	
16th	The Commanding Officer held an inspection of the Battalion at 10.30 a.m. today. Other parades as yesterday.	

Army Form C. 2118.

July 1915.

.13.

WAR DIARY

INTELLIGENCE SUMMARY.

(Erase heading not required.)

Instructions regarding War Diaries and Intelligence Summaries are contained in F.S. Regs., Part II. and the Staff Manual respectively. Title pages will be prepared in manuscript.

Hour, Date, Place	Summary of Events and Information	Remarks and references to Appendices
17th	The Battalion paraded at 10.30 a.m. for drill under the Adjutant. The Divisional Baths at SAILLY were having hours of 3 and 5 pm. No 1 and 4 Companies been allotted to the Battalion today between the paraded at 2 pm. under Captain McNAB for bathing occupying the Baths from 3 to 4 pm. and No 2 and 3 Companies at 3 pm. under Capt. MITCHELL occupying the Baths from 4 to 5 pm. A Working party of 200 men under the command of Captain W.L. MITCHELL was detailed from the Battalion tonight.	
18th	A Parade for Divine Service was held at 11 a.m. CHURCH of ENGLAND at 9 a.m. and ROMAN CATHOLICS at 8 a.m. The following appeared in Appointment, Commissions, and Rewards, List No. 37, dated 10th inst., received today:— "HONOURS and AWARDS":—	

14

July 1915

WAR DIARY

INTELLIGENCE SUMMARY.

(Erase heading not required.)

Army Form C. 2118.

Hour, Date, Place	Summary of Events and Information	Remarks and references to Appendices
18th (Continued).	"2nd Lieut. L.A. ELGOOD, 1/5th Battalion, ROYAL HIGHLANDERS, awarded the Military Cross." "APPOINTMENTS:- "2nd Lieut. J. KENNEDY (2nd Battalion, ROYAL HIGHLANDERS) 5th Battalion, ROYAL HIGHLANDERS granted the temporary rank of Captain whilst holding appointment as Adjutant. Dated 23rd April 1915." In accordance with instructions received from Brigade to supply one Company for a tour of trench duty with the 2nd Battalion NORTHAMPTON REGIMENT, No. 1 Company was detailed for this duty and proceeded to the trenches tonight.	
19th	Parades today were held as under:- 6.30am. - Physical training with arms and Musketry instruction. 10 a.m. - Route March. 2.30 p.m. Lecture by O.C., Companies on "Duties of Guards and Sentries". Two Working Parties, consisting of 120 men under the Command of Captain G.S. RAE and 100 men under the Command of Captain W.L. MITCHELL were detailed from the remainder of the Battalion tonight. /-	

July 1915.

WAR DIARY

INTELLIGENCE SUMMARY.

(Erase heading not required.)

Army Form C. 2118.

Hour, Date, Place	Summary of Events and Information	Remarks and references to Appendices
20th	Parades today were held as under:— 10 a.m. Adjutant's parade for drill. 2 p.m. Under Company arrangements for instruction in Bayonet Fighting.	
21st	As Yesterday, with the exception that a parade was held this morning at 6.30 a.m. under Company arrangements for Running drill. Two Working Parties consisting of 4 N.C.Os. and 150 men under the Command of Captain G.S. RAE and 4 N.C.Os. and 100 men under the Command of Captain W.L. MITCHELL respectively, were supplied by the Battalion tonight, including 30 men from Grenadier Coy.	
22nd	Parades today were held as under:— 10 a.m. Adjutant's parade for drill. 2 p.m. Instruction in Bayonet Fighting under Company arrangements.	

Army Form C. 2118.

July 1915.

WAR DIARY

INTELLIGENCE SUMMARY.

(Erase heading not required.)

Hour, Date, Place	Summary of Events and Information	Remarks and references to Appendices
23rd	Parades today were:- 6.30 a.m. Running drill under Company arrangements. 10 a.m. Route March. 2.30 p.m. Lecture by O.C. Companies. Two Working Parties were supplied by the Battalion tonight as follows:- 4 N.C.Os. and 150 men under the command of Captain G.S. RAE and 4 N.C.Os. and 100 men under the command of Captain W.L. MITCHELL, including 30 men from Transport. 1 man was killed and 1 man accidentally injured with pick. Parades were held as on 22nd inst. with the exception that the 2 p.m. parade was for Musketry instruction.	
24th	No.1 Company having completed their tour of trench duty with the 2nd NORTHANTS, returned to their former billets tonight. No casualties. Last to be recorded during their six days in the trenches.	
25th	The Battalion paraded for Divine Service as under:- Presbyterians at 10 a.m. in Orchard adjoining Headquarters. Roman Catholics at 8.15 a.m., under the Officer for Duty, for service in Catholic Church, SAILLY. Sn/.	

July 1915.

Army Form C. 2118.

WAR DIARY
INTELLIGENCE SUMMARY.
(Erase heading not required.)

Hour, Date, Place	Summary of Events and Information	Remarks and references to Appendices
25th (continued).	In accordance with instructions received from Brigade, to provide a fatigue party for work at Brigade Machine Gun Range, G.36.a. 2 N.C.Os. and 20 men were detailed from No. 2 Company and proceed there today. Tonight the Battalion supplied three Working Parties of 6 N.C.Os. and 136 men, 2 N.C.Os. and 64 men and 3 N.C.Os. and 50 men respectively.	
26th	The Battalion paraded today as under:- 6.30 am. Physical training under Company arrangements 10 am. Adjutant's Parade 2 pm. Instruction in Bayonet fighting under Company arrangements. Another four Officers joined the Battalion today and were taken on the Strength and were posted as follows:- Captain A.H.M. WEDDERBURN to No. 2 Company as O.C. Company. " J.A. MOFFAT to No. 4 " as O.C. " Lieut. J.M.S. DUKE to No. 2 " ; and 2nd Lieut. A. HANDYSIDE to No. 3 " Today and yesterday all N.C.Os. and men	

Army Form C. 2118.

/ 18 /

WAR DIARY
of
INTELLIGENCE SUMMARY.

July 1915

(Erase heading not required.)

Hour, Date, Place	Summary of Events and Information	Remarks and references to Appendices
26th (continued)	2 Nos. 1 and 2 Companies who had never been inoculated twice were inoculated for the second time by the Medical Officer.	
27th	The Battalion paraded as yesterday, the 2 p.m. parade being for instruction in Fire Control and Direction. Nos. 3 and 4 Companies provided a Working Party tonight of 100 men; 1 man wounded. Parades as yesterday.	
28th	Nos. 3 and 4 Companies paraded at 2pm. today, with the exception of those who had previously been inoculated twice, for inoculation by the Medical Officer. Tonight Nos. 1 and 2 Companies provided Working Parties consisting of 2 N.C.Os. and 50 men from each Company. This afternoon Inter-Battalion Sports were held at ESTAIRES the 2nd, 4th and 5th Battalions of the BLACK WATCH taking part in the proceedings. Over 80 competitors entered from the Battalion, for the different events, with very successful results. They	

-19-

= July 1915 =

WAR DIARY
or
INTELLIGENCE SUMMARY.
(Erase heading not required.)

Army Form C. 2118.

Hour, Date, Place	Summary of Events and Information	Remarks and references to Appendices
28th (continued)	They gained out of a total prize-list of 33 for 14 events, the very creditable total of 13 prizes. Officers, N.C.Os. and men figured in the following events with success:- Swimming Race 2nd Prize; 100 yards Race 1st Prize; Life-Saving 3rd Prize; Jacket and Cap Race 1st, 2nd, 4th & 6th prizes; Quarter Mile Race 1st & 2nd Prizes, Three-legged Race 1st & 3rd Prizes. The Battalion also won the Officers v. N.C.Os. Relay Race and the five-a-side competition. Considering the short time the competitors had at their disposal to prepare themselves, their performance today has given great satisfaction, and proved their fitness, and the good physical condition of the Battalion as a whole, after many months of strenuous campaigning.	
29th	Today parades were held as under:— 6.30 a.m. Bayonet Fighting under Company Officers. 10 a.m. Adjutants parade for Battalion drill. 2 p.m. Instruction in trench digging under Coy. Officers. The Battalion furnished a working party tonight of 150 men.	

20.

= July 1915. =

WAR DIARY

INTELLIGENCE SUMMARY.

(Erase heading not required.)

Army Form C. 2118.

Hour, Date, Place	Summary of Events and Information	Remarks and references to Appendices
30th	Parades were held today as under:- 6.30 a.m. As yesterday. 10 a.m. Route March. 2.30 p.m. Musketry instructions under O.C. Companies. A Working Party consisting of 2 N.C.Os and 50 men was furnished tonight by the Battalion.	
31st	The Battalion paraded today at 6.30 a.m. for Physical training. A party of 10 men detailed from the Battalion under the charge of 2nd Lieut. W.W. Ford. paraded at 10.45 a.m. today for the purpose of witnessing a demonstration of the uses of the "WEST Bomb-throwing Catapult" to be given by the inventor, Captain WEST, at 23rd Infantry Brigade Grenade School, BARLETTE FARM, (H.26.a) at 11.30 a.m. This evening in accordance with 24th Infantry Brigade Operation Order No. 28 dated 29th inst. the Battalion handed over the billets they had occupied during the month and proceeded/-	

Army Form C. 2118.

= July 1915. =

WAR DIARY

INTELLIGENCE SUMMARY.

(Erase heading not required.)

Instructions regarding War Diaries and Intelligence Summaries are contained in F. S. Regs., Part II. and the Staff Manual respectively. Title pages will be prepared in manuscript.

Hour, Date, Place	Summary of Events and Information	Remarks and references to Appendices
31st (continued).	Proceeded to the trenches for a further tour of trench duty, taking over Subsection 3.S., No 3 Section trenches from 2nd MIDDLESEX REGIMENT and Subsections 4.P. and 4.Q. T (No. 4 Section) from 2nd MIDDLESEX REGIMENT and No. 3 Section Head-Quarters from 2nd Battalion SCOTTISH RIFLES, 2 Platoons of the 1st WORCESTERS being in Support in Subsection 3.R. + 6 platoons of East Lancashire Reg. in support at CROIX BLANCHE. Nugent Blair Imrie Lieut-Col., Commanding 1/5th Bn. The Black Watch 3rd August 1915.	

8th, Division.

24th, Brigade.

I/5th, Black Watch.

August, 1915.

121/6737

S.G
20th Aug?

8th Division

1/5th Royal H.W
Vol VIII
August 15

August 1915.

Army Form C. 2118.

WAR DIARY
INTELLIGENCE SUMMARY.
(Erase heading not required.)

Hour, Date, Place	Summary of Events and Information	Remarks and references to Appendices
1st	As Yesterday. Very quiet and weather Good. The Brigade Commander inspected the lines this morning at 1.15 am. Base this evening and 11 men arrived from the and posted to their former Companies.	
2nd	As Yesterday. 2nd Lieut. G.S.M. WILKIE, No 3 Company, was severely wounded in the head today, while in the act of firing over the parapet with one of the men's rifles. Lieut. JOHN POLSON DAVIDSON, R.A.M.C., having been posted to take charge of the Medical and Sanitary duties, joined the Battalion tonight, and was taken on the strength. One of our snipers having taken up a position in rear of trenches, reported having dispersed an enemy working party, working on their wire under cover of a screen opposite our position.	
3rd	As Yesterday. Today the weather was very changeable and occasional heavy showers of rain rendered the trenches in a muddy condition. Lieut. F.W. MILNE, R.A.M.C. who had performed the duties of Medical Officer to the Battalion since 27th March:-	

Army Form C. 2118.

= August 1915. =
WAR DIARY
INTELLIGENCE SUMMARY.
(Erase heading not required.)

Instructions regarding War Diaries and Intelligence Summaries are contained in F.S. Regs., Part II. and the Staff Manual respectively. Title pages will be prepared in manuscript.

Hour, Date, Place	Summary of Events and Information	Remarks and references to Appendices
3rd (continued)	27th March 1915, left the Battalion this evening, having received instructions to report himself at No. 18 General Hospital, ETAPLES for duty. The duties of Medical Officer and Sanitary Officer were taken over by LIEUT. J. P. DAVIDSON today.	
4th	As Yesterday. Weather slightly improved during the day. Intimation was received this morning of the death of 2ND LIEUT. G. S. M. WILKIE from wounds received on the 2nd inst. Two bodies, both believed to be men of the Battalion killed on 9th May last, were discovered today at rear of trenches held by 2ND. NORTHANTS. A burial party consisting of 1 N.C.O. and 4 men from No. 1. Coy. buried the bodies this evening 150 yards behind firing line at N.9.a.9.4. On identification, one of the bodies, from the effects found on his person, proved to be that of 2580 Pte. D. MUIR, No. 2 Coy., the other body was unidentified, but from the uniform worn by the soldier, he appears to have been attached to some Regular Battalion. A Field / -	

Army Form C. 2118.

3/

= August 1915. =

WAR DIARY
or
INTELLIGENCE SUMMARY.
(Erase heading not required.)

Instructions regarding War Diaries and Intelligence Summaries are contained in F. S. Regs., Part II. and the Staff Manual respectively. Title pages will be prepared in manuscript.

Hour, Date, Place	Summary of Events and Information	Remarks and references to Appendices
4th (continued).	A Field General Court-Martial assembled today at EAST LANCS Headquarters at 10 a.m. for the trial of No. 2590 Pte. C. DONAGHEY and 2851 Pte. A. McCORD, both of No. 4 Company. The former having committed an offence under Army Act Section 6 (1.g), and the latter, offences under Army Act Section 6 (1.g) and (1.h). In accordance with 24th Infantry Brigade Operation Order No. 29 dated 4th inst., the Battalion was relieved tonight in 3S, H.P. and H.Q. and at French Headquarters by 2nd. Bn. EAST LANCS, and occupied billets on the road leading from RUE BIACHE to DU QUESNOY, H.19 and 25. Battalion Headquarters were established at 3E.25.d.9.8.	
5th.	The funeral of the late 2nd Lieut. WILKIE to Merville Cemetery was attended by Captain Rae and the officers of No. 3 Company today. Inspections / Inspections /	

Army Form C. 2118.

H — August 1918 —

WAR DIARY
INTELLIGENCE SUMMARY
(Erase heading not required.)

Hour, Date, Place	Summary of Events and Information	Remarks and references to Appendices
5th (continued)	Inspections of equipment and rifles were held today under Company arrangements. At a parade of the Battalion held at 2 p.m. the sentences of the Court held on 4th inst. for the trial of Ptes. DONAGHEY and McCORD, were promulgated, Pte. DONAGHEY being awarded 6 months imprisonment with Hard Labour and Pte. McCORD one year with Hard Labour.	
6th	Parades were held today as under:— 6:30 a.m. Physical Training under Coy. arrangements. 10 a.m. Parade for drill under the Adjutant. 2 p.m. Drill under Company arrangements. A Working/—	

5.

August 1915.

Army Form C. 2118.

WAR DIARY

INTELLIGENCE SUMMARY

(Erase heading not required.)

Instructions regarding War Diaries and Intelligence Summaries are contained in F. S. Regs., Part II. and the Staff Manual respectively. Title pages will be prepared in manuscript.

Hour, Date, Place	Summary of Events and Information	Remarks and references to Appendices
6th (continued).	A Working Party of 150 men was furnished by the Battalion this evening.	
7th	Bands as Yesterday. A Working Party of 100 men was furnished by the Battalion this evening.	
8th	Divine Services were held today as under:- Church of Scotland:- in Orchard at Battalion Headquarters at 12 noon. Roman Catholics:- at Farm H.31.d.3/2. Sheet 36, near Rue Du-Quesnes, at 9 a.m. Major R. THORNTON R.A.M.C. (T.F.) quite unexpectedly joined the Battalion today to take over the duties of Medical and Sanitary Officer, LIEUT. J.P. DAVIDSON, present Medical Officer, remaining with the Battalion for several days to instruct MAJOR THORNTON in his new duties. One of|.	

= August 1915 =

WAR DIARY

INTELLIGENCE SUMMARY.
(Erase heading not required.)

Army Form C. 2118.

Hour, Date, Place	Summary of Events and Information	Remarks and references to Appendices
8th (continued)	One of the men of No. 1 Coy. was accidentally wounded in the leg with a bullet from the incinerator at the rear of billet.	
	In accordance with Brigade Operation Order No. 30 dated 7th August 1915, The Battalion as a Unit of the Brigade, left their present billets this evening, and took over the billets allotted them in RUE DE BRUGES previously occupied by 2nd Battalion WEST YORK'S, the Brigade being in Divisional Reserve from 9th inst.	
9th	Battalion Headquarters were established at G24.c.6/8. The Divisional Baths SAILLY, having been allotted to the use of the Battalion today from 7a.m. to 12 noon, the companies bathed at intervals during this period for bathing purposes.	
	The Battalion paraded at 2 p.m. under Coy. arrangement. A working party of 200 men was provided by the Battalion this evening.	
10th	The Battalion paraded today as under:- 10 a.m. Adjutants Parade for drill. 2 p.m. Conferrer at disposal of O.S.C. Companies.	
	Lieutenant General	

WAR DIARY
INTELLIGENCE SUMMARY.
(Erase heading not required.)

August 1915

Army Form C. 2118.

Hour, Date, Place	Summary of Events and Information	Remarks and references to Appendices
10th (Continued)	Lieutenant General Sir W.P.PULTENEY. K.C.B. D.S.O. Commanding 3rd Army Corps made a tour of inspection of the Brigade today, visiting the Battalion at 3.30 pm and inspecting the different billets occupied by the Companies, who were also inspected outside their respective billets. The General was very satisfied with all he had inspected.	
11th	Parades were held today as under :- 6.30 a.m. Physical training. 10 a.m. Adjutant's Parade for drill. 2 p.m. Musketry Instruction under Coy. Arrangements. Lieut. J.P.DAVIDSON, Temporary Medical Officer, having received instructions to report himself for duty with the 2ND. Battalion LINCOLN REGIMENT left the Battalion today.	
12th	The 30 yards range at G.18.C.3.4. was allotted to the Battalion today for Musketry Practice as follows :- 6 a.m. to 7.30 a.m. No. 1 Company. 7.30 a.m. to 9 a.m. No. 2 Company. 9 a.m. to 10 a.m. No. 3 Company. 10 a.m. to 11 a.m. No. 4 Company.	

//= August 1915 =

WAR DIARY

INTELLIGENCE SUMMARY.
(Erase heading not required.)

Army Form C. 2118.

Instructions regarding War Diaries and Intelligence Summaries are contained in F.S. Regs, Part II. and the Staff Manual respectively. Title pages will be prepared in manuscript.

Hour, Date, Place		Summary of Events and Information	Remarks and references to Appendices
12th (continued)		A Field General Court Martial assembled today at the Headquarters of 1st Battalion SHERWOOD FORESTERS, G.30.a.2.1. at 11 a.m. for the trial of No 11½ Corporal T. WILLMOTT, No 14 Company, for an offence under Army Act(s)(2).	
13th		Parades were held today as on 11th inst. The shooting Range was allotted to the Machine Gun Detachment between the hours of 11 a.m. and 2 p.m. today. As arranged, the recently formed Divisional Band played a select programme of music, in the Orchard adjoining Battalion Headquarters, this evening, between the hours of 5 and 7 p.m. The music was much appreciated by all ranks present.	
14th		Parades were held today as under:— 6.30 a.m. Bayonet fighting under Coy Arrangements. Other parades as yesterday. At the Divisional Horse Show held at Sailly this afternoon from /—	

Army Form C. 2118.

WAR DIARY
or
INTELLIGENCE SUMMARY.
(Erase heading not required.)

August 1915.

Hour, Date, Place	Summary of Events and Information	Remarks and references to Appendices
14th (Continued)	From 2 to 5 p.m. the Battalion gained three first prizes for "best pack animal", "best heavy draught horse", and "single horse turnout" respectively. The sentence of the court held on 12th inst. for the trial of No. 1192 Corporal T. WILLMOTT was promulgated today, Corporal WILLMOTT being reduced to the ranks.	
15th	Divine Services were held today as under:— CHURCH OF SCOTLAND:- at 10 a.m. in the field adjoining Battalion Headquarters. ROMAN CATHOLICS at 8.15 a.m. at Battalion Headquarters under Coy. S.M. D. BURGESS for service in SAILLY Church at 9 a.m. Owing to the unsettled state of the weather today, the Church Service at 10 a.m. had to be cancelled.	
16th	5 Officers and 115 Other Ranks attended a Gas Demonstration given by Lieut. McCROMBIE, Gas Expert, 1st ARMY, today at THE PASTURE POST at 11.30 a.m. Parades today were as under:— 6.30 a.m. Physical Training —	

WAR DIARY

~~INTELLIGENCE SUMMARY.~~
(Erase heading not required.)

Army Form C. 2118.

= August 1915. =

Hour, Date, Place	Summary of Events and Information	Remarks and references to Appendices
16th (continued).	6:30 a.m. Physical Training under Coy. arrangements. 10 a.m. Adjutant's Parade for drill. This evening the 24th INFANTRY BRIGADE's period in Divisional Reserve expired, and the Battalion in accordance with Brigade Operation Order No. 31 dated 15th inst. moved from present billets No.1 and 2 Companies, under the Command of Captain McNAB and Captain WEDDERBURN respectively took over portion front line trenches in Nº 4 SECTION from 1ST LONDON REGIMENT namely from BOUTILLERIE communication trench exclusive in Sub-section H.Q. to left of Sub-section H.R. One platoon, 20 men strong, was detailed to occupy BOTTLEY POST from No. 2 Company. Trench Headquarters were established at A.LA.TRANQUILLITÉ. H.34.d.9/6. No. 3 Company garrisoned CROIX MARECHAL POST with No. 4 Company in reserve in farm at H.21.a.3.3. Battalion Headquarters being established in large farm at H.20.d.7/6. RUE BIACHE and Brigade Headquarters at H.21.c.9.9.	

Army Form C. 2118.

= August 1915 =

WAR DIARY

INTELLIGENCE SUMMARY.
(Erase heading not required.)

Hour, Date, Place	Summary of Events and Information	Remarks and references to Appendices
17th	As Yesterday. No 3 Company provided a Working Party of 50 men this morning.	
18th	As Yesterday. No 3 and 4 Companies provided a Working Party of 100 men this morning. While several of the signallers were running out telephone wire this afternoon, at rear of trenches, the Sergeant Signaller in charge was severely wounded by an enemy sniper. One man of No. 1 Company was slightly injured in the head with a pick while working in the trenches this evening but remained at duty. In accordance with Brigade Operation Order No. 32 dated 18th inst. the line was re-adjusted this evening. Nos. 1 and 2 Companies were relieved in Sub section H.Q. up to the point where BOUTILLERIE Communication Trench meets Front Trench (west of the GRANDE RUE de la BOUTILLERIE) and in BOUTLERY Post by the 1st WORCESTERS and took over/-	

= August 1915. =

WAR DIARY

INTELLIGENCE SUMMARY.
(Erase heading not required.)

Army Form C. 2118.

Hour, Date, Place	Summary of Events and Information	Remarks and references to Appendices
18th (continued)	and took over part of the trench from the cabin of 3 S to DEAD DOG AVENUE (exclusive) and the Machine Gun Section took over the Machine Gun in left of 3 R from The 7th MIDDLESEX and the 2ND. SCOTTISH RIFLES respectively French Headquarters remaining at A LA TRANQUILITE.	
19th	As Yesterday. One man wounded No. 1 Company. No. 4 Coy. occupied the Brigade Reserve Range at G.I.&.c. 36. for Musketry Practice today, between the hours of 2pm and 4pm.	
20th	As Yesterday. In accordance with Battalion Operation Order of today's date, No. 1 and 2 Companies were relieved in the trenches this evening, by No. 3 and 4 Companies under the command of Captains MITCHELL and MOFFAT respectively. No. 1 Company occupying the billet previously occupied by No. 4 Company and No. 2 Company taking over CROIX MARÉCHAL POST previously garrisoned by	

/ August 1915

Army Form C. 2118.

WAR DIARY

INTELLIGENCE SUMMARY

(Erase heading not required.)

Hour, Date, Place	Summary of Events and Information	Remarks and references to Appendices
20th (Continued)	Garrisoned by No.3 Company. During their tour of trenches duty for the past four days No.1 and 2 Companies experienced a very quiet time, there being nothing to report.	
21st	As Yesterday. No.2 Company provided a Working Party of 50 men this morning for work under 2nd Field Company R.E. Two men of No.1 Coy. were admitted to hospital sick. No.1 Company were at the Brigade Reserve Range at G.18.C.36. this morning between the hours of 9 and 11 a.m. for Musketry Practice. Two of the enemy were shot by one of the Battalion Snipers this morning, from sniping post at N.5.a.8.1. These two men were seen working on a suspected machine gun emplacement at N.11.a.7.5. The night being very quiet some new loopholes were constructed.	
22nd	Dispositions as yesterday. Church Service.	

1 August 1915.

Army Form C. 2118.

WAR DIARY

INTELLIGENCE SUMMARY.
(Erase heading not required.)

Hour, Date, Place	Summary of Events and Information	Remarks and references to Appendices
2nd (continued)	Church Spruce was held at No.1 Coy's billets at 10 a.m. No. 1150 Pte. A. Nicoll of No. 4 Coy. reported having seen one of the enemy working on parapet opposite 3.S.2. at 11.20 a.m. this morning and that he accounted for him with a shot from sniping rifle. Scheme for firing on enemy's roads, devised by 2nd Lieut. YARROW in command of the Sniping Section of the left half battalion, was put into operation this evening. Suitable positions having been selected and constructed for this night firing fire was directed mainly on the road leading to FERME DE LA MARLAGUE. Work done — Snipers posts improved and alternative positions constructed. Another German was observed, this afternoon by our Snipers working at back of enemy trench about Point 84 (N.10.6.9.3) but was out of range of effective rifle fire. He also presented a difficult target, wearing a white coat and black cap against a background of sandbags of similar colours. One of our aeroplanes was brought down by the enemy at 5.10 p.m.	

= August 1915. =

15

Army Form C. 2118.

WAR DIARY
INTELLIGENCE SUMMARY.
(Erase heading not required.)

Instructions regarding War Diaries and Intelligence Summaries are contained in F.S. Regs., Part II. and the Staff Manual respectively. Title pages will be prepared in manuscript.

Hour, Date, Place	Summary of Events and Information	Remarks and references to Appendices
22nd (Continued)	At 5.10 p.m. this evening 1 of/spire 3R, falling within their lines. Dispositions as yesterday.	
23rd	During the night 22nd–23rd firing was kept up by our snipers on the BOIS MAISNIL – LE TOUQUET road and on the road stated yesterday. One of our snipers hit one of enemy's periscopes this morning. Work done:— firing positions constructed for night firing in 1872 and southern continuation of scheme. Enemy were very quiet during the day in consequence of which our snipers were inactive.	
24th	Dispositions as yesterday. No. 1 Company were out for a route march this morning. Very quiet day with Companies in trenches, nothing unusual happening. In the ordinary course Nos. 3 and 4 Companies should have been relieved from trench duty this evening by Nos. 1 and 2 Companies, but information having been received that the Brigade would be relieved on 26th inst. it was decided that they should remain in the trenches until that date.	
25th	As yesterday. No. 1 Company provided a Working Party this morning of 20 men. One man	

= August 1915. =

WAR DIARY

INTELLIGENCE SUMMARY.
(Erase heading not required.)

Army Form C. 2118.

Hour, Date, Place	Summary of Events and Information	Remarks and references to Appendices
25th (continued)	One man of Machine Gun Section was killed this morning while in the act of washing himself and one of No. 4 Company's snipers seriously wounded in the head, otherwise nothing unusual occurred during the day. Dispositions as yesterday.	
26th	No. 1 Company and all d employed men paraded at 9 a.m. for bathing purposes, the Divisional Baths, SAILLY, having been allotted to the Battalion today. Orders having been received from the Brigade that the Brigade relief would not take place this evening No. 1 and 2 Companies relieved No. 3 and 4 Companies in the trenches in accordance with Battalion Operation Order dated 25th inst. No. 4 Company took over CROIX MARECHAL POST and No. 3 Coy. the reserve billets vacated by No. 1 Company. Dispositions as yesterday.	
27th	The Companies stationed in the trenches experienced a very quiet time today & nothing unusual happening. As yesterday.	
28th	2nd Lieut. J.W. HUSBAND joined the Battalion today from the 2/5th Battalion, was taken on the strength and posted to No. 3 Company for duty. No. 3 Company were at Brigade Reserve Range at G.18.c.3.b. today between the hours /—	

Army Form C. 2118.

= August 1915. =

WAR DIARY

INTELLIGENCE SUMMARY.
(Erase heading not required.)

Instructions regarding War Diaries and Intelligence Summaries are contained in F.S. Regs., Part II. and the Staff Manual respectively. Title pages will be prepared in manuscript.

Hour, Date, Place	Summary of Events and Information	Remarks and references to Appendices
28th (Continued).	Between the hours of 2 and 5 p.m. for Musketry Practice. Nothing unusual occurred during the day and the two Companies in the trenches spent another quiet day.	
29th	As Yesterday. No 3 Company and Machine Gun Reserve team billeted at Battalion Headquarters paraded for Divine Service at No. 3 Company's billet at 10.30 a.m. today. 2 N.C.O.s and 1 man of No. 3 Company and 1 man of No. 2 Company proceeded to the Base today to be discharged, their period of engagement having expired. The two Companies in the trenches again experienced a quiet day.	
30th	As yesterday. No 3 Company paraded for a route march at 10 a.m. 2nd Lieut. J.C. FORSYTH joined the Battalion today from 2/5th Battalion, was taken on the strength and posted to No. 1 Company for duty. The Companies in the trenches again experienced a quiet day. The usual night firing was carried on at intervals between 8 and 10 p.m. and Machine Gun fire was opened on the road BAS MAISNIL and made junction N.12.a.1.2. One man of

= August 1915 =

WAR DIARY
INTELLIGENCE SUMMARY.
(Erase heading not required.)

Army Form C. 2118.

Hour, Date, Place	Summary of Events and Information	Remarks and references to Appendices
30th (continued)	One man of No.1 Company was slightly injured in the face with the bolt of his rifle while firing. As yesterday.	
31st	No.3 Company paraded this morning at 10a.m. for a route march. The two companies in trenches experienced a quiet time during the day but in the evening the enemy were more active and exploded a mine short of No.2 Section trenches with little effect, nothing further resulted. No.3 Company provided a Working Party of 50 men this evening for work under 2nd Field Company R.E.	

SUMMARY OF FIGHTING STRENGTH.

```
                                    O.    O.R.
Fighting Strength at beginning of month   28    474.
         "          "       "    end     27    446.
```

WAR DIARY
INTELLIGENCE SUMMARY

(Erase heading not required.)

Army Form C. 2118.

August 1915.

Hour, Date, Place	Summary of Events and Information	Remarks and references to Appendices
31st (continued).	**SUMMARY OF CASUALTIES &c during month.** **Killed.** / **Wounded.** / **Hospital Admissions.** / **Total.** Died of Wounds O. O.R. / O. O.R. / O. O.R. / O. O.R. 1. 1. / *. 6. / Nil. 74. / 2. 81. * 3 slight, remained at duty. + 48 returned to duty. Great prevalence of Scabies during month, 75% of hospital cases being due to this complaint, which seems to originate from lack of vegetable meat. **SUMMARY OF CASUALTIES since Battalion disembarked 2-11-14.** **Killed.** / **Wounded.** / **Missing.** / **Hospital Admissions less returned to duty** / **TOTAL.** Died of Wounds & Disease O. O.R. / O. O.R. / O. O.R. / O. O.R. / O. O.R. 3. 84. / 19. 310. / Nil. 5. / 5. 307. / 27. 701. With reference to above figures, 4 Officers were only slightly wounded and remained at duty and 1 Officer returned to duty after treatment. Of the 310 Other Ranks wounded, 31 were slight and remained at duty, and 70 returned to duty after treatment for hospital in this country, the remainder were all transferred to England with a few exceptions, the same remark applies to the figure under the heading "Hospital Admissions". Regarding the figures under "Hospital Admissions" to obtain the	

August 1915.

Army Form C. 2118.

WAR DIARY
INTELLIGENCE SUMMARY.
(Erase heading not required.)

Hour, Date, Place	Summary of Events and Information	Remarks and references to Appendices
31st (continued)	to obtain the true total that really have been admitted, those returned to duty after treatment in this Country must be added, namely 4 Officers and 272 Other Ranks. It may be mentioned that of the total of 84 Other Ranks under the heading "KILLED etc" only 1 died of disease.	

4th September 1915.

McCrae Captain,
for Lieut.-Col.,
Comdg. 15th B. The Black Watch.

<u>8th. Division.</u>

<u>24th. Brigade.</u>

<u>I/5th. Black Watch.</u>

<u>September, 1915.</u>

8th Dragoons

1/5th Royal West
Kent IX
Sep 15.

28/10/15

September 1915.

WAR DIARY

INTELLIGENCE SUMMARY.
(Erase heading not required.)

Army Form C. 2118.

Hour, Date, Place	Summary of Events and Information	Remarks and references to Appendices
1st	As yesterday. Nothing unusual occurred during the day. In accordance with Brigade Operation Order No. 34 dated 30th August 1915 and Battalion Operation Order No. 2 dated 31st August 1915, the Brigade went into Reserve, and the Battalion as part of the Brigade was relieved in the trenches and defences, both by 1st Battalion LONDON REGIMENT, and at Battalion Head-Quarters and reserve billet, Rue Biache, by 8th Battalion MIDDLESEX REGIMENT, and took over Rue De Bruges reserve billets from 1st LONDON REGIMENT as formerly occupied from 8th to 19th August 1915, with the same Battalion Head-Quarters. No casualties occurred during relief.	
2nd	The companies were engaged today completing deficiencies in ammunition etc., and cleaning equipment, rifle inspection being held in the afternoon. The Adjutant, Captain Kennedy J. whilst proceeding back to Battalion, met with a mishap on the way, the horse	

September 1915

WAR DIARY
INTELLIGENCE SUMMARY
(Erase heading not required.)

Army Form C. 2118.

Hour, Date, Place		Summary of Events and Information	Remarks and references to Appendices
2nd (contd.)		horse stumbling and severely crushing his left foot. He was removed to Hospital to-day. The Battalion this morning provided a Working Party of 100 men. 1 man, stretcher-bearer, wounded. Parades were held to-day as under:—	
3rd	7 a.m.	Bayonet Fighting	
	9-30 a.m.	Route March.	
	2 p.m.	Parade under Company arrangements. This morning No 1 Coy. provided a Working Party of 50 men but owing to the unsettled state of the weather very little work could be done.	
4th		Parades were held to-day as yesterday. A draft of 48 Other Ranks joined the Battalion to-day, consisting of 41 from 3/5th BLACK WATCH and 7 from Base. The Draft was taken on the strength and posted as follows:—	

Army Form C. 2118.

September 1915
WAR DIARY

INTELLIGENCE SUMMARY.
(Erase heading not required.)

Hour, Date, Place	Summary of Events and Information	Remarks and references to Appendices
4th (contd)	1 N.C.O. and 19 men to No 2 Coy.	
	1 man to No 1 Coy.	
	1 N.C.O. and 12 men to No 3 Coy.	
	1 N.C.O. and 13 men to No 4 Coy.	
	1 N.C.O. and 4 O.R. were admitted to hospital to-day sick.	
	The Divisional Band paid another visit to the Battalion Headquarters this evening, arrangements having been made to play a selected programme of music between 4 p.m. and 6 p.m. in the Orchard at séfte. Unfortunately the weather conditions prevented the Bandsmen playing, heavy showers of rain falling all day.	
	The Brigade Reserve Range was allotted to the Battalion to-day, and No 1 Coy. were at the Range from 2 p.m. to 4 p.m. and 5 p.m. to 7 p.m. to 8 a.m. for musketry practice	
5th	The Battalion paraded for Divine Service as under :—	
	Church of England. 8 a.m. for Communion Service in Cemetery	
	Military Church, BAC ST. MAUR.	

Army Form C. 2118.

October 1915

WAR DIARY
OF
INTELLIGENCE SUMMARY.
(Erase heading not required.)

Instructions regarding War Diaries and Intelligence Summaries are contained in F.S. Regs., Part II. and the Staff Manual respectively. Title pages will be prepared in manuscript.

Hour, Date, Place		Summary of Events and Information	Remarks and references to Appendices
5th (cont.)	Church of England Head-Quarters. Roman Catholics Church.	11 a.m. in Orchard adjoining Battalion. 9 a.m. for service in BAC ST. MAUR Catholic Church. 1 Man was admitted to Hospital sick to-day, and 3 rejoined.	
6-		To-day the Battalion paraded as on 4th inst. No 2 Coy. provided a Working Party of 20 men this morning under 15th Field Coy. R.E.s. 1 man was admitted to Hospital sick to-day.	
7-		5 O.R. were admitted to Hospital sick to-day. Parades were held to-day at 7a.m. 10a.m. and 2p.m. under Coy. arrangements, the 10 a.m. parade being for practice in extended Order Drill. No 3 Coy. provided a Working Party of 1 N.C.O. and 25 men at 9 a.m. this morning for work under 1st HOME COUNTIES FIELD COY. R.E. 2nd Lieut. J.W. HUSBAND being in command of the party. The Brigade Reserve Range was allotted to the Battalion to-day for musketry practice between the hours of 11a.m. and 2p.m. Nos. 2, 3, and 4 Coys. occupying the Range productively for 1 hour.	

WAR DIARY
INTELLIGENCE SUMMARY

September 1915.

Army Form C. 2118.

Hour, Date, Place	Summary of Events and Information	Remarks and references to Appendices
7th (cont'd)	A Working Party of 100 men was provided by the Battalion this evening. 1 man of No. 3 Company being seriously wounded. 1 Officer and 3 O.R. were admitted to Hospital to-day sick, and 5 O.R. returned from Hospital.	
8th	As yesterday. The C.O. inspected the Battalion at 11-30 a.m. The Brigadier-General, Commanding 24th INFANTRY BRIGADE inspected the Draft which joined in 4th inst. at Battalion Headquarters at 10 a.m. A Working Party of 50 O.R. was provided by the Battalion this morning. The Machine Gun Detachment was at the Brigade Reserve Range to-day for practice, from 11 a.m. to 2 p.m. The Divisional Baths, SAILLY having been allotted to the Battalion to-day for bathing purpose, the Companies occupied same as follows:- 2 to 3 p.m. No. 1 Coy, 3 to 4 p.m. No. 2 Coy, 4 to 5 p.m. No. 3 Coy, 5 to 6 p.m. No. 4 Coy.	
9th	Parades were held to-day as on 3rd inst.	
10th	The Battalion was still resting. Pte PARKER wounded on the 7th inst., died of Wounds. Fine weather. Battalion still in billets. Parades as before.	

September 1915

WAR DIARY
INTELLIGENCE SUMMARY
(Erase heading not required.)

Army Form C. 2118.

Hour, Date, Place	Summary of Events and Information	Remarks and references to Appendices
11th	Battalion still in billets. Parades as before. C.S.O. boys paying particular attention to Physical Drill, jumping etc. Lieut. McINTYRE takes charge of bombing platoon. Blocking cartridges under box arrangements. Bombing platoon formed by 8 trained I.N.C.O. from each coy. Weather still fine. Working Party to day under Lieut. DUKE, carrying party no casualties.	
12th	Parades:- Church Parade at 10.30 a.m. Revd. Thomson says good-bye to officers and men as he was leaving for home on the 15th. Coys. were also at the Range.	
13th	Battalion still in billets, usual parades.	
14th	Battalion trained in Physical exercises, jumping etc. As yesterday. The Battalion Football team played the Sherwood Foresters and, after a very keen and exciting match, won 2-1. The whole team played well, and the match was played in a very friendly spirit.	
15th	As yesterday. The C.O. inspected 7th & 3rd Coys. in marching order and also inspected the Kit and	

September 1915.
WAR DIARY
INTELLIGENCE SUMMARY.

Army Form C. 2118.

Hour, Date, Place	Summary of Events and Information	Remarks and references to Appendices
15th (cont'd)	and contents of the packs. 2nd Lieut. FORSYTH was in charge of a small Working Party. Revd J. M. Clark, successor to Revd L. Thomson is taken on the strength of the Battalion. The Battalion goes into Brigade Reserve.	
16th	The Battalion paraded to-day as under:- 7 a.m. Physical Training under Coy. arrangements. 10 a.m. 1, 304 Coys. under Coy. arrangements. No 2 Coy. was inspected by the C.O. in Full Marching Order at 2 p.m., and No 1 Coy at 2-30 p.m. 3 O.R. were admitted to Hospital, sick, and 2 rejoined.	
17th	Parades were held to-day as under:- 7 a.m. Physical Training. 10 a.m. Instruction in Bombing & Blocking under Coy. arrangements. 2 p.m. Under Coy. arrangements. Machine Gun Section were at Brigade Reserve Range to-day from 2 p.m. for practice.	

WAR DIARY
INTELLIGENCE SUMMARY
(Erase heading not required.)

Army Form C. 2118.

September 1915

Hour, Date, Place	Summary of Events and Information	Remarks and references to Appendices
17th (contd)	No 583 Pte. A. McBride was sent to the Base to be discharged, his engagement expiring on 29th inst. 1 man admitted to Hospital sick, 3 rejoined	
18=	At yesterday. The Battalion was allotted the use of the Brigade Reserve Range, which was occupied as follows:- 2-3 a.m. by No 4 Coy, 3-4 p.m. by No 3 Coy, 4-5 p.m. by No 2 Coy, 5-6 p.m. by No 1 Coy. 2 men admitted to Hospital sick, 2 men rejoined from Hospital. 1 man of No 4 Coy. was accidentally wounded to-day with detonator of grenade at Brigade Bomb School.	
19th	Divine Service was held to-day as under:- 10 a.m. Church of England at NORTHANTS Headquarters, parade at No 4 Coys Billets. at 9-30 a.m. under Officer for duty. 10-30 a.m. Church of Scotland at Battalion Headquarters. 9 a.m. Roman Catholics in Bac ST MAUR Catholic Church, party paraded at No 1 Coys billets at 8.30 a.m. under 6 S.M. No 4 Coy. 1 man of No 3 Coy was wounded this morning with shrapnel from Anti-aircraft shell. 6 men admitted to Hospital sick, 1 rejoined. In accordance with instructions received from Brigade the Battalion left the billets in RUE DE BRUGES this evening and took over the front line trenches from WESTERN WALL of CONVENT to BOUTILLERIE ROAD (inclusive) from 1st SHERWOOD FORESTERS, Battalion Headquarters being established at RUE DAVID H.34.d.6.8.	
20=	Bn. in trenches - Breastworks were shelled by enemy, who had three direct hits on parapet but did little damage, no casualties.	

Army Form C. 2118.

WAR DIARY
INTELLIGENCE SUMMARY.
(Erase heading not required.)

September 1915.

Instructions regarding War Diaries and Intelligence Summaries are contained in F.S. Regs., Part II. and the Staff Manual respectively. Title pages will be prepared in manuscript.

Hour, Date, Place	Summary of Events and Information	Remarks and references to Appendices
20th (contd.)	Bn. was relieved by 1st SHERWOOD FORESTERS and marched back to billets in RUE DE BRUGES. Situation report, normal, enemy quiet. No casualties.	
21st	Bn. in billets. Parades as usual. Working parties continuing. 225 men were out at night. There were no casualties. First day of bombardment.	
22nd	As before. Bn. practising assault and bayonet charges. 25 men under 2nd Lieut. HUSBAND employed as working party under 15th Field Coy. R.E. Second day of bombardment.	
23rd	Bombardment of enemy's trenches increases. Bn. parades as before.	
24th	Bn. parades at 7 a.m. and 10 a.m. Physical training. At 7.56 p.m. the Bn. moves from RUE DE BRUGES and takes up assembly position in LIMIT POST. Weather dull, warm and inclining to rain. Bn. strength was as follows:- 20 Officers 400 Other Ranks.	
25th	At 4-25 a.m. the bombardment of the enemy's lines commenced together with demonstrations of smoke to represent gas on the right flank and at 4-30 a.m. the 25th Inf. Brigade assaulted the enemy's lines between the WELL FARM SALIENT and the BRIDOUX ROAD. At 6-50 a.m. orders were received for the Bn. Grenadier Platoon to report to 25th Inf. Brigade, & 2nd. Lieut. MACINTYRE proceeded with them in	

September 1915.

WAR DIARY
INTELLIGENCE SUMMARY.
(Erase heading not required.)

Army Form C. 2118.

Hour, Date, Place	Summary of Events and Information	Remarks and references to Appendices
25th (cont'd)	in fighting kit to 25th Brigade H.Q. at the TEMPLE of CITY ROAD where he received orders to report to O.C. 2nd BERKSHIRE REGT. in 1st line German trench and was given a guide. On arrival in the 1st line German trench LIEUT. MACINTYRE reported to O.C. 2nd BERKSHIRE REGT. and was sent to 2nd line trenches to bomb the ANGLE FORT. After throwing all their bombs the Platoon was forced to retire and LIEUT. MACINTYRE returned to the Battalion. At 9.28 a.m. 8th Division wired as follows:- "25th INF. BDE Bns. have all joined up in 2nd line". During the forenoon various wires were received from 1st Army and also from French G.H.Q. stating that attack by 47th, 15th, 1st, 7th & 2nd Divisions & also MEERUT Division were all progressing well. Wire received at 2.30 p.m. stated that French in CHAMPAGNE "maintained their progress and have made between seven & eight thousand prisoners." At the same time "1st Army had taken 2353 prisoners." At 12.49 p.m. an S.O.S. message was received from 24th Inf Bde. assumes H.Q. as follows:- "S.O.S. BRIDOUX FORT. The Bn. stood to arms. At 1-27 p.m. the following was received:- "Strong counter attacks have developed against the 25th Inf. Bde. in enemys trenches, but we are still holding enemys front line trenches." At 4-10 p.m. the following was received:- "S.O.S. both flanks RIFLE BDE." Again the Bn. stood to arms, but were not called upon. The 25th Inf. Bde. retired to former position in our front line trenches. Casualties during action: 5 wounded (mining) all bombers.	

Forms/C. 2118/10

Army Form C. 2118.

September 1915.
WAR DIARY
INTELLIGENCE SUMMARY.
(Erase heading not required.)

Hour, Date, Place	Summary of Events and Information	Remarks and references to Appendices
26th	Bn. in reserve behind first line breastwork. H.Q. at TEMPLE FARM. In afternoon Bn. was ordered to take over trenches held by SHERWOOD FORESTERS in the CONVENT WALL SECTION. Enemy quiet, but shelling behind the trenches.	
27th	Bn. in trenches - quiet. During the night 26/27th morning of the 27th frequent bursts of gun fire with machine gun and rifle fire were ordered. The enemy replying. Bn. relieved by 7th MIDDLESEX. We had no casualties. Bn. took over billets in RUE DE QUESNES and finding guards in FERRET, CAIN & ABEL posts. Bn. employed in clearing up arms & equipment after their trying time from the 25th - 28th, owing to trenches and avenues being in a very muddy state.	
28th	We found a working party of 150 men under Capt. WEDDERBURN. This party worked on the new line formed after the attacks on the 25th.	
29th	Bn. found working party of 100 men under Capt. MOFFAT working on the new chord line.	
30th	Bn. moved into front line breastwork occupied by 1st ROYAL IRISH RIFLES in sections 50 - 51. Bn. Headquarters being in MOAT FARM.	

Summary/-

September 1915.

Army Form C. 2118.

WAR DIARY
or
INTELLIGENCE SUMMARY.
(Erase heading not required.)

Hour, Date, Place	Summary of Events and Information	Remarks and references to Appendices

Summary of casualties during the month of September 1915.

Killed or Died of wounds		Wounded		Missing		Admitted to Hospital sick		Total	
O.	O.R.	O.	O.R.	O.	O.R.	O.	O.R.	O.	O.R.
nil -	1	nil -	9 - 74	-	1	- 5 -	50 -	- 5 -	61 -

Revived from Hospital during the month :- — 2 — 55
Draft received from 3/5th The Black Watch :- — 1 — 41 —

Amr. Blair-Irvine Lieut-Col.,
O. Comdg., 5th The Black Watch.

10th October 1915.

<u>8th, Division.</u>

<u>24th, Brigade.</u>

1/5th, Black Watch.

<u>October, 1915.</u>

121/7470

10.G
5 sheet

8th Division

1/5th R. Higher.

Dec '15

Ice dome S'ir Romero
18.10.15

Vol IX

Army Form C. 2118.

WAR DIARY
INTELLIGENCE SUMMARY.
(Erase heading not required.)

Instructions regarding War Diaries and Intelligence Summaries are contained in F. S. Regs., Part II. and the Staff Manual respectively. Title pages will be prepared in manuscript.

October 1915.

Place	Date	Hour	Summary of Events and Information	Remarks and references to Appendices
In the Field	1st		Battalion in trenches - weather fine. Situation reports - Enemy quiet. 2nd Lieut. G. AIRTH GRANT. was transferred to England sick on 29th Sept. and struck off the strength of Battalion from that date.	
	2nd		Situation report - conditions normal. - Enemy quiet. Battalion relieved by LINCOLN REGT. There were no casualties. Battalion returned to Billets, formerly occupied in RUE DE BRUGES.	
	3rd		Church parade was held today at 4 P.M.	
	4th		Battalion paraded as follows :- 10.a.m. Physical Drill, 10 a.m & 2 P.m under company arrangements. Machine gun section at Ranges.	
	5th		Battalion in billets as before. Parades as usual. Capt. MITCHELL attached to 8th Division signal Coy.	
	6th		Parades as before. Machine gun section at Ranges.	
	7th		Parades as usual. Eight O.R. granted leave all 14 in the Capt. T. AUBERTIN and Lieut. A.W DUKE joined Battalion today from 3/5th Bn. The BLACK WATCH. Capt. AUBERTIN being posted to temporary command of no 3 Coy., vice Capt. W.I. MITCHELL attached to 8th Division signal company for instruction. Lieut DUKE assuming command of machine gun section.	
	8th		Parades as usual. Battalion allotted Baths from 2 - 6 P.M.	
	9th		Battalion paraded as follows :- 10am Physical Training 12-150 m Inspection by Y.O.C. 8th Division - Marching Order. Draft joined the Battalion and allocated as follows :- no 1.- 11. O.R. no 2.- 13. O.R. no 3. 22. O.R. no 4. 20. O.R.	
	10th		Battalion paraded for Divine Service at 10.30 a.m. Battalion moved to trenches N 41. + N 51. taking over from 1st MIDDLESEX. and 2nd SCOTTISH RIFLES. (no 1 and 2 bys). no 3 at CROIX BIANCHE. no 4 at CROIX BIANCHE billets.	

Army Form C. 2118.

October 1915

WAR DIARY
or
INTELLIGENCE SUMMARY.

(Erase heading not required.)

Place	Date	Hour	Summary of Events and Information	Remarks and references to Appendices
In the Field	11th		Battalion in the trenches was heavily shelled by 4.2 & 5.9 howitzers, and much damage to Parapet was done. The bombardment was particularly heavy in N°4 and N°1 Company had 9 casualties. Now of which were serious. Battalion was employed in reconstructing and repairing the broken work.	
	12th		As before - there was a little shelling, but little or no damage was done to material or personnel.	
	13th		As before - Battalion employed again on repair and reconstruction of trench	
	14th		Draft of 150 R joined Battalion today from 3/5th The Black Watch and were taken on the strength and posted as follows: 100 R to N°1 Coy; 40 R to N°2 Coy; and 10 R to N°3 Coy. In the trenches - N°1 and 2 Companies relieved by N°3 and 4 Companies respectively. Enemy very quiet and nothing unusual to report.	
	15th		As before - Enemy quiet.	
	16th		As before - Work continued and half from 1 & 2 companies given to Lewin repairs etc.	
	17th		Battalion relieved by 1st MIDDLESEX and marched to billets in RUE DE BRUGES	
	18th		Battalion in billets was inspected by Brigadier General commanding 24th Infantry Brigade. Battalion became Divisional troops, and is to be made into Pioneer Battalion:- Companies to be employed as follows: N°1 Coy. with 15th Field Coy. R.E. on Avenues in Right Brigade area. N°2 Coy. on roads in Divisional area. N°3 Coy. with 181st Tunnelling Coy. R.E. and N°4 Coy. with 2nd Field Coy. R.E. on left Brigade area. N°3 Company at CROIX BLANCHE and N°4 Coy. in billets near COMMAND POST. 12 other ranks were retained at end of current month, proceeded to the Base today, to be discharged from the Service.	
	19th		No work was started today. Coy Officers employed going over work to be done in the future. Machine gun Section with the exception of 1 Sergt. and 4 men returned to their Companies.	

Army Form C. 2118.

October 1915.

WAR DIARY
INTELLIGENCE SUMMARY.
(Erase heading not required.)

Instructions regarding War Diaries and Intelligence Summaries are contained in F. S. Regs., Part II. and the Staff Manual respectively. Title pages will be prepared in manuscript.

Place	Date	Hour	Summary of Events and Information	Remarks and references to Appendices
In the Field	20th		No 3 Company commence work with the Mining Coy R.E. 1 N.C.O. and 16 men on continuous fatigues for the 24 hours, working in four shifts of 6 hours. Rest of Battalion in billets and paraded as follows:- 7 a.m. Physical Drill. 10 a.m. & 2 p.m. under Company arrangements. 2 Officers provided on leave for 8 days to-day.	
	21st		1 N.C.O. and 4 Sappers from R.E. Boys attached to each Coy for work under Company. No 542 L/Cpl G. ANDERSON awarded medal of St George 3rd class. Parades as yesterday.	
	22nd		As yesterday. Companies employed with R.E. in the different areas as previously stated. 1 N.C.O. and 2 men of No 1 Coy. and 1 N.C.O. of No 2 Coy. proceeded to the M.T. Base ROUEN today on probation for transfer to Mechanical Transport Branch. Army Service Corps.	
	23rd		As yesterday. No 622 Drummer. A. W. AITKEN proceeded to the Base today for transference to Home Establishment. 1 N.C.O of No 1 Coy. proceeded to the Base today to be discharged from the service, his engagement expiring on 8th Nov. The Battalion handed today for Divine Service as under :-	
	24th	10-30 a.m.	Presbyterians at Battalion Head-Quarters.	
		10-30 a.m.	Church of England at No 1 Company's billets. Holy Communion at 8 a.m.	
		9 a.m.	Roman Catholics under B.S.M. D BURGESS at No 1 Company's billets.	
	25th 26th		1 N.C.Os + men granted leave of absence for 4 days, proceeded to United Kingdom today. 1 N.C.O of No 1 Coy wounded in the head, while with working party. Companies employed under R.E. as previously. As yesterday.	

Army Form C. 2118.

October 1915

WAR DIARY

INTELLIGENCE SUMMARY.

(Erase heading not required.)

Instructions regarding War Diaries and Intelligence Summaries are contained in F. S. Regs., Part II. and the Staff Manual respectively. Title pages will be prepared in manuscript.

Place	Date	Hour	Summary of Events and Information	Remarks and references to Appendices
In the Field	27th		As yesterday. No 2009 L.Q.M.Sgt. S.S.D. MILNE No 2 Company proceeded to England today to join 3/5th Bn. The BLACK WATCH having been nominated for a commission in that Battalion and gazetted 2nd Lieut.	
	28th		Companies employed as yesterday under R.E.	
	29th		Companies employed as yesterday. 1 N.C.O. of No 1 Coy. and 1 N.C.O. and 3 men of No 3 Company proceeded to England today on recommendation as candidates for Commission.	
	30th		As yesterday.	
	31st	12 noon	The Battalion paraded for Divine Service today as under:- Church of Scotland at temporary Head Quarters.	
		10.30 a.m.	Church of England at temporary military Church, BAC ST MAUR.	
		9 a.m.	Roman Catholics in Catholic Church BAC ST MAUR. 1 Officer and 18 other ranks having been granted leave of absence from 31.10.15 to 7.11.15 proceeded on leave today. Major R.H. MILLAR joined the Battalion today from 3/5th Battalion, to take over command.	

Summary of Casualties for month of October 1915.

	Wounded		Missing		Sick		Total	
	O	O.R.	O	O.R.	O	O.R.	O	O.R.
Admitted to Hospital		6		1	2	59	2	65
Rejoined from Hospital		2		1	1	50	1	52

No fatal casualties occurred during the month.

October 1915.

Army Form C. 2118.

WAR DIARY
INTELLIGENCE SUMMARY
(Erase heading not required.)

Place	Date	Hour	Summary of Events and Information	Remarks and references to Appendices

Strength of Battalion at beginning of month :- O. 29   O.R. 513.

Strength of Battalion at end of month :- 32.   515.

R H Milner
C.C. 5th Bn. The Black Watch
Major

5th November 1915.

8TH DIVISION

24 BDE

5TH BN ROY. HDRS (BLK WATCH)
NOV - DEC 1915

Pioneers.
8th Div.

Battn. transferred
from 24th Inf.Bde.
8th Div. 18.10.15.

5th BATTN. THE BLACK WATCH (ROYAL HIGHLANDERS).

N O V E M B E R

1 9 1 5

Army Form C. 2118.

November 1915.
WAR DIARY
INTELLIGENCE SUMMARY
(Erase heading not required.)

Instructions regarding War Diaries and Intelligence Summaries are contained in F.S. Regs., Part II. and the Staff Manual respectively. Title pages will be prepared in manuscript.

Place	Date	Hour	Summary of Events and Information	Remarks and references to Appendices
In the Field.	1st	Nov 1915	Companies employed under R.E. as usual.	
	2nd		3 Officers proceeded on short leave to United Kingdom to-day. As yesterday. Lieut-Col. Hen. F. BLAIR-IMRIE having received instructions to proceed to England to assume duty with Home Establishment left the Battalion to-day. Major R.H. MILLAR assumed command of the Battalion from to-day's date. The following address by Lieut-Col. BLAIR-IMRIE, on leaving the Battalion, was published in Battalion Orders of to-day's date:- ADDRESS. "Lieut-Col. Hen. F. BLAIR-IMRIE, on being relieved in the command of the Battalion by Major R.H. MILLAR, wishes to convey to all Officers, Warrant Officers, N.C.O.s, and Men his deep and heartfelt gratitude for the staunch and soldier like manner in which all ranks have supported him while he has had the honour to be their Commanding Officer, and he trusts they will now extend the same support to Major R.H. MILLAR." As yesterday, Companies employed as usual.	
	3rd		One man of No. 1 Company proceeded to the Base to-day, to be discharged from the Service, his period of engagement expiring on 17th inst.	

Army Form C. 2118.

November, 1915.
WAR DIARY
INTELLIGENCE SUMMARY.
(Erase heading not required.)

Instructions regarding War Diaries and Intelligence Summaries are contained in F.S. Regs., Part II. and the Staff Manual respectively. Title pages will be prepared in manuscript.

Place	Date	Hour	Summary of Events and Information	Remarks and references to Appendices
In the Field.	4th		As yesterday. Companies working under R.E.s as usual.	
	5th		As yesterday.	
	6th		As yesterday.	
	7th		The Battalion paraded to-day for Divine service as under:—	
		12 noon.	Church of Scotland at Battalion Headquarters.	
		10-30 a.m.	Church of England at Temporary Military Church BAC ST MAUR.	
		9 a.m.	Roman Catholics in BAC ST MAUR. Roman Catholic Church.	
			2+ Other ranks proceeding on short leave to-days.	
	8th		Battalion working under R.E.s as usual. No 2236 Pte. D.J.A. NEISH. No 3 Coy. proceeding to ENGLAND to-day on being nominated for a commission in the 3/5th Battalion THE BLACK WATCH.	
	9th		As yesterday. + Officers proceeded on leave to-day.	
	10th		As yesterday. 1 N.C.O. of No 4 Coy proceeded to the Base to-day to be discharged owing to expiry of engagement on 23rd inst. 13 N.C.Os. and men were discharged from Territorial force this day owing to expiry of engagement.	
	11th		As yesterday.	
	12th		As yesterday.	
	13th		As yesterday. 1 man of No 4 Coy. accidentally shot in billets at COMMAND POST.	

November, 1915.
WAR DIARY
INTELLIGENCE SUMMARY.

Army Form C. 2118.

Place	Date	Hour	Summary of Events and Information	Remarks and references to Appendices
In the Field.	14th		The Battalion paraded for Divine Service to-day as on 7th inst.	
	15th		One N.C.O. of No 3 Company and two men of No 2 and 4 Coys respectively proceeded to the Base to-day to be discharged from the Service owing to expiry of engagement on 29th, 28th and 29th inst., respectively. Battalion working under R.E. as usual.	
	16th		As yesterday.	
	17th		As yesterday. 4 Officers proceeded on short leave to-day.	
	18th		As yesterday.	
	19th		As yesterday.	
	20th		As yesterday.	
	21st		The Battalion paraded for Divine Service to-day as under:-	
		12 noon.	Church of Scotland at Battalion Headquarters.	
		11.30 a.m.	Church of England at No 1 Coy's billets under the Sgt. on duty.	
		9 a.m.	Roman Catholics under the Officer for duty, parading at No 1 Coy's billet. 20 Other ranks proceed to United Kingdom on short leave to-day for seven days.	
	22nd		Companies employed under 6.R.E. as usual. No 4 Company returned to billets in RUE DE BRUGES from COMMAND POST.	

Army Form C. 2118.

November, 1915.

WAR DIARY
INTELLIGENCE SUMMARY.
(Erase heading not required.)

Place	Date	Hour	Summary of Events and Information	Remarks and references to Appendices
In the Field.	23rd		Nos 1 & 2 Companies paraded at 12 noon in full marching order for inspection by the Commanding Officer. The C.O. also held an inspection of billets at 12-30 p.m. to-day. 1 man of No. 4 Company proceeded to the Base, Rouen, to-day to be discharged from the Service, his period of engagement expiring on 7th Decr next. No 3 Coy moved from Croix Blanche to Rue De Bruges this evening. The Battalion as part of the 8th Division went into Corps Reserve	
	24th		to-day. The Battalion paraded at 8 a.m. full marching order, and marched via Rue De Bruges, Sailly, Estaires, Neuf Berquin, Vieux Berquin, arriving at the latter place at 12 noon. The Battalion then halted in a field adjoining the road at Vieux Berquin and dinner was served out to the men. Nos 3 & 4 Companies having been detailed to work under C.C. IIIrd Corps. in the forest of Nieppe, left in advance for the billets allotted them on the La Rue du Bois, E.22 a. and b. Reference Map Belgium 1.40,000 sheet 36A. Nos 1 & 2 Companies and Headquarters proceeded at 2.0.m. to Point Sec Bois, E.9.a.4. en route for Corps Reserve Area, resting for the night there having covered during the day roughly 18 Kilometres or 13 miles.	

Army Form C. 2118.

November, 1915.
WAR DIARY
INTELLIGENCE SUMMARY.
(Erase heading not required.)

Instructions regarding War Diaries and Intelligence Summaries are contained in F.S. Regs. Part II. and the Staff Manual respectively. Title pages will be prepared in manuscript.

Place	Date	Hour	Summary of Events and Information	Remarks and references to Appendices
In the Field.	24th (cont.)		The march was resumed at 9 a.m. via La Rue Du Bois, La Motte to outskirts of Steenbecque, area allotted Battalion south side of railway 12 kilometres Nº 1 Company taking over the billets at J.1.d.10.5. and Nº 2 Company taking over billets at J.1.d.10.3. and J.1.d.8.2. Battalion Headquarters were established at I.12.6.7.4. (Sheet 36A (1/40,000).) Roads dry, weather fine.	
	25th		Dispositions as yesterday. Nºs 3 & 4 Companies engaged at work under O.C. IIIrd Corps in Forest of Nieppe. Nºs 1 & 2 Companies were employed to-day cleaning billets and kit.	
	26th		Dispositions as yesterday. Nºs 1 & 2 Companies paraded to-day at 12 noon for inspection by Field Marshall Sir John French, Commander-in-Chief of the Forces, but owing to the unsettled state of the weather, the inspection was cancelled. 4 Officers proceeded on leave to-day. Weather dry and frosty.	
	27th		Dispositions as yesterday. Parades were held to-day as under:-	
		10 a.m.	Nº 1 Coy. Feet inspection in billets. Nº 2 Coy. Inspection of arms, equipment, clothing etc.	
		2 p.m.	Nº 1 Coy. Inspection of arms, equipment, clothing etc. Nº 2 Coy. Feet inspection in billets.	

Army Form C. 2118.

November, 1915.
WAR DIARY
INTELLIGENCE SUMMARY.
(Erase heading not required.)

Instructions regarding War Diaries and Intelligence Summaries are contained in F. S. Regs., Part II. and the Staff Manual respectively. Title pages will be prepared in manuscript.

Place	Date	Hour	Summary of Events and Information	Remarks and references to Appendices
In the Field	28th		Nos 1 & 2 Companies paraded for Divine Service as under:- Presbyterians at the Quarter-Master's stores at J.1.c.6.8.	
		10 a.m.	1 Officer and 12 other ranks proceeded on leave to United Kingdom to-day. 1 N.C.O. of No 1 Coy proceeded to England to-day on being nominated for a commission in the 3/5th BLACK WATCH.	
	29th		Dispositions as yesterday. Nos 1 & 2 Companies commenced company training in accordance with programme approved of by G.R.E. 8th Division. 1 N.C.O. and 2 men and 1 N.C.O. of No 1 & 3 Companies respectively proceeded to the Base, ROUEN, to-day, to be transferred to England for discharge owing to expiry of engagement.	
	30th		Dispositions as yesterday. Nos 1 & 2 Companies paraded for training as per programme. Weather dry and frosty.	

WAR DIARY

INTELLIGENCE SUMMARY

November, 1915.

Army Form C. 2118.

Place	Date	Hour	Summary of Events and Information	Remarks and references to Appendices
In the Field.	30th (contd).		Summary of Casualties during the month of November, 1915.	

	Wounded.		Sick.		Total.	
	O.	O.R.	O.	O.R.	O.	O.R.
Admitted to Hospital	-	1	-	34	-	35
Rejoined from Hospital	-	1	-	22	-	23

No fatal casualties occurred during the month.

Strength of Battalion at Beginning of month, (including attached). O. 32 O.R. 590
" " " end " " " 32 565

3rd December 1915.

R. H. Milner, Major,
O.C. 5th Bn. The Black Watch.

Pioneers.
8th Div.

Battn. transferred
to 154th Inf.Bde.
51st Div. 6.1.16.

5th BATTN. THE BLACK WATCH (ROYAL HIGHLANDERS).

D E C E M B E R

1 9 1 5

Page 1.   Original.

1/5th Bn; The Black Watch.

WAR DIARY

INTELLIGENCE SUMMARY.

(Erase heading not required.)

December 1915.

Army Form C. 2118.

Place	Date	Hour	Summary of Events and Information	Remarks and references to Appendices
In the Field	Decr 1st		Dispositions as yesterday. Numbers 1 and 2 Companies paraded for training in continuation of the programme drawn up.	
	2nd		As before. The weather was against training, but Companies were employed in the Infantry training laid down in programme. 1 Man. R.A.M.C. (T.F.), was attached to detachment at LA QUE DE BOIS, LA MOTTE, from 2/4th FIELD AMBULANCE, for medical duties. Companies were unable to go for route march owing to the wet weather.	
	3rd		No. 2 Company were employed in R.E. yards.	
	4th		The weather having improved Companies continued infantry training – the Companies were weak, however, as parties had to be found for work in R.E. yards. 13 N.C.Os and men proceeded to England this evening – leave having been granted them for 8 days. A Reading and Writing Room was opened for use of Numbers 1 and 2 Companies and Transport section. Two men of Number 2 Company re-engaged for a further period of service, with the Battalion.	

Army Form C. 2118.

WAR DIARY
INTELLIGENCE SUMMARY.
(Erase heading not required.)

December 1915 (cont).

Place	Date	Hour	Summary of Events and Information	Remarks and references to Appendices
In the Field	5th		Nos. 1 and 2 Companies paraded for Church Parade at 10.15 a.m., and Nos. 3 and 4 Companies at 12 noon.	
	6th		Number 2 Company commenced their Engineer Training with 2nd FIELD COMPANY R.E. to-day, being employed in the construction of Bridges. Four Officers rejoined Battalion to-day, having been on leave. 1 N.C.O. & nos. 1 Coy. was evacuated out of Divisional Area to-day.	
	7th		Number 1 Company commenced their Engineer Training with 15th FIELD COMPANY R.E. to-day, one half of that Company being employed in bridge work, the other half in trench digging instruction etc. No. 2 Company continued their training. The weather was good in the morning and very wet in the afternoon and evening. 1 Officer and 12 other ranks rejoined to-day, their short leave having terminated. 1 n.c.o. of no.4 Company rejoined to-day from military Police, his sentence having been remitted.	
	8th		Engineer Training of Companies continued. The weather showing very little improvement. A Medical Board was held to-day at 23rd FIELD AMBULANCE MORBECQUE, which was attended by 6 N.C.O. and men unfit for trench duty, of these 6 were certified as unfit for service with the Battalion, and were admitted to Hospital for evacuation to the Base.	

WAR DIARY
INTELLIGENCE SUMMARY

Page 3.   Army Form C. 2118.
December 1915 cntd.

Place	Date	Hour	Summary of Events and Information	Remarks and references to Appendices
In the Field	9th		Training as before, was interfered with by bad weather.	
	10th		Companies paraded for training as before. The weather was very bad, but training continued so far as was possible. Lecture on Gas in STEENBECQUE School was attended by C.O. and Officers Commanding Companies.	
	11th		1 N.C.O. and 2 other ranks passed as unfit by medical Board, were evacuated out of Divisional Area to-day. 2 N.C.O.'s proceeded on one month's leave to United Kingdom to-day. Heavy rain accompanied by a strong wind, making the conditions very disagreeable. Number 2 Company ceased work at the Bridge, by instructions from C.R.E.	
	12th		The Battalion less two Companies paraded for Divine Service at 10 a.m.	
	13th		12 Other ranks proceeded on leave to United Kingdom to-day. 1 N.C.O. passed as unfit for further service, was evacuated out of Divisional Area to-day. Nos. 1 and 2 Companies paraded at 7.30 a.m., 10 a.m. and 2 p.m. Infantry training was again started under Company arrangements. The weather was fine and dry	

Page 4.

Army Form C. 2118.

WAR DIARY
INTELLIGENCE SUMMARY
December 1915 (contd)

(Erase heading not required.)

Place	Date	Hour	Summary of Events and Information	Remarks and references to Appendices
In the Field	13th (contd).		1 Man of No. 2 Company on Transport duty was seriously injured about the head by a kick from a horse at Transport Lines, during "Evening Stables" to-day. 1 Officer granted extension of leave on medical certificate, reported to-day.	
	14th		As before – 19 O.R. (13 for 7 days as stated on 12th inst. and 6 recouped men for 1 month), proceeded on leave to United Kingdom to-day. 1 O.R. rejoined from leave to-day. 1 Officer proceeded on leave to-day.	
	15th		1 Platoon from each Company employed constructing huts for expected drafts. Parades as before – but interfered with by bad weather. 2 underage men were to-day transferred to the 23rd FIELD AMBULANCE to-day for transfer to Base for transfer to Home Establishment.	
	16th		Parades as before – weather improved. No. 3217 Pte. Thomson No. 3 Coy. Medium 23rd FIELD AMBULANCE to-day from Epilepsy. Inter Company Football Competition – First Round:- Draw for Inter Company Football Competition – First Round:- No. 4 Coy v. No. 1 Coy – Result 1 – 0 for No. 1 Coy. No. 3 Coy v. Transport – Result 3 – 0 for No. 3 Coy.	

Page 5

WAR DIARY
INTELLIGENCE SUMMARY

November 1915 (contd)

Army Form C. 2118.

Place	Date	Hour	Summary of Events and Information	Remarks and references to Appendices
In the Field	16th (contd)		Bayeo in Football Competition - Head Quarters and No. 2 Company. 1 N.C.O. re-engaged for a further period of service with 1st Battalion.	
	17th		Parades as before. 1 N.C.O. granted extension of leave on medical certificate, rejoined to-day.	
	18th		Parades as before. Lieut. A.W. DUKE and 6 O.R. proceeded to WISQUES for four days' course of instruction in working of LEWIS RIFLE GUN.	
	19th		Nos. 1 and 2 Companies paraded for Divine Service at 10.30 a.m.	
	20th		Battalion (less Nos. 3 and 4 Companies) left billets and paraded at Railway Crossing, STEENBECQUE Station at 8 a.m. and marched via LA BELLE HOTESSE, MOULIN CROQUET to PONT D'ASQUIN, thereafter joining 8th Division Column at 12.25 p.m. Battalion then marched as part of the 8th Division and billeted for the night at WARNE. Weather fine.	
	21st			

Army Form C. 2118.

WAR DIARY
INTELLIGENCE SUMMARY

December 1915 (contd)

Page 6.

Place	Date	Hour	Summary of Events and Information	Remarks and references to Appendices
In the field	21st		Division resumed march and the Battalion paraded at 8 a.m. and marched as part of the Division through CLARQUES – THEROUANNE – on approaching DELETTE Battalion was ordered to retire and cover the retire of troops over the THEROUANNE – ST AUGUSTINE bridge – taking up still position on the heights around CLARQUES. Should the Battalion returned to Billets in CLARQUES. Weather very wet and cold.	
	22nd		1 Officer and 3 other Ranks granted one month's leave on re-engaging for further Service) proceeded on leave to United Kingdom this evening. Orders were received for an early start but these were cancelled and instead given to put the villages of CLARQUES and HERBELLE in a state of defence. No. 1 Company proceeded to HERBELLE and Lieut. R.F.D. BRUCE prepared plans of defences – Lieut. J.M.S. DUKE acting as O.C. No 2 Company did the same at CLARQUES. At 4 p.m. orders were received to proceed to ROQUETOIRE and take over billets there. Billets for the night were at LA ST SLONERIE. Weather bad. Heavy Showers of snow and cold.	
	23rd		Battalion paraded and marched to cross Roads East of ROQUETOIRE, then marching	

Army Form C. 2118.

WAR DIARY or INTELLIGENCE SUMMARY.

(Erase heading not required.)

December 1915 (contd)

Place	Date	Hour	Summary of Events and Information	Remarks and references to Appendices
In the Field	23rd (contd).		Marching out the Head-Quarter group to billets, Marching via COHEM L WITTES - BLARINGHEM, LA BELLE HOTESSE - STEENBECQUE. All these places mentioned are found on map HAZEBROUCK 1/100,000.	
			The Battalion (less the 2 Companies at LA MOTTE) marched and conducted themselves splendidly during the Divisional Manoeuvres. Only 1 man was sent to Hospital sick - and 1 man dropped out. Very fine and dry weather today. Battalion to night their period of short leave having terminated. 13 O.R. rejoined.	
	24th		No 1 and 2 Companies and other details, who were on the manoeuvres, were inspected on parade at 11.45 a.m. by the C.O. Companies were employed during the rest of the day storing up clothing and equipment. 1 O.R. rejoined at Transport Lines and Evacuated out of Divisional Area in 14th inst.	
	25th		Christmas Day. A draft of 112 O.R. joined the Battalion from 3/5th Battalion, THE BLACK WATCH today. They marched to No 1 Company's parade ground and billetted for the night at the huts Numbers 1 and 2 Companies had erected for them.	
	26th		Battalion paraded at 11 a.m. for Divine Service.	

Army Form C. 2118.

Page 8.

WAR DIARY / INTELLIGENCE SUMMARY

December 1915. (Cont'd).

(Erase heading not required.)

Place	Date	Hour	Summary of Events and Information	Remarks and references to Appendices
In the Field	26th (ctd).		Draft was inspected to-day at 10 a.m. by the C.O. and M.O., and were billeted for the night in the huts. C.O.'s addressed the Companies as follows:- "The C.O. is very glad he will be able to report to Lieut-Colonel HEW F. BLAIR, IMRIE, C.M.G. that the marching and conduct of the Battalion on Divisional Manoeuvres this week has been splendid." "He wishes all ranks a very Happy Christmas."	
	27th		Draft received on 25th inst: was posted as follows:- No.I Company - 24 O.R.; No.II Company - 24 O.R.; No.III Company - 42 O.R.; No.IV Company - 24 O.R.'s Draft joined the Companies to which they had been posted to-day.	
	28th		Nos. 1 and 2 Companies paraded at 10 a.m. and 2 p.m. under Company arrangements. Captain J.A. MOFFAT, O.C. No 4 Company, who proceeded on leave to United Kingdom on 17th November last was struck off the strength of the Battalion having been passed fit for Home Service only. (Authority A.G.'s No.4418 dated 25/2/15).	

Page 9.

WAR DIARY
INTELLIGENCE SUMMARY

December 1915 (cont).

Army Form C. 2118.

Hour, Date, Place	Summary of Events and Information	Remarks and references to Appendices
In the field, 28th (cont).	3 Officers and 20 O.R. (3 for 1 month), proceeded on Leave to United Kingdom to-day.	
29th	Parades as yesterday. Weather fine - slight showers. 1 N.C.O. of No. 2 Company re-engaged for a further period of service with Battalion. Result of Semi Final ties of football competition played on 26th inst. No. III Company v. Head Quarters - No. III Coy. won by 3 goals to 0. No. I Coy. v. No. 2 Coy. - No. 1 Coy. won by 2 goals to 1 (after extra time).	
30th	The final game between Nos. 1 and 3 Companies was played to-day at System Field adjoining RUE NEUVE. No. 1 Coy beating No. 3 Company by 3 goals to 1. It was a splendidly contested game, and No. 1 proved worthy winners of a grand match. Nos. 1 and 2 Companies paraded for musketry instruction at 10 a.m.	
31st	1 Officer proceeded on leave to United Kingdom to-day. Parades as yesterday. 14 O.R. proceeded on Leave to United Kingdom to-day.	

Page 10.

WAR DIARY
INTELLIGENCE SUMMARY.
(Erase heading not required.)

Army Form C. 2118.

December 1915.

Hour, Date, Place	Summary of Events and Information	Remarks and references to Appendices
In the Field. 31st (contd).	The Battalion was favoured with a visit of the Divisional Band this afternoon which played between the hours of 2 o'clock and 3.30 P.M. Unfortunately the Band had to stop playing before the programme was finished, owing to the bad state of the weather.	

Strength of Battalion at beginning of month :-
O. 0 O.R. 562
Do. at end of month :-
O. 32 O.R. 659

Summary of Casualties during month.

	Died of Wounds		Wounded		Sick		TOTAL	
	O.	O.R.	O.	O.R.	O.	O.R.	O.	O.R.
Admitted to Hosp.	-	*1	-	1	-	33	-	34
Rejoined from Hosp.	-	-	-	-	-	21	-	21

* Including 1 man who ultimately died in Hospital.

In the Field.
2/1/16

A. W. Millar Major
O.C. 1/5th Bn. The Black Watch.

3095/719/2

8 Div
24th BDE
2 East Lancs Reg
1914 Nov - 1916 Jun

BEF

8 DIV

24 BDE

2 EAST LANCS

1914 NOV — 1916 JUNE

To Box 1720

8th Division
24th Inf.Bde

Battn. disembarked
Havre from England
7.11.14.

WAR DIARY

2nd EAST LANCS.

November

1914.

Army Form C. 2118.

WAR DIARY
or
INTELLIGENCE SUMMARY.
(Erase heading not required.)

Instructions regarding War Diaries and Intelligence Summaries are contained in F.S. Regs., Part II. and the Staff Manual respectively. Title pages will be prepared in manuscript.

Hour, Date, Place	Summary of Events and Information	Remarks and references to Appendices
Southampton 30th October 1914 11 a.m.	Arrived from South Africa and commenced to disembark. Received orders to proceed to HURSLEY Camp near WINCHESTER to form part of 24th Bde 8th Divn.	
4-30 p.m.	Entrained in two trains at Southampton	
7-30 p.m. HURSLEY PARK 5 p.m. 8 p.m.	Arrived Winchester and marched to HURSLEY Park arriving two hours later. Weather wet especially during the march to HURSLEY PARK	
31st October	Commenced mobilization and continued throughout the day, making up to strength with drafts from 3rd Battn S.R. and a few returning sick and wounded of 1st Battn.	
1st November to 4th November 9 a.m.	Continued mobilization, weather wet. Mobilization completed Received orders warning order to be prepared to	

Army Form C. 2118.

WAR DIARY
or
INTELLIGENCE SUMMARY.
(Erase heading not required.)

Instructions regarding War Diaries and Intelligence Summaries are contained in F.S. Regs., Part II. and the Staff Manual respectively. Title pages will be prepared in manuscript.

Hour, Date, Place	Summary of Events and Information	Remarks and references to Appendices
H.Q Ror? 9. a.m	To be prepared to embark at short notice.	
4. p.m.	Received orders to move at 12 noon 6th November.	
6th November 11.30 a.m	Left HURSLEY.PARK by march	
4 p.m.	Arrived Southampton and embarked on board S.S. LAKE. MICHIGAN. Weather very wet	
At Sea 6th November	Left Southampton.	
7 - 8.0 p.m	Arrived off HAVRE. From entrance Bay, Army	
HAVRE 7th November 1 a.m	Entered HAVRE. DOCK.	
12. noon	Commenced to disembark	
3 p.m	Marched from Docks to No 6 Rest Camp. Drew tents and pitched Camp.	
8th - 9th November	Remained in Rest Camp.	
10th November	Marched at 12 noon entrained and left HAVRE by Goods train 7 p.m.	

(9 29 6) W 4141—63 100,000 9/14 H W V Forms/C. 2118/10

Army Form C. 2118.

WAR DIARY
or
INTELLIGENCE SUMMARY.
(Erase heading not required.)

Instructions regarding War Diaries and Intelligence Summaries are contained in F. S. Regs., Part II. and the Staff Manual respectively. Title pages will be prepared in manuscript.

Hour, Date, Place	Summary of Events and Information	Remarks and references to Appendices
11th November	Arrived MERVILLE 4 p.m. Marched to NEUF.BER-QUIN and went into Billet there with remainder of 24th Bde.	1 man injured on train. Left at Boulogne sick.
NEUF.BERQUIN 12th November	Remained in Billet	
13th November	Remained in Billet	
8 p.m.	Received orders to be ready to move next day.	
14th November 7 p.m.	Marched at 2 p.m. via ESTAIRES to POINT du HEM. Detailed two companies A & B to take over trenches under orders of G.O.C. 25th Bde. left on the road junction S.E. corner of Sq. M.23. Head Quarters and remainder of Batt. billeted at POINT du HEM.	From this onwards, Reference for Sheet 36 Belgium 1/40000. The line of trench received on 14th-18th Nov? was the right portion of what was subsequently known as C. Lines. sent?
15th November	Head Quarters and remainder of Batt. with 2 Companies Sherwood Foresters relieved FEROZEPORE Brigade in trenches, left in prolongation of that taken up by the two detached Coys above mentioned, right about Road Junction on S.E. corner of Sq. M.28. The two detached Coys again came under the orders of 24th Bde. Weather very wet and trenches and communications very muddy. Local attacks were made on the two left Companies	

(9 29 6) W 4141—463 100,000 9/14 H W V Forms/C. 2118/10

Army Form C. 2118.

WAR DIARY
or
INTELLIGENCE SUMMARY.
(Erase heading not required.)

Instructions regarding War Diaries and Intelligence Summaries are contained in F. S. Regs., Part II. and the Staff Manual respectively. Title pages will be prepared in manuscript.

Hour, Date, Place	Summary of Events and Information	Remarks and References to Appendices
6 pm	During the night sniping, but were not pushed home, and were easily repulsed.	
16th November	Remained in same position. An exchange of occasional shots continued throughout the day between trenches. The C.O.'s Coy was shelled and also was Bde H.Qrs situated on the RUE DE BACQUEROT NEMNIN. Weather continued wet.	1 Killed 7 Wounded
17th November	A repetition of the preceding day. A partial attack was made by the enemy on the right of the line, but was not pushed home, but was easily repulsed.	4 Killed 13 Wounded
18th November	A repetition of the two preceding days. Except that no attacks were made by the enemy. The Batts and 2 Coys 1st Sherwood Forester were relieved by 2 Coys Devonshire Regt. and the whole of the West Yorkshire Regt. The Batt went into Billets NW of POINT DU HEM Sq	1 killed 2 Wounded. 1 killed

Form/C. 2118/11.

WAR DIARY
or
INTELLIGENCE SUMMARY.
(Erase heading not required.)

Army Form C. 2118.

Hour, Date, Place	Summary of Events and Information	Remarks and references to Appendices
18th Nov? 5.p.m	Sgt. M. 114. Remained in Billet.	
POINT DUHEM 19th November 4 p.m.	Marched to relieve 2/NORTHAMPTONSHIRE Bn. in trenches on a line right on POINT No6V. Sq M 34, left on the right of 6 Leics. Snow fell during the afternoon, but cleared about 11 p.m, when a hard frost set in	1 Wounded. The Battalion was consequently known as "B". The line was divided into 4 sections numbered 1, 2, 3. 4 from right to left, each section being held by 1 Company. 4 Killed 5 Wounded.
20th November	Nothing occurred along the front beyond the usual interchange of casual shots between trenches. Frost continued.	
21st November	The usual interchange of shots between trenches continued. The right, "A" Coy. and Left centre Coy "E" were shelled for short periods during the afternoon, casualties were slight. The frost continued.	6 Wounded
22nd November	As on the 21st except that the enemy artillery did not shell the trenches A thaw set in	
" 5 p.m.	Battn. was relieved by 2/NORTHAMPTONSHIRE	5 Wounded (about 2.5/11/14)

Army Form C. 2118.

WAR DIARY
or
INTELLIGENCE SUMMARY.
(Erase heading not required.)

[ ] (original ... Army for ...)

Instructions regarding War Diaries and Intelligence Summaries are contained in F.S. Regs., Part II. and the Staff Manual respectively. Title pages will be prepared in manuscript.

Hour, Date, Place	Summary of Events and Information	Remarks and references to Appendices
28th Nov 5 pm	Reserve	When in Brigade Reserve two Coys remained in constant readiness to turn out and a standing Patrol kept at ROUGE CROIX x-rd
29th – 30th November	Battalion remained in Billets.	

Confidential

WAR DIARY

2nd Bn. Northamptonshire Regt.
from
DEC 1- 1914 = DEC 31. 1914

8th Division
24th Inf. Bde

WAR DIARY

2nd EAST LANCS.

December

1914.

WAR DIARY
or
INTELLIGENCE SUMMARY.
(Erase heading not required.)

Army Form C. 2118.

Hour, Date, Place	Summary of Events and Information	Remarks and references to Appendices
28th Nov? 5 p.m. 29th – 30th November. 1st December. 4 p.m.	Richene. Battalion remained in Billets	Whilst in Brigade Reserve two Coys remain in exceptions readiness to turn out and a Housing Patrol 6 nightly at ROUGE CROIX. N°21.O.
	Battalion removed in Billets moved to B lines and relieved 2nd Northamptonshire in trenches. "C" Coy 5th Black Watch accompanied the Bttn and occupied N°3 section of the line then relieving "B" Coy 1st Battalion Rahn and working parties. The "C" Coy 1st Battalion Rahn was in a bad state requiring much repairs to parapets. Nothing but the usual interchange of shots between trenches occurred during the night	1 Wounded 1 Killed Wounded
2nd December	N°s 1 and 3 sections of the lines were shelled by the enemy for an hour between 11 & 12 without recent except for slight damage to parapets. [Beyond this nothing but the usual interchange of rifle shots occurred.]	
3rd December	N° 1 section was shelled with high explosive shells between 11 a.m and 12 noon, slight damage to parapets only. Baton H.Q°s was shelled with percussion shrapnel between 3·15 p.m & 3·45 p.m. No damage except to adjacent houses. During the afternoon the enemy's trenches in front of N°1 section were shelled by our Artillery	8 Wounded

Instructions regarding War Diaries and Intelligence Summaries are contained in F.S.Regns: Part 2, and the Staff Manual Respectively. Title pages will be prepared in manuscript.

WAR DIARY.

A.F. C.2118.

Hour, Date Places	SUMMARY OF EVENTS AND INFORMATION.	REMARKS AND REFERENCES TO APPENDICES.
8th December 6.p.m.	A feeble attack by about 50 of the enemy was made on No 1 Platoon, this was not pressed & was easily repulsed by the fire of 1 Platoon. Heavy rain fell during the night, causing considerable damage to parapet.	5 Wounded (died 9/12/14) Men
9th December	The usual rifle fire continued between trenches. There was an outbreak of shouting accompanied by a burst of rapid fire from the German trenches. No attacks was made and the fire rapidly subsided.	1 Wounded Men
10th December	Nothing occurred beyond the usual interchange of short rifle fire between trenches. A notice board. Barbed wire in front of the German trenches was observed.	4 Wounded Men
" 5.p.m.	Battalion was relieved by 2/ Northumptonshire Regt & proceeded to RED BARN as Bde Reserve	
11th & 12th December	Battalion remained in Billets.	1 Wounded Men
13th December	Battalion remained in Billets	Men
" 11-30 a.m	Orders to be ready to move were received	
14th December	Battalion marched to EST̄AIRES and went into Billets in the Main Street	See Appendix A Men

Instructions regarding War Diaries and Intelligence Summaries are contained in F.S. Regns: Part 2, and the Staff Manual Respectively. Title pages will be prepared in manuscript.

WAR DIARY. A.F. C.2118.

Hour, Date Place	SUMMARY OF EVENTS AND INFORMATION.	REMARKS AND REFERENCES TO APPENDICES.
15th, 17th December	Remained in Billets at ESTAIRES	
18th December 12-30 p.m.	Received verbal orders from Brigadier 24th Bde to be ready to move at 2 p.m. in support of 23rd Bde. This was confirmed at 1 p.m.	
" 2 p.m.	Battalion left ESTAIRES and marched to man trenches along the RUE DE BACQUEROT right on the main LA BASSEE road left on the road Junction M.32.c.	
" 4 p.m.	The Batln. occupying the position assigned to it and came under the orders of the G.O.C. 23rd Bde.	
" 11-30 p.m.	Verbal orders received to move to the M.I.N. (M.32d) with ½ Coy & 2 Coys, sending 2 Coys 800 yds S.E. of the M.I.N. in close support of the DEVON-SHIRE and WEST YORKSHIRE Regts. which had carried a German trench and repelled counter attacks.	
19 December 2 a.m.	The Battn reached the position assigned to it.	6 Wounded (Lieut B. Velor, R.A.M.C. and 5 men)
" 7 a.m.	The two advanced Coys were withdrawn to trenches on the RUE DE BACQUEROT N.W. of the M.I.N. Battn remained at the M.I.N. & on the RUE de BACQUEROT during the day	

Instructions regarding War Diaries and Intelligence Summaries
are contained in F.S. Regns: Part 2, and the Staff Manual
Respectively. Title pages will be prepared in manuscript.

WAR DIARY.
A.F. C.2118.

Hour, Date Places	SUMMARY OF EVENTS AND INFORMATION.	REMARKS AND REFERENCES TO APPENDICES.
19th December 12 midnight	Orders were received to leave one coy in covered madeira at the M1N and move the remainder to billets at RED BARN.	
20th December 2 a.m.	The move to RED BARN was completed, the Batt" again came under the orders of the G.O.C. 24th Brigade	
" 9 a.m.	The Coy left at the M1N rejoined H.Qrs.	5.9"
" 9.30 a.m.	An attack on A" & "B" lines was reported & orders received for the Battn to stand by ready to move out under cover. Normal conditions were resumed.	10 a.m.
" 2 p.m.		
21st December	Batt" remained in billets at RED BARN	1 wounded
22nd December 10 a.m.	Orders were received to be ready to turn out at a moment's notice to go to support of the enemy were reported by an airman to be moving about 3,000 yds East of NEUVE CHAPELLE.	This line was known as A: line. They were divided into sections as in A: line. Generally speaking the trenches ran along the western edge of the main LA BASSEE Road with a prominent salient abutting 4 platoons on the right and an advance Post Maureau. Platoon just N.E. of the Moulin
" 4 p.m.	Batt" marched to relieve 1/Sherwood Foresters in trenches on the line. Road junction at & NEUVE CHAPELLE (M.34 d Road junction 5.4.2.	Road junction (in 5.4.8

Instructions regarding War Diaries and Intelligence Summaries are contained in F.S.Regns: Part 2, and the Staff Manual Respectively. Title pages will be prepared in manuscript.

WAR DIARY. A.F. C.2118.

Hour, Date Places	SUMMARY OF EVENTS AND INFORMATION.	REMARKS AND REFERENCES TO APPENDICES.
25th December	outpost	
" 5. p.m.	20¹ section to bury some German dead which had been lying there for some time. Batt'n was relieved in trenches by 1st Hampshire Fusiliers and marched to Billets at POINT ROCHON or part of Divisional Reserve. Battalion remained in Billets.	Appx. A
26th December		
" 11-15 p.m.	Orders received to turn out at once & march to RED BARN.	Appx. B*
27th December 1-15 a.m.	Arrived at RED BARN & formed up in fields on either side of LA BASSÉE Road	*It was subsequently ascertained that the troops for this movement were a considerable support that an attack on the whole 8th Division line were planned.
" 2-15 a.m.	Ordered to move about ½ a mile north along the road & go into billets in the houses. Movement completed.	
" 3-30 a.m.		
" 7- a.m.	Orders received to resume normal conditions & return to Billets.	Appx. C
" 8-30 a.m.	Batt'n complete in Billets where it remained for the day.	5-9
28th December	Batt'n remained in Billets.	
" 3-30 p.m.	Batt'n marched by Coy's at 15 minutes interval to A. lying & relieved 1st Hampshire Fusiliers in trenches. Relief completed by 8-30 p.m.	

Instructions regarding War Diaries and Intelligence Summaries
are contained in F.S.Regns: Part 2, and the Staff Manual
Respectively. Title pages will be prepared in manuscript.

WAR DIARY. A. F. C. 2118.

Hour, Date Place	SUMMARY OF EVENTS AND INFORMATION.	REMARKS AND REFERENCES TO APPENDICES.
28th December 3.30 p.m.	Enemy was very inactive during the night & all available men were employed in fire & communication trenches to stop influx of water.	
29th December	The enemy continued to be very inactive. The influx of water continuously increased in spite of pumping.	8 Killed 4 Wounded (closes 3/12/14)
30th December	Water increased rapidly in S.P.1 Section during the night, & the support trenches of S.P.1 & 2 sections had to be abandoned. The enemy remained very inactive	2 Wounded
31st December	The water continues to rise & the right face of the salient in S.P.1 Section was completely cut off. The communications with the whole of the salient were also impassable. The enemy continues machine throughout the day except they a couple of small bombs were thrown into the No 2. Section without damage. Relief of the Battn. By 1/ Stafford Forresters commenced but owing to difficulties of communication was not completed until 10.30 p.m.	4 Wounded (2 died 1.21/1/15 1.4/1/15)
" 5 p.m.		

Instructions regarding War Diaries and Intelligence Summaries
are contained in F.S.Regns: Part 2, and the Staff Manual
Respectively. Title pages will be prepared in manuscript.

WAR DIARY. A.F. C.2118.

SUMMARY OF EVENTS AND INFORMATION.   REMARKS AND REFERENCES TO APPENDICES.

Hour, Date Places		
31st December 11-30 p.m	10-30 p.m Battalion complete in Billets at RED BARN as Bde Reserve.	

B.M. 486

APPENDIX "A"

To
 Officer Commanding
  2nd East Lancashire Regt.

Following from Fourth Corps begins, Eight Division will hold a Brigade of Infantry in readiness to move out at twenty four hours notice a.a.a. message ends.

24th Brigade has been selected and detailed instructions in case of move follow.

From
 24th Infantry Bde

APPENDIX "B"

To
O Commanding
2nd East Lancashire Regt.
24th Brigade

Divisional mounted Troops with Yeomanry dismounted and Cyclists with Cycles to move via LE MARAIS Farm and BOUT DEVILLE to CROIX BARBEE cross roads A.A.A. Middlesex Regt and East Lancashire Regts in Divisional Reserve move via PONT DU HEM to RED BARN on LA BASSEE road. A.A.A. Royal Irish Rifles and half battalion Kensington move to LA FLINQUE Cross Roads A.A.A. Moves to take place forthwith and report arrival at points mentioned where Units will form up off roads. A.A.A. Acknowledge.

Addressed all Units in Divisional Reserve; repeated Infty Bdes

From 8th Division

"C" Form (Original). Army Form C. 2123.
MESSAGES AND SIGNALS.

Prefix **SM** Code **DLPM** Words **116**
From **ZW**
By **Chumley M**
At **19 . 2 . 14**

Service Instructions: **ZW**

TO **2ND EAST LANCASHIRE REGT**

Sender's Number: **BM 634** Day of Month: **19TH** AAA

In continuation of my BM 631 of today AAA Your battalion will remain in its present position until after relief of B LINES has been completed which may not be until 11 pm but hour will be communicated to you from here AAA You will then leave one company at MIN FARM in support of C LINES until you receive an order from this Brigade to dismiss it AAA After being informed from this office that B LINES as been relieved you may take your battalion

"D" Form (Original). Army Form C. 2121.
MESSAGES AND SIGNALS
No. of Message

Prefix ____ Code ____ Words ____ 36
Received From ____
Charges to collect ____ To Church(ill)
Service Instructions: ZW

Handed in at the ZW Office at 4.20 P.m. Received here at 4.40 P.m.

TO 2/ EAST LANCS R (THROUGH
    (2/ W YORK R)

B.M. 63   19TH   AAA

Please hold one company
under arms in readiness to
turn out instantly during the
night and acknowledge

From   GEN INF BDE
Place
Time   4.10 P.M.

"A" Form.   Army Form C. 2121.

MESSAGES AND SIGNALS.

TO: 2nd East Lancs.

Sender's Number: Bm 528   **Day of Month:** Nineteenth   **AAA**

You will move from your present position under orders of G.O.C 23rd Inf Bde. aaa When you move you will come to RED BARN where you will remain in billets as Bde Reserve aaa 1st Worcesters 1/Sherwood Foresters & 2/Northants move back to their billets in and near ESTAIRES at 7am aaa 1st Worcesters are relieving 2/Sco Rifles in B lines and 1/Sherwood Foresters the 2/Middlesex in A line this evening aaa 2/Northants remain in Dive Reserve near ESTAIRES aaa Please acknowledge.

From: Twenty fourth Inf Bde
Place:
Time: 2.14 am

"A" Form.   Army Form C. 2121.

MESSAGES AND SIGNALS.

TO: 2nd East Lancs.

Sender's Number: BM 531
Day of Month: Nineteenth
AAA

~~to Sherwood Forest~~ Please arrange that you machine guns in limbered wagon are at RED BARN at 4 pm so that they can accompany machine Section of 1st Sherwood Forresters to A lines aaa This is providing that the GOC 23rd Inf. Bde does not require them aaa The limbered wagon to return to you after machine guns have been taken off at Hqrs A lines

From: Twentyfourth Inf. Bde.
Time: 10.12 pm

"C" Form (Original). Army Form C. 2122.
MESSAGES AND SIGNALS.   No. of Message 2

Prefix SM Code IHct Words
Received From ZX By E Jukes
Sent, or sent out At ___ m. To ___ By ___
Office Stamp. 29/12/14

Charges to collect
Service Instructions. ZX

Handed in at HQ ZX Office 9.30 a.m. Received 9.28 a.m.

TO SECOND E LANCS

| Sender's Number | Day of Month | In reply to Number | AAA |
| BM 547 | Twentieth | | |

attack reported on A and
B. lines aaa stand by
with your Bn ready but
under your cover

FROM / PLACE & TIME Twenty-fourth Inf Bde
9.30 am

Army Form C. 2123

MESSAGES AND SIGNALS. No. of Message 8

Prefix — Received From ZX By S. [illegible]
Sent, or sent out At — To — By —
Office Stamp 20/12/14 ZX

Service Instructions: 2 x 4 addresses

Handed in at HQ ZX Office 3.20 P.m. Received 3.37 P.m.

TO: First Worcesters second E Lancs first Sherwood Foresters fifth Black Watch

Sender's Number: BM 566
Day of Month: Twent[ieth]
AAA

following message has been Received by fourth Corps From O H Q begins C-IN-C congratulates you on good hard work carried out by fourth Corps yesterday ends addressed first Worcesters repeated second E Lancs first Sherwood Foresters fifth Black Watch and second Northants

FROM PLACE & TIME: Twentyfourth inf Bde 3.20 Pm

"C" Form (Original). Army Form C. 2123.
MESSAGES AND SIGNALS.

| Prefix | Code | Words 60 | Received From By | Sent, or sent out At To By | Office Stamp. |

Charges to collect £ s. d.

Service Instructions.

Handed in at the ___ Office, at ___ m. Received here at ___ m.

TO: 2/ EAST LANCS

| Sender's Number. | Day of Month. | In reply to Number. | AAA |

BM 544 | 20T/11

Relief Releive the lines completed AAA Move your 3 companies and battalion HQ to RED BARN AAA Remaining coy to stay at the MIN AAA Brigadier wishes you to keep 3 companies at RED BARN in state of readiness as it it is expected that enemy may attack our lines tonight

FROM: 4.24TH INF BDE
PLACE:
TIME: 12 midnight

SIGNALS.

Service Instructions: 2 X Pte Crockett

Handed in at Bde Office 35 ... Received 8.60 p.m.

TO: FIRST WORCESTERS FIRST SHERWOOD FORESTERS SECOND E LANCS FIFTH BLACK WATCH

Sender's Number: BM 586   Day of Month: twenty first   AAA

indian corps airman reports that german trenches near NEUVE CHAPELLE and BOIS DE BIEZ were strongly held this afternoon aaa eighth div arty have been ordered to strongly engage them aaa addressed first worcesters repeated first sherwood foresters second E Lancs and fifth black watch

FROM / PLACE & TIME: TWENTY FOURTH INF BDE 8.35 pm

MESSAGES AND SIGNALS.

Army Form C. 2123 A.

First Worcesters Second E Lancs.
Fifth Black Watch

FROM: 24th Inf Bde
PLACE:
TIME: 10.10 am

Army Form C. 2123.

AND SIGNALS. No. of Message

Charges to Pay. £ s. d. | Office Stamp.

Service Instructions.

Handed in at .... Office .... m. Received ...... p.m.

TO: [illegible] Worcesters [illegible] forward
[illegible]
5th Black Watch

Sender's Number	Day of Month	In reply to Number	AAA
BM 564	[illegible]		

following message received from [illegible]
[illegible] twenty-third inf Bde
[illegible] attack on [illegible] lines this
morning aaa [illegible] wounded [illegible] has
been reported by the [illegible]
[illegible] place [illegible] [illegible] and
addressed [illegible] [illegible] reported [illegible]
[illegible] [illegible] [illegible] forward
[illegible] [illegible] [illegible] and 5th
Black Watch.

FROM: Twenty fourth inf Bde
PLACE & TIME:

"C" Form (Triplicate). Army Form C. 2123 A.

MESSAGES AND SIGNALS.   No. of Message 1

DS DHPM 61

| Charges to Pay | Office Stamp |
| £ s. d. | 22/12 |

Service Instructions: 2 × Pte Crockett

Handed in at the .... Office, at 2.42 p.m. Received here at 2.55 p.m.

TO SECOND E LANCS

| Sender's Number | Day of Month | In reply to Number | AAA |
| DM 607 | 22nd | | |

Telegraph from 8th Div begins we are heavily attacked at QUINQUE RUE aaa continue to do everything possible to keep enemy in our front in their trenches ends aaa please tell general aaa have warned A and B lines and asked them to intensify rifle and machine gun fire

FROM: 24th Inf Bde
PLACE:
TIME: 2.30 pm

"C" Form (Quadruplicate).   Army Form C. 2123 A.

MESSAGES AND SIGNALS.

No. of Message: 6

8M   KCA   126

Charges to Pay   £   s.   d.

Office Stamp.

Pte Crockett

Service Instructions. 2× 4 addresses

Handed in at the Pole office Office, at 10.15 A.m. Received here at 10.45 A.m.

TO: First Sherwood Forresters First Worcesters Second E Lancs Fifth Black Watch (Four addresses)

Sender's Number	Day of Month	In reply to Number	AAA
BM 594	Twenty second		

Airman reports six batties of enemy concentrated in readiness in bend of railway south of BAS POMMEREAU reference LILLE maps 1/80000 aaa Fifth Black Watch will send two coys at once to haps A lines where they will be under orders of OC 1st Sherwood Forresters aaa Remainder Fifth Black Watch will stand to arms under cover in billets aaa Second E Lancs will stand to arms under cover in billets at Red Barn aaa A and B lines will take what precautions they consider necessary aaa acknowledge addressed First Sherwood Forresters repeated

FROM

PLACE

TIME

"C" Form (Original). Army Form C. 2123.
MESSAGES AND SIGNALS.

less the company mentioned above to billets at the RED BARN

FROM: 23 RD INF BDE
TIME: 4.50 p.m.

8th, Division.

24th, Brigade.

2nd, East Lancs.

January, 1915.

Oct 1915

Miss West.   T.9

24th Brigade   121/4330

2nd East Lancs.

Vol II. 1 — 31.1.15

Army Form C. 2118.

WAR DIARY
of
INTELLIGENCE SUMMARY
(Erase heading not required.)

Instructions regarding War Diaries and Intelligence Summaries are contained in F.S. Regs., Part II. and the Staff Manual respectively. Title pages will be prepared in manuscript.

Hour, Date, Place	Summary of Events and Information	Remarks and references to Appendices
1st & 2nd January	Battalion remained in Billets at RED BARN	
3rd January 3-30 p.m.	Battalion remained in Billets.	
9 p.m.	Battalion marched by Companies at 15 minutes interval to relieve 1/Hertford forches in A Lines	1 Wounded (acc)
	Relief complete	
	Dispositions on the right of the line were slightly altered to close gap between the right and the left of the 5th Brigade, one Platoon being posted in a retrenchment about 200 yards in rear of the right against leaving a standing patrol on the RUE DE BOIS.	2 Wounded
	On the left of the line a Maxim Gun was placed in position to cover the gap between A & B Lines.	
	Nothing occurred during the night but the usual rifle fire.	
4th January	There was the usual amount of rifle fire. Two of our trench Mortars endeavoured to knock down anything houses in front of the advanced post in No 3 section but without success. One of three mortars in No 4 section was shelled in the afternoon but no damage was done.	
	Rifle bombs were fired by the enemy into No 2 section in the evening but no damage was done.	5 Killed 4 Wounded
	Generally speaking the water throughout the line except in No 4 section was subsiding.	

WAR DIARY
or
INTELLIGENCE SUMMARY

Army Form C. 2118.

(Erase heading not required.)

Hour, Date, Place	Summary of Events and Information	Remarks and references to Appendices
5th January 9.50–10.80 a.m.	Enemy shelled a point on the road running between PK & JCos and Coy of N°4 Station. Also fired Motor Bombs into Hog Station in Lyth Coes without damage. The usual intermittent rifle fire continued throughout the day.	
4 p.m.	An Officer from B Lines pointed out to the Machine Gun on the left a new German trench, in front of the centre of B Lines. The Machine Gun enfiladed this trench at a range of 550 yards and obtained hits.	
8 p.m.–9 p.m.	Trench Mortar fired two rounds at sniper's house in front of advanced post in N°3 Section and made one direct hit. The usual intermittent rifle fire continued throughout the day.	
6th January	The usual intermittent rifle fire continued throughout the day.	2 Killed (Pvt. P.S. Linder + 1 other) 3 Wounded
1 p.m.	Enemy sent paint into the Advanced Post of N°3 Sans into the trench of N°3 Station but without damage.	
5 a.m.	Afternoon trench began to relieve trenches.	
8.30 p.m.	Relief completed.	
11.30 p.m.	Battalion complete in Billets at PONT ROUCHON as Divisional Reserve.	

Army Form C. 2118.

WAR DIARY
or
INTELLIGENCE SUMMARY

(Erase heading not required.)

Hour, Date, Place	Summary of Events and Information	Remarks and references to Appendices
7th January	Battalion remained in Beluik. Orders received that we were to form IV Corps Battalion Vanguard. Heavy rain and high wind all day.	
8th January	Remained in Beluik. High wind and heavy rain storms.	
9th January 3.30 p.m.	Marched to relieve 1st The Buffs in trenches in A Lines. Owing to difficulty of communications and darkness of night, relief was not completed until 9.45 pm. Winters still occurred. Heavy rain storms.	1 Wounded
10th January	The usual interchange of rifle fire between trenches. Trenches in a very bad state with mud and water. Part of a trench in No 1 Section was abandoned at daylight. Enemy fired Bombs and pneumatic shrapnel into No 2 Section's trench. 11 pm and 7 pm.	2 Killed 12 Wounded
11th January	Working parties employed from 7pm to 5am completing breastworks in rear of the trenches as soon as it became necessary to abandon trenches. Enemy shelled the road in rear of 2/5 of Line with retreat. Between 12 noon and 1 pm. Heavy Rapid & Musketry fire in front of right of Line which however died down. The usual interchange of rifle fire between trenches continued throughout the day. Water increased in trenches especially in the A1 section.	6 Wounded

Army Form C. 2118.

WAR DIARY
or
INTELLIGENCE SUMMARY
(Erase heading not required.)

Instructions regarding War Diaries and Intelligence Summaries are contained in F. S. Regs., Part II. and the Staff Manual respectively. Title pages will be prepared in manuscript.

Hour, Date, Place	Summary of Events and Information	Remarks and references to Appendices
11th January 7 p.m.	Working Parties continued work on breastworks. Fine clear day until 5 p.m. when slight rain fell.	
12th January	Nothing beyond the usual interchange of rifle fire between trenches occurred during the day. The water in the trenches showed little change.	2 wounded
" 5 p.m.	Relief by 1/ Sherwood Foresters commenced. Owing to difficulties of communication, the relief took a long time. Notts.	
13th January 12.35 a.m.	Battalion was anything in Brigade Brigade Reserve Billets at RED BARN with one company North of ROUGE CROIX in close support of B Lines. Battalion remains in Billets.	
14th January	Battalion remains in Billets. A good deal of rain during the day.	
15th January 4.30 p.m.	Battalion remained in Billets. Began to relieve 1/ Sherwood Foresters in trenches. Leaving RED BARN Relief by Companies. Relief was delayed by state of ground and bad weather, and was not completed until 11 p.m.	1 killed 8 wounded
" 10 p.m.	Work on breastworks continued. High wind rising to a gale during the night & heavy showers of rain.	

WAR DIARY
or
INTELLIGENCE SUMMARY

(Erase heading not required.)

Army Form C. 2118.

Instructions regarding War Diaries and Intelligence Summaries are contained in F. S. Regs., Part II. and the Staff Manual respectively. Title pages will be prepared in manuscript.

Hour, Date, Place	Summary of Events and Information	Remarks and references to Appendices
16th January	Sniping continued throughout the day. Work was continued on the breastworks at night commencing 7 p.m.	6 wounded
17th January	A party consisting of 2nd Lieut Burnett and 20 men of "A" Coy bombed with a rifle grenade near the LA BASSÉE and 5 wounded (Lieut L.G. Sheroley & 4 men) South of the sign of No 1 Section. Sniping was carried on throughout the day. The Breastwork in rear of No 1 Section was shelled by the enemy without result.	5 wounded (Lieut L.G. Sheroley & 4 men)
7pm – 12 Midnight	Work on the Breastworks was continued.	
18th January 12 Midnight to 5 a.m.	Work on the Breastworks continued. Sniping was carried on between trenches continued throughout the day out. Nothing beyond the usual sniping occurred during the day.	2 killed (Sergt Ellis & priv) 3 wounded
5.15 p.m.	Relief by the 1/ Sherwood Foresters commenced	
8.30 p.m.	Relief completed without casualties	
11.45 p.m.	Battalion assembled in Boyce Barre Billets & PONT ROBCHON. Men were brought back the latter half of the way in wagons.	
19th & 20th January	Battalion remained in Billets. Sniping went on both days	

1247 W 3299 200,000 (E) 8/14 J.B.C. & A. Forms/C. 2118/11.

Army Form C. 2118.

WAR DIARY
or
INTELLIGENCE SUMMARY

(Erase heading not required.)

Instructions regarding War Diaries and Intelligence Summaries are contained in F. S. Regs., Part II. and the Staff Manual respectively. Title pages will be prepared in manuscript.

Hour, Date, Place	Summary of Events and Information	Remarks and references to Appendices
16th January	The usual sniping continued throughout the day. Work was continued on the breastworks at night commencing 7 p.m.	6 Wounded
17th January 12 Midnight – 10 am	A party consisting of Capt Knott and 20 men placed wire entanglements across the R. of BASSÉE and S of Keelin (Bay Sy Hill & 4 men). The usual sniping continued throughout the day. The Breastwork in rear of No 1 Section was shelled by the enemy without result.	
1 pm – 12 Midnight	Work on the breastworks was continued.	
18th January 12 Midnight to 5 am	Work on the breastworks continued. The usual sniping between trenches continued throughout the day. Beyond the usual sniping occurred every the day there is nothing was no activity fire.	2 Killed (Lieut E.W. Siske & 1 Pvt) 3 Wounded
5.15 p.m.	Relief by the 1/Sherwood Foresters commenced.	
8.50 p.m.	Relief completed without casualties.	
11.45 p.m.	Battalion assembled in Boyes Davoue Billets at PONT ROUCHON. Men were brought back the latter half of the way in wagons.	
19th & 20th January	Battalion remained in Billets. Bathing was on both days.	

Army Form C. 2118.

WAR DIARY:

Instructions regarding War Diaries and Intelligence Summaries and contained in F.S. Regs., Part II. and the Staff Manual respectively. Title pages will be prepared in manuscript.

Hour, Date, Place	Summary of Events and Information	Remarks and References to Appendices
23rd January	Work on breastworks continued till 7 p.m. Front did not hold. Rapid thaw set in	
24th January	The enemy sniping continued throughout the day and No. 4 section were shelled for a short time, but no damage was done.	3 Wounded
" 10-30 p.m.	Owing to the thaw, relief did not commence until 10-30 p.m. when the Lewis Company 1/Sherwood Foresters arrived	
25th January 2-30 a.m.	Relief complete.	
" 3-15 a.m.	Battalion complete in Bryant River Billets	1 Killed
"	"B" Company in close support of B Coys.	1 Wounded
8-00 a.m.	Orders received to stand to arms ready to turn out in support of attack on 1st Corps	
7 p.m.	Orders cancelled. Normal conditions resumed.	
26th January	Battalion remained in Billets	
27th January	Battalion remained in Billets	
" 6 p.m.	Battery at RED BARN by Capt Bradlow 1/ Sherwood Foresters in A Lines	11 Wounded
" 10-45 p.m.	Relief complete	59

Army Form C. 2118.

WAR DIARY:

Instructions regarding War Diaries and Intelligence Summaries and contained in F.S. Regs., Part II. and the Staff Manual respectively. Title pages will be prepared in manuscript.

HOUR, DATE, PLACE	SUMMARY OF EVENTS AND INFORMATION	REMARKS AND REFERENCES TO APPENDICES
29th January	Working Parties employed by night on the new line in Loverden Road and preparation on the right flank. Orders received not to withdraw troops from firing line by day.	
30th January	We were interchange of rifle fire between trenches. Enemy fired 37 H.E. shells near the right salient only 7 burst & no casualties occurred. There were a few casualties from shell fire in the same place in the afternoon and on the left of the line. 1/Hertford Regiment commenced relief. Relief completed. Battalion complete in Corps Reserve Billets near LA GORGUE. A few commuters in the morning which caused all day.	1 Killed 8 Wounded
31st January	Battalion remained in Billets. Nights fine with cold wind & occasional snow showers.	

Muirhead Lt Col
9th Essex Regt
31.1.15

8th, Division.

24th, Brigade.

2nd, East Lancs.

February, 1915.

T.4

24th Brigade

2nd East Lancs.

$\frac{121}{4582}$

Vol III 1 - 28.2.15

WAR DIARY

Army Form C. 2118

Hour, Date, Place	Summary of Events and Information	Remarks and References to Appendices
1st February 1915	Battalion remained in Billets. Fine day.	—
2nd February	Battalion remained in Billets	
" 4 p.m.	Marched to relieve 1/Hereford Foresters in Army trenches at 20 minutes interval	1 killed 2 wounded
" 10 p.m.	Relief complete. 1 Company 5th Black Watch in No 4 Section. Headquarters and "B" Company in A.I. Redoubt & adjoining farm. Fine day.	—
3rd February	Usual interchange of rifle fire between trenches and slight increase of enemy's artillery fire on different points of the line. Fine clear day.	Lewis McDermott killed 8 wounded
4th February	Never interchange of rifle fire between trenches.	—
" 6 p.m.	Enemy shelled Redoubt and adjoining farm during the afternoon without causing any casualties.	2 killed 5 wounded
" 6 p.m.	Headquarters & A Coy moved to storey billet. Enemy keeping up rapid outburst. Fine day	—

Army Form C. 2118.

WAR DIARY:

Instructions regarding War Diaries and Intelligence Summaries and contained in F.S. Regs., Part II. and the Staff Manual respectively. Title pages will be prepared in manuscript.

HOUR, DATE, PLACE	SUMMARY OF EVENTS AND INFORMATION	REMARKS AND REFERENCES TO APPENDICES
5th February 1916	Usual interchange of rifle fire between trenches	
" - 9.30-10 a.m.	Enemy shelled French [being] on new trench	3 killed, 5 wounded
" - 10.45 a.m.	Enemy working party on German working party	
" - 11 a.m.	Enemy fired a couple shell at the Retand	
" - 6 p.m.	Being 3 duds and remaining 3 shells in the without not caused in causalities	5th
" - 9 p.m.	Afternoon further commenced coy	
" - 10.15 p.m.	Relief completed. Battalion completed in Brigade Reserve. "C" & "D" Coys in Quinque Rue in close support of "B" Line.	
6th February	Battalion remained in Reserve "D" Company remained at Ritsu to a stand time on account of enemy artillery fire	1 wounded
7th February	Battalion remained in Billets	nil
8th February - 5.30 p.m.	Battalion remained in Billets. Marched by Companies at 30 minutes interval to relieve 1/Northamp. Regt in firing	nil

WAR DIARY:

Army Form C. 2118

Instructions regarding War Diaries and Intelligence Summaries and contained in F.S. Regs., Part II. and the Staff Manual respectively. Title pages will be prepared in manuscript.

Hour, Date, Place	Summary of Events and Information	Remarks and References to Appendices
8th February 1915 9.45 p.m.	Relief complete. High cold wind all day. Withdrawn to bivouac	1 Killed 3 Wounded
9th February	Working parties engaged by night on Rue des Berceaux Road and new parapet near MAISON BLUE.	1 Killed 6 Wounded 5 —
	The usual interchange of rifle fire between trenches continued throughout the day. Working Parties as before at night.	
10th February	Rifle fire was less than usual especially in the afternoon. It recommenced about 6 p.m. and continued rather increasing the normal amount until 2 a.m. night. Parties on the Berceaux night.	2 killed 1 wounded
11th February	Very light to relieve. First Kings Own & 2nd Battn in little attacking.	1 wounded
— 6.50 p.m.	11th Division Fourteen commence to relieve.	
— 9.35 p.m.	Relief complete.	
— 11.30 p.m.	Battalion complete in Sapper Avenue Billets	—

Army Form C. 2118.

WAR DIARY:

Instructions regarding War Diaries and Intelligence Summaries and contained in F.S. Regs., Part II. and the Staff Manual respectively. Title pages will be prepared in manuscript.

HOUR, DATE, PLACE	SUMMARY OF EVENTS AND INFORMATION	REMARKS AND REFERENCES TO APPENDICES
12th February 1915	Battalion received in Billets.	
13th February "	High wind and heavy rain all day. Battalion remained in Billets.	5.9ft.
14th February "	High winds and heavy rain. Battalion remained in Billets.	
" 4.15 P.M.	Battalion left Billets by Coys, at 5 minute intervals to relieve [illegible] in the trenches.	
" 6.35 P.M.	Leading Company left to take up trenches.	2 Wounded (Coms 15/2/15)
" 10.30 P.M.	Relief complete, much delay in [illegible] darkness of night and heavy going, also [illegible] almost pathless through less during the day.	
	1 Coy. of [illegible] was killed 80 & 2nd Lieut. "D" Coy, 2nd Battalion Regt. being on Piquet.	
15th February 12.30 P	[illegible] Enemy sniping continues from 24 M Bde, [illegible] to effect that [illegible] from enemy reported attack trenches on 13/2/15.	Appendix A

Army Form C. 2118

WAR DIARY:

Instructions regarding War Diaries and Intelligence Summaries and contained in F.S. Regs., Part II. and the Staff Manual respectively. Title pages will be prepared in manuscript.

Hour, Date, Place	Summary of Events and Information	Remarks and references to Appendices
15th February 1915 12.30 p.m.	One Company of 3rd Bn. British moved up by motor to relieve Headquarters of Bn in the vicinity of [illegible]. Very quiet day. B/5 the tenure hours [illegible] were [illegible]	2 killed 1 wounded
		57 [?]
16th February	[illegible] was very quiet. Sniping continued [illegible] the relieved an A, B & 2 sections were [illegible] during the afternoon to assemble. A bright clear day.	3 wounded (one 73/10)
— 9 P.M.	Heavy rifle & machine gun fire on trench of the Brigade on the right of Bn of [illegible]. Lasted for 15 minutes.	only
17th February	Rifle fire between 9 p.m. 1, 2 & 8 Artillery activity.	5 wounded
	[illegible] in the afternoon.	
— 6.30 p.m.	Relief by 2nd [illegible] further commenced	
— 10.30 p.m.	Relief completed.	

WAR DIARY:

Army Form C. 2118.

Instructions regarding War Diaries and Intelligence Summaries and contained in F.S. Regs., Part II. and the Staff Manual respectively. Title pages will be prepared in manuscript.

Hour, Date, Place	Summary of Events and Information	Remarks and references to Appendices
17th February, 1915. 11.50 p.m	Battalion complete in Brigade Reserve Billets. "A" & "B" Coys in Command Billets. High wind and heavy rain storm during the day.	
18th February "	Battalion remained in Billets	
19th " "	Battalion remained in Billets. Liaison Day.	
20th " "	Battalion remained in Billets.	
" 5.30 p.m	Left Billet by Coy/Coys as Rimels Toulouse/Shrapnel Wood Trenches in 4 Lines	
" 6.30 " "	Relief commenced	
" 9.35 " "	Relief completed	
21st February " Midnight to 6.2 a.m	Still day with one heavy hail storm. Working parties employed on Trenches road work & new communication trench.	1 wounded
" 10 a.m	Information received that Germans had removed wire entanglements from their front opposite left of "B" Lines. A Platoon of "D" Coy from Post H.I. and 1 Machine Gun from No 3 Section ordered to reinforce No 4 Section which was held by 1 weak Company 5th Black Watch.	2 wounded
" 11.30 a.m	Movement completed.	
" 12 noon to 1 p.m	Enemy shelled Right Redout. No casualties	

Army Form C. 2118.

WAR DIARY:

Instructions regarding War Diaries and Intelligence Summaries and contained in F.S. Regs., Part II. and the Staff Manual respectively. Title pages will be prepared in manuscript.

Hour, Date, Place	Summary of Events and Information	Remarks and references to Appendices
22nd February 1915.	Normal conditions were resumed. Nothing of importance occurred during the day.	2 killed. (Lieut H.F. Hersley & 1 man) 4 wounded
23rd " 6 p.m.	1/Sherwood Foresters commenced relief of A Turns.	
" 9.30 p.m.	Relief complete.	
" 11.30 "	Battalion complete in Corps Reserve Billets. Fine frost at night.	
24th February 1915.	Battalion moved in Billets. Slight snowfall.	Very blustery wind (Transfer to Pte "B"Coy)
25th " — "	Battalion moved in Billets. Heavy snowfall at night, which rapidly thawed.	
26th " — "		1 Recruit to join 9 Longuniae Fue (Tf (transferred to no 15 Coy's respectively)
" 1.30 p.m.	Shelled by Bys at 20 minute interval to relieve 1/ Sherwood Foresters in A Turns.	1 killed 3 wounded
" 9 p.m. "	Relief complete.	
27th February "	Some interchange of Rifle fire between trenches.	
28th February "	Heavy shelled Rifle shelled and B° & Vespers without result. Rifle fire less than usual. Orders received that Sherwood quite be taken over by the 1/ Seaforth Highlanders and 6th Gordt. that night and that the Battalion would proceed into Box Reserve at LA FLINGUE.	1 killed 2 wounded

Army Form C. 2118.

WAR DIARY:

Instructions regarding War Diaries and Intelligence Summaries and contained in F.S. Regs., Part II. and the Staff Manual respectively. Title pages will be prepared in manuscript.

Hour, Date, Place	Summary of Events and Information	Remarks and references to Appendices
28th February 1915.		
6.30 p.m	No.s 1 & 2 sections relieved by the 1/Seaforth Highlanders &	
7.30 p.m	No.s 3 & 4 sections relieved by the 6/Jats.	
10 p.m	Relief complete.	
11 p.m	Battalion complete in Bas Rouge Billets at La Gorgue	Casualties for month
	FRINQUE.	2 + 17 W 51.

8th, Division.

24th, Brigade.

2nd, East Lancs.

March, 1915.

T.5

18/4/39

24th Brigade

2nd East Lancs:

Vol IV 1-31. 3/15

Army Form C. 2113.

WAR DIARY
or
INTELLIGENCE SUMMARY

(Erase heading not required.)

Instructions regarding War Diaries and Intelligence Summaries are contained in F.S. Regs., Part II. and the Staff Manual respectively. Title pages will be prepared in manuscript.

Hour, Date, Place	Summary of Events and Information	Remarks and references to Appendices
9th March 1915 3:30 p.m.	Operation orders received	
" 7:25 p.m.	Battalion MARCHED A FLINQUE and proceeded into stores ROUGE CROIX	
" 8 p.m.	Battalion complete in front of ROUGE CROIX cross roads T.5.4.6.	
10th March 7:30 a.m.	Artillery bombardment of German trench commences	Strength 22 Officers
" 9 a.m.	Rochestown arrived in Bn HQ. B Coy Bunkers	5 Officers killed
" 10:30 a.m.	8 – 9 Coys meeting in support ... SIGN POST Road. Remaining 2 Coys in ... St. Omer Rd. and "HIGH STREET."	4 Officers wounded
		Major W.A. SANDERS Capt. W.T. GALLAGHER Lieut S.M. ALLISON Lieut C.F.J. WOLSELEY killed
" 10:50 a.m.	Information received that 23rd Bde had taken first line trenches 46 German Rds in all	6 Officers wounded Major Col C.K. Hazzard Capt Kent Captain Capt P.O. Robinson (wd) Lieut P.L. E. Allen Lieut F.N. Thompson Lieut Lowe (attached)
" 11:10 a.m.	Orders received to move ... (copy)	Staff attached 2/East Lancs
" 12:51 p.m.	B Coy. To lead in order 14-21. B & D Coys in order 18-65 in rear	Other Ranks killed 147 (3 since died) wounded 21 missing
" 1:25 p.m.	Battalion moved to HIGH ST. Line 18-21-16 and a Platoon Royal West Regiment 8 Coys in rear of B Coy and 2 Pl. East Surrey in reserve ... Information from Brig. Gen. ... Bois de BIEZ occupied	

WAR DIARY or INTELLIGENCE SUMMARY

Army Form C. 2118.

(Erase heading not required.)

Hour, Date, Place	Summary of Events and Information	Remarks and references to Appendices

10th March 1915

3.0 p.m. — Orders received to collect Battalion at Rue Tilleloy in Reserve.

4.0 p.m. — A"& C" Coys withdrawn to RUE TILLELOY in Res: Reserve. B" Coy to join same, one Coy remaining in F.T. in close support. "D" Coy to remain in support N. of E. Lane, reinforcing 1st Batt: NORTHANTS on R. SHERWOODS on L.

6 p.m. — Right 2 Coys of "D" reinforcing 1st Batt: NORTHANTS with 2 Coys E Lancs R SHERWOODS and NORTHANTS advanced.

9 p.m. — Sherwoods on right, SHERWOODS and 2 Coys E of Pont 2 Coys NORTHANTS in front of same R and moving forward to them.

10 p.m. — 2 Coys E LANCS Reinf: on right, 2 Coys of 1st Batt: on right of SHERWOODS. "D" Coy behind same 15 x 66. "A" "B" "C" Coys approached in reserve. B" in D" "D" or ground in rear.

11th March

1.50 a.m. — The following orders have been approved: Commence 7 a.m. Heavy Bombardment to the front itself to 9.33 from 6.45 a.m. Infantry take Mauquissart through BOIS DU BIEZ to VERY DE GRAND. 3rd Division to LA CLIQUETTERIE. 7th Division on AUBERS. 2nd Div: on LA PLOUICH. 4 Brs: to support 23 Brs: in Reserve in Position. 8 & Reserve supplies by 23rd Bn. 23.0 Back in Reserve Billets at LA RUSSIE PIETRE.

WAR DIARY
or
INTELLIGENCE SUMMARY

(Erase heading not required.)

Army Form C. 2118.

Instructions regarding War Diaries and Intelligence Summaries are contained in F. S. Regs., Part II. and the Staff Manual respectively. Title pages will be prepared in manuscript.

Hour, Date, Place	Summary of Events and Information	Remarks and references to Appendices
11th March 1915 4:30 a.m.	SHERWOODS on right, NORTHANTS on left, both in line. WORCESTERS in support. NORTHANTS/E.LANCS have 2 Coys in support of SHERWOODS. 2 Coys E.LANCS and Field Coy R.E. in reserve in RUETILELOY.	
" 7 a.m.	Advance commenced but Sherwoods were sufficient magazine unable to advance and sustained heavy losses in the endeavour. The day was wet, the E.Lancs further sustained about 300 pts in Rear. The Batn. then had orders to dig in to consolidate the line. Orders were for Bn. to enable support.	
" 7.15 p.m.	NORTHANTS	WORCESTERS	SHERWOOD FORESTERS 3 Coys E.LANCS with a view to the whole Bn. attacking next morning.	
12th March 2 a.m.	3 Coys E.LANCS were in position to attack in rear of NORTHANTS and WORCESTERS who they were to advance through in the assault.	
" 5 a.m.	Orders given for the attack to commence at 10:30 a.m. after an hours bombardment by Artillery.	
" 6 a.m.	Enemy counter attacked 2nd & 4th Bde between airoplane flew over front of NORTHANTS. The SHERWOODS however... were driven back however and is reported they...afterwards	

Army Form C. 2118.

WAR DIARY
or
INTELLIGENCE SUMMARY
(Erase heading not required.)

Instructions regarding War Diaries and Intelligence Summaries are contained in F. S. Regs., Part II. and the Staff Manual respectively. Title pages will be prepared in manuscript.

Hour, Date, Place	Summary of Events and Information	Remarks and references to Appendices
12th March 1915 6.45 a.m.	2nd Hrs NORTHANTS, WORCESTERS & LANCS suddenly surprised by a German trench about 400 yds in front of the NORTHANTS trenches running up to old trenches which the NORTHANTS & men [?] found impossible to retake. The attempt cost us many casualties. 9th Bde were sent to the scene & [held?] up by [?] concentric fire [?] [?] Preparations were made to [?] night attack by 13th & 14th Bde at 1.00 a.m. on the 13th. This was postponed.	[?] ordered from 2nd [?] to [?] R.
13th March 2 a.m.	23rd Bde ordered to [?] to [?] by mortar [?] at [?] 7.14.6.70.Y	
1.10 p.m.	24 [?] aged [?] N & W Polish to [?] [?] [?] to ROUGE CROIX	
2.30 p.m.	Division ordered to proceed to POINT 206 and get [?] [?] with a view to participating [?] [?] attack.	
5 p.m.	Proceeded to [?]	
"	No Battn in reserve N of ROUGE CROIX	
14th March 2.30 p.m.	H.E. shell exploded [?] [?] on the [?] near H.Q. D Coy billet. [?] 24 killed [?] [?]	24 killed. 37 wounded (11 severely) Lieut A. Robinson 4th Yorks Shire Attached Northumberland Fusiliers wounded 14/3/15
" 7 p.m.	37 [?] [?] Killed & 37 [?]	
	[?] [?] with 2 myselves [?] A [?] [?] [?] [?] at [?] 29 & 21 Fa pond [?] S.E.	1 killed
	[?] [?] S. West of LINQUE and PIETRE Rd.	

WAR DIARY:

Army Form C. 2118.

Instructions regarding War Diaries and Intelligence Summaries are contained in F.S. Regs., Part II. and the Staff Manual respectively. Title pages will be prepared in manuscript.

Hour, Date, Place	Summary of Events and Information	Remarks and references to Appendices
March 24th 1915. 5.47 p.m.	The Battalion marched off strong in Billets at 6.30 p.m. [Weather cold & showery]	
March 25th "	The 24th Brigade moved into Billets viz:- B+G. St. M A U R & SAILLY [The Battalion marching off at 5 p.m. arrives in their Billets on the RUE BATAILLE at 8.8 p.m.] Marches extra & wet day	
March 26th 6.30 p.m.	Battalion in Billets at RUE BATAILLE. "A" "B" Coys and 2 Coys 5th Black Watch were in trenches visited by the CO. C consisted of "C" & "D" Coys were in Billet in Bergues Ferme at RUE DUQUESNIS. The enemy's Trench (in many very much damaged very complete) was very heavily shelled by the 18th. The enemy in front also much shaken. Practically no firing between Trenches. Fine cold night altogether.	Trenches of Trenches visited by Brig's of the No 3 Battn H/M 24th Div and now occupied by the Battn went into trenches 3.P.3. & 1.3.R. B Coy in No 5 crater. 10 A.9.4 - No 5 crater. 3Q.3.R. in 3 R. two plys in a B Coy C Coy in No 5 C 2.6 The 1st Platoon was passing a unavoid pool. "B" Coy went in Trench [L] Plats on Trench No 3 central. 2 Platoons in Butt N + A G.1. 1 Platoon in 2nd line in Trench 11 + A 12.
March 27th "	Day in the 27th. Platoon of "A" Coy went up from trench to reinforce "B" Coy which was very weak for the length of line held.	
March 28th "	Operations on the March 26th. L "D" Coy relieved by 2 Coys 5th Black Watch in trenches 3.Q. & 3.R. 2 "B" Coy relieved by 2 Coys 5th Black Watch into	
March 29th " 7.15 "		

Army Form C. 2118.

WAR DIARY
or
INTELLIGENCE SUMMARY

(Erase heading not required.)

Instructions regarding War Diaries and Intelligence Summaries are contained in F.S. Regs., Part II. and the Staff Manual respectively. Title pages will be prepared in manuscript.

Hour, Date, Place	Summary of Events and Information	Remarks and references to Appendices
March 29th 1915 7 p.m.	and returned to Billets on RUE DU QUESNES.	
" 9 p.m.	Ceremony of trooping by "C" & "D" Coys. Remainder of Bn. on fatigue.	
March 30th "	"C" & "D" Coys in trenches and "A" & "B" Coys in Billets in Brigade Reserve.	
	Very little firing, fine & std.	1 Wounded
March 31st "	As on March 30th.	

1247 W 3299 200,000 (E) 8/14 J.B.C. & A. Forms/C. 2118/11.

APPENDIX 1.

H.Q. IV Corps.
445 (G)

H.Q. 8th Div'n.
164. K.

8th Division.

The Lieutenant General Commanding the Army Corps wishes you to convey the following message to the General Officer Commanding 24th Bde for communication to the Battalions concerned:-

"On handing over A Lines by the Sherwood Foresters and East Lancashire Regt, the Corps Commander wishes to place on record his high appreciation of the gallant and soldierlike manner in which these Battalions have defended their lines during the past 4 months. Their casualties have been high (Sherwood Foresters 76 killed 281 wounded East Lancashire 59 killed 224 wounded) but they have stuck to a difficult and dangerous task with a determination worthy of all praise and have expended an amount of physical labour in the construction of the lines which does them high credit."

sd/A.G.Dallas
Brig-General
H.Q. IVth Corps   General Staff IVth Corps.
27/2/15

APPENDIX 2.

To
    O.Commdg
        2nd East Lancashire Rgt.

B.M. 167
d/13/3/15

Following message received from General Davies Commdg 8th Division begins:-

I wish to express to all ranks of the 8th Division my profound admiration for their heroic conduct during the last few days.

            sd/R.W.Luckock Captain,
                Brigade Major.

APPENDIX B.

To
O.C. 2nd East Lancashire.

B.M. 155.
13/5/15.

The Brigadier General congratulates all Officers, N.C.O's & Men of the Battalions of the 24th Infantry Bde on the magnificent fight they fought for three continuous days and nights under the most trying and arduous circumstances. He deeply regrets the heavy losses in Officers, N.C.O's and men but no men have suffered in a better cause or in a nobler manner than those of the Battalions of the 24th Infantry Bde.

sd/R.V.Lockett Captain,
Brigade Major.

The attack which we are about to undertake is of the first importance to the Allied Cause. The Army and the Nation are watching the result, and Sir John French is confident that every individual in the IV. Corps will do his duty and inflict a crushing defeat on the German VII. Corps which is opposed to us.

H. RAWLINSON, Lieut.-General,
Commanding IV. Corps.

Headquarters, IV. Corps,
9-8-15.

2/E. LANCASHIRE

Summary of events March 9th to 14th inclusive.

March 9th.
- 3.30.pm. Operation Orders received.
- 7.25.pm. Battn. left billets at LAFLINQUE and proceeded into close billets at ROUGECROIX.
- 8.pm. Battn. complete in billets at ROUGECROIX and in forts 5 and 6.

March 10th.
- 7.59.am. Artillery bombardment of German trench commenced.
- 9am. Instructions received for the Battn. to move up to B lines trenches.
- 10.30.am. B and C coys. were in B lines trenches having their left on SIGN POST rd. Remaining 2 coys. in big orchard between SIGN POST rd. and "HIGH STREET".
- 10.50.am. Information received that 23rd Bde had been partly held up and that the Battn. were to be prepared to close the gap between 23rd and 25th bdes.
- 11.10.am. Orders received to move at once to cross roads (P.T 18) at M 35 A. in support of Irish Rifles.
- 12.5pm "A" and C" coys on line 13-31 "B" and "C" coys on line 18-65 in support.
- 1.20.pm Situation as follows. Line 18-31-30 and German trench east of 50 held by Irish Rifles and 2 coys E. Lancs. remainder E. Lancs. in support. Troops of 23rd bde in trenches 18-53-54. These had been shelled out by our own guns but returned. Edge of BOIS DU BIEZ appeared to be strongly held.
- 3.0.pm Orders received to collect Battn. in preparation for further advance.

24th Bde were about to advance as follows. Northants on left Sherwoods on right supported respectively by Worcesters and 2 Coy's E. Lancs.

- 6 p.m. Sherwoods and Northants advanced.
- 9 p.m. Situation as follows, Sherwoods 200 yds S.E. of

March 14th 7 p.m. The Bn: relieved the 2nd Gordons, Scots Fusiliers and Bedfords in trenches on a line from Ditch running S.E. & N.W. between points 89 & 91 to a Point in D.Lines 150 yds S.W. of LA FLINQUE and Pietre Rd.

18/3/15

APPENDIX 1.

To O.C 2nd East Lancashire Regt.

B.M.668.

The Brigadier is delighted to be able to forward the above. No one appreciates more than he does the excellent work done by the Battalions, more especially during the anxious flood times since Christmas. All Battn's have played the game thoroughly and worked splendidly. The Corps Commdr had a long talk with the Brigadier on the 26th on this subject, i.e. floods, work, defence and casualties, and he thoroughly appreciates the extraordinarily hard and good work done by Regtl Officers and men throughout the past trying time. The Brigadier warmly congratulates all ranks.

sd/R.M.Luckock Capt,

28/2/15

Brigade Major,
24th Inf Bde.

8th, Division.

24th, Brigade.

2nd, East Lancs.

April, 1915.

121/5363

8th Division.

2nd East Lancs

Vol V 1 – 30.4.15

T. 6

WAR DIARY:

Army Form C. 2118

Instructions regarding War Diaries and Intelligence Summaries and contained in F.S. Regs., Part II. and the Staff Manual respectively. Title pages will be prepared in manuscript.

Hour, Date, Place	Summary of Events and Information	Remarks and References to Appendices
April 1st 1915	As in March 31st	
3.30 p.m.	A" & "B" Coy marches into Billets at Bac St Maurice	
	BAC ST MAUR.	
7.15 p.m.	Rest of Bn. & "D" Coys by the 13th London Regt as remainder	
12 Midnight	The whole of the Battalion were in Billets in Bac Maur	
	at BAC ST MAUR.	
April 2nd	Battalion remained in Billets	
April 3rd	Battalion remained in Billets	
April 4th	Battalion remained in Billets	
April 5th	Battalion remained in Billets all day	
April 6th	Battalion in Billets.	
	24. A. Tow E. A. see Reft. as above & the works from the 23" date on this day	Enemy Aeroplanes flying. Broken. Very little activity. Trigonel fighting dies. Fair dry weather in some. Casualties.
4.15 p.m.	"B" & "D" Coys moved to FLEUR BAIX taking over billets	
	over Reserve from the 7th Middlesex	
6.15 p.m.	"A" & "C" Coys left BAC ST MAUR to take over Reserve	
	Pt. 5 Section from the 2nd Middlesex - Battalion HQrs	
	in FLEUR BAIX.	
	"B" & "D" Coys in Trenches T6 & T7 (Capt Barton) (ZWastwood)	
April 7th		
April 8th	As on April 7th. Fine & Warm	
April 9th	As on April 8th. Fine & Warm	

WAR DIARY:

Army Form C. 2118

Instructions regarding War Diaries and Intelligence Summaries and contained in F.S. Regs, Part II. and the Staff Manual respectively. Title pages will be prepared in manuscript.

Hour, Date, Place	Summary of Events and Information	Remarks and references to Appendices
April 9th 1915 7.p.m	"C" & "D" Coys relieved "A" & "B" Coys in the Trenches. The latter moved back into Rue Becker on the RUE DELPIERRE. Fine.	dug day and at 5.0 p.m night
April 10th "	"B" in Trenches. "A" & "B" in Rue Becker. Fine. Machine guns firing from enemy in Trenches streaming	115. O.R. Reinforcement. Joined
April 11th "	condition on April 10th. Fine.	(W wounded)
April 12th "	On April 11th	1.W. wounded
" 7 a.m "	"A" & "B" Coys relieves "C" & "D" Coys in the Trenches. The Enemy ishing over the Rilley recaptured by "C" & "D" Coys. Fine.	
April 13th "	"A" & "B" Coys in Trenches. "C" & "D" in Rue Becker. Enemy shelled our trenches firing about 30 shells. Men slightly wounded. Fine. Rein with firing between Trenches. Stormy day	2 wounded 1st RWF (same Div) 2/H.L.I. 1 Bgl ofker (at Duty)
April 14th " 3 p.m	On April 14th.	
April 15th " 7.p.m	"C" & "D" Coy relieves "A" & "B" in Trenches. The latter placed in Rue Becker. occupied by "C" & "D" Coy. Fine.	Bgn/E.M.HILL slightly wounded (at Duty)
April 15th " 8 p.m	"C" & "D" Coys in Trenches. "A" & "B" in Rue Becker Communication established with Rue du Kargo. Considerable firing throughout the night. Fine	2 Killed

WAR DIARY:

Army Form C. 2118.

Instructions regarding War Diaries and Intelligence Summaries and contained in F.S. Regs., Part II. and the Staff Manual respectively. Title pages will be prepared in manuscript.

Hour, Date, Place	Summary of Events and Information	Remarks and References to Appendices
April 17th 1915.	C & B Coys in Trenches. A & D in Bde Reserve. A good deal of firing from German Trenches which shew a day at night. Line & Coys at night	2 Wounded
April 18th "	C & D Coys in Trenches. A & B in Bde Reserve.	
" 5.40 P.m. "	A & D Coys marche into Billets in 51st Divne at BAC ST. MAUR.	2 Officers 72 O.Ranks
" 7.30 P.m. "	C & B Coys were relieved in the Trenches by the Rifle Brigade.	During the time in the Trenches training and exercises as usual.
" 10 P.m. "	The whole Batt" were in Billets in Divnl. Reserve at BAC ST MAUR. Fine & warm day.	
April 19th "	Battalion in Billets	
April 20th "	Battalion in Billets	
April 21st "	Battalion in Billets	
" 2.30 P.m. "	The Battalion were Reviewed by Major General and addressed by Field Marshall Sir John French who complimented them on the Part they had taken in the Action of NEUVE CHAPELLE and also in their work in the Trenches during the twelve months they have been in the Front Line.	
April 22nd		

Army Form C. 2118.

WAR DIARY:

Instructions regarding War Diaries and Intelligence Summaries and contained in F.S. Regs., Part II. and the Staff Manual respectively. Title pages will be prepared in manuscript.

Hour, Date, Place	Summary of Events and Information	Remarks and references to Appendices
April 19th 1915	Battalion in Billet	1st Seaforths & 1st Wiltshires 55. OR Rifle Brigade
6.45 p.m.	Ord. Batta marched out of Billet to take over the sector of trenches held by the 2nd Middlesex	not conforming. Details of other Battalions from B. & W.
9 p.m.	R.l.o. Complete	N.G. C.O.I.
April 25th	A good deal of firing from German trenches in the	1.P.18. 1.R. & 1.S. Relf M
8 a.m.	early morning	2. & 3. Lg. Eng. W.
	30 small shells (H.E.) fired at B7B Coys Trenches. No Casualties. No Dmg.	Ballry Coy in Billet N.6 & 17
April 26th		
11.55 am	Battalion in trenches. Enemy fired 8 shells at 8 Coys Trench trench doing any damage	in Reserve 1.B. N.9.A.4/6. 2 Wounded (name died 25/4/15) Battn N9 Brnr. RUE PETIL-
1 p.m.		ON. N.9. & 9/5. while the 2
	Enemy shelled the RUE PETILLON strong point in town with Shrapnel & small H.E. Shells. No dmg.	Reft Platoon of Seforths
	Battalion in trenches	champ. R. Leg trench.
April 27th		
	2 Wounded	
4 p.m.	3 wing shells RUE PETILLON from some time without dmg.	Reft. Reserve coy now on position & supplying the any
8 p.m.	Battalion relieved by the 5th Black Watch and Seaforth to Billet on the RUE DU BOIS in Rue Riviere.	Ammunition & Bombs in front trenches on the trenches.
April 28th	Battalion in Billet in RUE DU BOIS in vicinity of A Coys first Day	Reserve.
11.30 pm	Enemy shelled RUE DU BOIS in vicinity of A Coys Billet. No damage.	

Army Form C. 2118.

WAR DIARY:

Instructions regarding War Diaries and Intelligence Summaries and contained in F.S. Regs., Part II. and the Staff Manual respectively. Title pages will be prepared in manuscript.

Hour, Date, Place	Summary of Events and Information	Remarks and references to Appendices
April 29th 1915	Battalion in Billets in RUE DU BOIS. Enemy shelled RUE DU BOIS. No damage done.	185 ommdrs (Working Party)
" 30th "	Battalion in Billets.	2/Lieut B.E. HOOPER Killed 2 wounded
" 7-40 p.m. "	Battalion commenced relieving 3/Black Watch in Trenches.	
" 11 p.m. "	Relief complete	For month K 1 + 4 W 1 + 11

8th, Division.

24th, Brigade.

2nd, East Lancs.

May, 1915.

137/5610

2/ 5th Division

2nd Lieut Lewis.

Vol VI — 1 — 31.5.15.

T7

Army Form C. 2

WAR DIARY:

Instructions regarding War Diaries and Intelligence Summaries and contained in F.S. Regs., Part II. and the Staff Manual respectively. Title pages will be prepared in manuscript.

Hour, Date, Place	Summary of Events and Information	Remarks and references to Appendices
1st May	Battalion in trenches in No 1 Section. H. Qrs. S.W. end of Rue PETILLON. H. Qrs. and trenches shelled in the morning and afternoon	2 Wounded
2nd May / 3rd May	As on 1st May	2 Wounded
	Battalion relieved by 1st Worcester Regt and moved to Billets in the RUE DE BRUGES.	1 Wounded
	At 2 p.m. Battalion moved to Billets 1½ miles N.W. of Sailly.	
4th May	Battalion in Billets	
5th May	Battalion in Billets	1 Killed (working party) 1 Injured
6th May	Battalion moved to move at 10 p.m. to assembly trenches on the FROMELLES – SAILLY Rd. opposite ROUGE BANCS. Orders to stand-fast for 24 hours received.	— " — 1 Wounded — " — 1 Seven Days — " — 1 Killed (—) 35. Reinforcements.
7th May		
8th May	Battalion moved off at 10 p.m. to assembly trenches on the FROMELLES-SAILLY Road, opposite the German position at ROUGE BANCS.	
9th May	Battalion ordered to assault line from Pries 884 to 875 at 5.40 a.m. 40 minutes after the commencement of artillery bombardment. "A" and "B" Companies followed by "D" Company with "C" Company in reserve, moved off through the Sally hafts. They immediately came under a very heavy cross fire from the German machine guns and rifles. Hardly heavy before they reached the FROMELLES Rd. "C" and "B" Companies followed by "D" Company & urged	Officers Killed. 10 Major L. RUSSELL Captain Y.F. RICHARDSON Lieut J.H. DAW 2nd Lieut E. BLIGH " G.M.L. GOODALL " H.E. HOWELL " T.G. NORTON " P.H.C. ALLEN " E.A. DOTHIE " A. de la P. MARSHALL
5:20 a.m.		
5:40 a.m.		63 Other Ranks Killed

HOUR, DATE, PLACE	SUMMARY OF EVENTS AND INFORMATION	REMARKS AND REFERENCES TO APPENDICES
9th May 5:40 am	charged, but were at once mown down by Machine Gun and rifle fire. Those few who had gone 25 yards, the survivors crying back to the trench and sap on FROMELLES Rd & further Artillery bombardment asked for and firing line re-organised with a view to second assault.	Officers wounded Capt & Adjutant R.H. ARNOTT Lieut R.S. BOOTHBY " R.K. CANNAN 2nd Lieut L. ANDERSSON " H.L. OWEN " E.J. HENDERSON " E.L.A. COPE " H.T. GORST " W.O. HEAPE 325 Other Ranks Wounded 42 — Missing
11 am	Artillery bombardment commenced, but our Artillery fell short, bursting in the advanced trench on FROMELLES Rd, in the target to rear and in the assembly trenches behind the target do the Regt. was being rapidly annihilated. Our own Artillery it was further known the target to the West side of the FROMELLES Rd. (1P and 1Q) Failure of assault attributed to:- (a) Distance Regt had to get across the open — 300 yds. (b) Assembly trench at right angles to objective thus involving a left wheel (c) Total failure of our artillery to shake the German trenches, so the enemy maintained a heavy machine gun and rifle fire during the attempted assault.	
10th May	Battalion moved at 1 am via Picatin to ROUGE DE BOUT and bivouacked for the day. Brigadier came round in the afternoon and thanks.	1 wounded

WAR DIARY:

Army Form C.

Instructions regarding War Diaries and Intelligence Summaries and contained in F.S. Regs., Part II. and the Staff Manual respectively. Title pages will be prepared in manuscript.

Hour, Date, Place	Summary of Events and Information	Remarks and references to Appendices
10th May	Thanking the Regt. for their gallant effort and said that no troops could possibly have done more.	
11th May 1:20 am	Battalion moved to Billets in CAMERON LANE	1 Officer & 89 Reinforcement
12th May	Battalion moved to Billets between LAVENTIE and LA FLINQUE.	
13th May	Battalion in Billets.	
14th May	Battalion in Billets	
15th May	Battalion moved to Billets at LE FRANC Factory ESTAIRES.	
16th May	In same Billets	
17th May	Battalion left LE FRANC Factory at 2:30 pm and moved into Billets in the North end of LAVENTIE.	
18th May	In same Billets.	
19th May 7:40 pm	Battalion left LAVENTIE and took over left half of "D" Lines from 1st London Regt.	Left Lt D Lewis is at CHAPIGNY 1 Officer promoted
20th May	Enemy shelled the right of "A" Coy and trench 9th Ont. at intervals from 11 and to 5 pm.	2 Officers joined
21st May	Fairly quiet	1 Killed

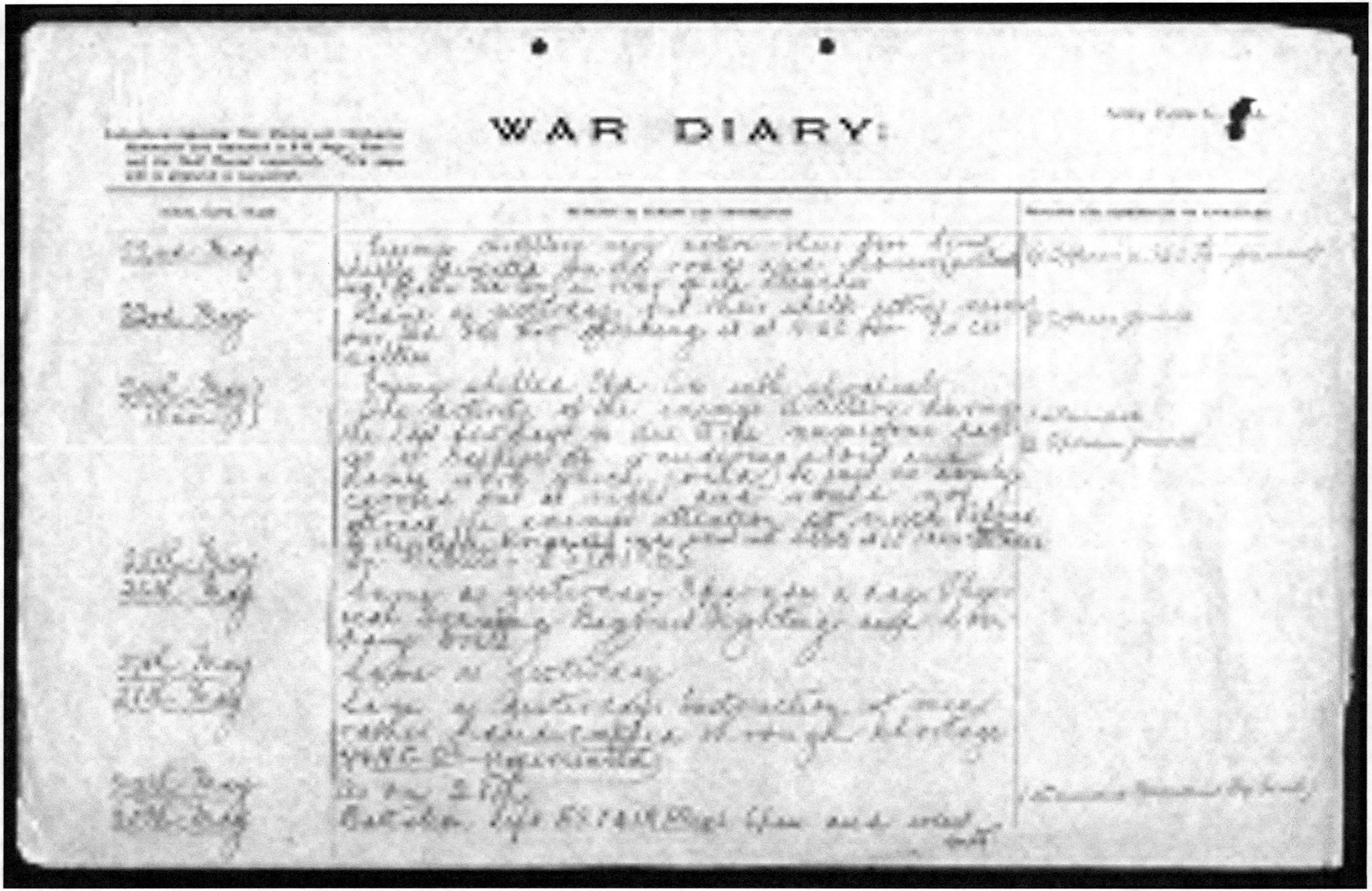

WAR DIARY

WAR DIARY:

Army Form C.2118.

HOUR, DATE, PLACE	SUMMARY OF EVENTS AND INFORMATION	REMARKS AND REFERENCES TO APPENDICES
30th May.	into Brigade Reserve Billets North of PONT DU HEM. 10(ten) men wounded by a German shell, 1000 yards N. of PONT DU HEM, whilst on the line of march.	10 wounded by enemy shell whilst on line of march.
31st May.	In above Billets. Regt. very crowded. Billets bad.	

8th, Division.

24th, Brigade.

2nd, East Lancs.

June, 1915.

Miss West

T 8

181/5991

8th Division

2nd East Lanc'd

Vol VII 1 — 30.6.15.

WAR DIARY

Army Form C. 2118.

Instructions regarding War Diaries and Intelligence Summaries and contained in F.S. Regs., Part II. and the Staff Manual respectively. Title pages will be prepared in manuscript.

Hour, Date, Place	Summary of Events and Information	Remarks and references to Appendices
1st June 1915.	Took over some more farms on the LA BASSEE Road which made the Billets less crowded.	
2nd June —	At same Billets. Parades three times a day under Gun of Majors. Physical training, Arms Drill & Bayonet fighting.	
3rd June —	As for 2nd June.	1st Rajput (Workers Bengaluru) (RE)
4th June —	Same as yesterday. Orders received to take over B Lines Coyt. and C.1. South of NEUVE CHAPELLE	
5th June —	Remained in Billets.	
" — 8.45 a.m	Battalion marched by Coys at 5 minute intervals via LA BASSEE Road and returned to NEUVE CHAPELLE and relieved 2/Northants Regt and 5/Black Watch who were working as one Battalion	The Coy received yesterday — Lewis Coy one C Coy one T. Coy. Length of line occupied 1100 yds. Support trench 3 Cellar near Piccard Coy by 1 Coy. The 6th Coy was divided between the Redoubt and Ruins Trench at "Moat Farm" Trench.
" — 12 Midnight	Relay complete. Lieut Col B.L. Rideford resumed command of the battalion. Relieved Command of the Battalion (temporarily)	Further support in Piccard Coy by 2 Coys at every bar ay 9pm. The Coy in reserve at Richebourg St Vaast furnished Ration Parties as many about 12 noon as before. DUCKS BILL.
6th June 1915.	Very little firing between trenches during the day. Enough ordering the night, trenches were not shelled. Very Hot still day.	La Tourelle
7th June —	Conditions as for previous day.	
" — 9 p.m — 12 M.N.	R.E. Working party worked out a new trench to cut off a	

Army Form C. 2118.

WAR DIARY:

Instructions regarding War Diaries and Intelligence Summaries and contained in F.S. Regs., Part II. and the Staff Manual respectively. Title pages will be prepared in manuscript.

HOUR, DATE, PLACE	SUMMARY OF EVENTS AND INFORMATION	REMARKS AND REFERENCES TO APPENDICES
8th June 1915.	The usual sniping between trenches continued wearing at night.	
9th June —	Very hot day until 1p.m. when there was a heavy thunder storm with a good deal of rain. Weather cooler.	
" 9-30 p.m	The usual conditions obtained. A working party of 80 men 2/N'humbd. Fus. under R.E. supervision commenced a new trench closing a salient in the divisional sector of the line. Working party covered by party of the 7th Fus. and wire entanglement installed by Capt. Perowne.	
10th June 1.55 a.m	Working parties & covering parties withdrawn. There was little sniping during work and no casualties incurred. Scots. Batt. was bombed by a trench mortar on the left sector without result.	
" — 9-30 p.m	Took over our Trench occurrences 45mm & 7.7 cm shellings. R.E. supervision heavy & sundays.	
11th June 1. a.m.	A wet wild & dark night. Working parties withdrawn no casualties.	
	A wet day. (today) 1st. sunny June. Quiet day today — enemy not sniping anything — no casualties upon weather.	
— " 9.30 p.m	Trench was relieved in trenches by 2/N'humbd F.T./Black Watch, but relief not completed till 12-30 a.m. so counting.	Relieved took over from Turnley Vy 2/N'humbd. Welsh Chukes & Re.tt.Watch. [illegible] machine gun officers Vy in Sapping & chukes over [illegible] to Rothwell & Myth.
12th June 12-30 a.m	Coys. marched independently on way to billets between LE NOUVEAU MONDE and SAILLY, last party arriving 2-50 a.m	

Army Form C. 2118.

WAR DIARY:

Instructions regarding War Diaries and Intelligence Summaries and contained in F.S. Regs., Part II. and the Staff Manual respectively. Title pages will be prepared in manuscript.

Hour, Date, Place	Summary of Events and Information	Remarks and references to Appendices
12th June 1915	Battalion resuming in Billets resting and cleaning up which were comfortable.	
13th June (Sunday)	Battalion received in Billets as last before. Weather fine.	Reinforcement 1 Off + 29 F. Ranks
14th June 1915.	Br Trieste. Bath bathed 100 at a time in baths at SAILLY Parade at 7. 10.30 a.m. 2.30 p.m. 5th Divn drill musketry etc. under Coy Officers.	Arrangements for Pont du Lys Hindenburg to take over trenches of 16th Bde.
15th June "	Br Trieste. K.O.C. 8th Divn Presents ribbon of D.C.M. to No 10504 Pte Rushworth on Batt. Parade at 10-30 a.m. — Route march until about 8 miles. Hot day, cover bivouac evening Five working parties of 50 men each sent to trenches of 16th Bde. Eng. Parades at 7 p.m. 10.30 a.m & 2.30 p.m.	
16th June —	Hun at Rickssen travel over constructed to Wayon S.S. Somrtey & Sgt Day on motor car to take over 16 h bde POR, hot day. Two working parties sent to trenches 1 man killed.	1 killed
17th June 8 p.m	Coy Parades as usual in billets. Batt in marched by LA BASSEE Road to PONT BUHEM and thence by Coys to former trenches in front of NEUVE CHAR-ELLE in relief of 2/ Rothants & 2/Hant Regt.	Reinforcement 1 Off 23 Rank & 4 Cos. + BUCKS B111 B Coys B Lines C coys Day Chateau redoubt etc. Garden
— 12 N.N.	Relief complete no casualties everything quiet night. 1 first Draft of men of DUCKS BILL without effect.	
18th June	Very little firing during the day. Trenches not shelled. Drew 3 toronadoes 1 Pyrus.	

WAR DIARY:

Army Form C. 2118

Instructions regarding War Diaries and Intelligence Summaries are contained in F.S. Regs., Part II. and the Staff Manual respectively. Title pages will be prepared in manuscript.

Hour, Date, Place	Summary of Events and Information	Remarks and references to Appendices
18th June 1915. 4 p.m.	Johnson Observation Balloon seen. Enemy busy with working parties. "New cut" parapet [Ponards?] completely improved by working party of R.E. Black watch Coy & Coy.	During the evening the glass began to fall fast. Brown in great distress was a copious sweat. Felt so ill & we could not continue...
19th June 1915.	Wind 7-40 p.m. Enemy's train from ROMBELLES heard.	Work on stokes [pit?] complete. Dear Brown others buried in sand, rubbed & jumped...
" 12-30 a.m.	Enemy to various outposts. Enemy snipers party up with rifle DUCKS BILL 61st Bty R.F.A. fired 7 shots	Two factory doorways...
" 1 p.m.	Enemy's Artillery replied with 8 shots. None fell in our trenches.	
" 4 p.m.	Hot day. Very little firing till 4 p.m. when 8 heavy shrapnel shells burst yard in one line, one falling within 50 yards of Bn Headquarters. No casualties.	
" 9-30 p.m.	Enemy trench mortar and Parapet grenades continued.	
20th June 1-30 a.m.	R.E. commenced new trench in Ducks Bill. No casualties.	Lieut J.E. FALBY, Transport
" 3 a.m - 6 a.m.	Work on support trenches during night. Snipetrapping - Very little firing. Storm at 4 a.m.	
" 6 p.m.	Enemy rifle shrapnel or party working on support trench in rear of C.T. No casualties.	
" 8 p.m - 12 M.N.	Work on new cut trench parapet grenades continued. Enemy trench mortar machine guns at times burst. Casualties occurred. Battalion sick report M.27. W.9.2. shelled by enemy.	Standart B.G. and 11.3 p.f. fires to Whitecord Farm from 2-30 p.m. to 5 p.m. [and?] 300 yds enemy seen left at 5 p.m.
21st June 2-30 a.m.	Bridges and huts. No casualties.	
	Medical Ramier Repels sound by artillery.	

WAR DIARY:

Army Form C. 2118.

Instructions regarding War Diaries and Intelligence Summaries and contained in F.S. Regs., Part II. and the Staff Manual respectively. Title pages will be prepared in manuscript.

Hour, Date, Place	Summary of Events and Information	Remarks and references to Appendices
21st June 1 p.m.	Orders received to Relieve 6th Batt. Goodenoughs M.35, 6,7,8 shelled — Warm still day. A good deal of activity in trenches. A German rifles & Trench grenades. Work & grain cutting etc. as before.	A German aeroplane came over to reconnoitre. Fired after we were in trenches. — 1 wounded
— 10 p.m.	Working party of 3/Black Watch elephants covered and tunnel	Lieut. Col. Bailey D.S.O. arrived from rest camp 8 p.m.
22nd June 1 a.m.	R.E. entered work in DUCKS BILL. Warm day. Conditions normal.	
— 11 — 9 a.m.	Brig-Genl Derham (69th Bde) visited lines in town.	
— 11 — 5–8 p.m.	1500 Sandbags filled during day & used after dark.	— 1 wounded
— 11 — 10 p.m. – 12 m.	Parapet of new trench almost completed, two tunnels in right of experiment. Other dugout on left of our parapet German right flank of DUCKS BILL much wired and grass cut. Work on new bastion in DUCKS BILL continues. Some rifle arm after dark	
23rd June 8 a.m.	Brig-Genl Penny (Actg G.O.C. 1st Div.) and Brig Genl Roberghem (or Bros) visited trenches — Fine day. Relief of Battn by 2/NORTHANTS & 3/BLACK WATCH cancelled. Nothing unusual occurred during the day. Lieut O. H. Penny reported from England.	Lieut Col Bailey left for Rest Stn on 9.30 p.m.

Army Form C. 2118.

WAR DIARY:

Instructions regarding War Diaries and Intelligence Summaries and contained in F.S. Regs., Part II. and the Staff Manual respectively. Title pages will be prepared in manuscript.

Hour, Date, Place	Summary of Events and Information	Remarks and References to Appendices
24 June 1915. 7 a.m.	Major R. Laurie proceeded to Brigade Headquarters to take command of ROTE (21B) 21st Heavy Howitzer on west bay.	
12 noon	Lt. G. Stanhope R.N. Any Officer arrived to take on the Battery (B by. 61. E1. E2. &B) Very quiet up to 5.2-3 p.m. Jet round when enemy renewed shelling with small gun and throwing bombs.	
4 p.m.	Rain'd at 5 p.m.	
	DUCKS BILL bombers on sentries.	
12 M.N.	1/ Warwicks relieved the Berks. Quiet night.	
25th June 1915. 3-30 a.m.	Battalion bivouacked for the night in orchard sw. of 29. L. 7/9.	
3 p.m.	Very heavy thunderstorm.	
3.30 a.m.	Battn. moved to billets in RUE DU QUESNES. H. Qrs. and C & B Coys. B Coy at CROIX BLANCHE occupying	
	Posn 26.9.22 gunners / Platoon, Later 1 Section,	
9 p.m.	were emptied up 5/7 m.	
	A Coy returned to trenches to assist O.C 1/5 Glouc	
	Watch to hold their own	
26 June 1915. 9 a.m.	Fine day, B. coy billets to RUE DU BOIS.	
	Bivre emptied at 10-15 p.m.	

Army Form C. 2118.

WAR DIARY:

Instructions regarding War Diaries and Intelligence Summaries and contained in F.S. Regs., Part II. and the Staff Manual respectively. Title pages will be prepared in manuscript.

Hour, Date, Place	Summary of Events and Information	Remarks and references to Appendices
26th June 1915 9 pm – 10.15 pm	Completing "A" Coy relieved from the trenches by him & 8 Platoons of 16 [?] returned from Bomb school	1 wounded
27th June 1915.	Lt Tillett, & Lieut Lewis & 16 men returned to arms depot. Lieut D.B Craig. R.A.M.C. rejoined from sick leave. Bale nature. One boy the Constant casualties"	1 injured
28th June —	Lt Tillett. Brigadier (Lt Col Lambert) came to Hobbs and discussed return of Officers. OC Officers programme. Off.s journey from the trenches to the trenches. Lieut Eley Huntingdon, much colder.	
29th June —	Lt Tillett. Capt L. King Howell and Capt Foss of the Bath's killed on a busy morning. Burial arranged. Glass day with thunder about.	
30th June —	Lt Tillett. Both armies to take over 1/R.I.Q.I.R. trenches from 1/Sandow Division. All Officers of Capt visited trenches. Heavy rain in the evening.	

8th, Division.

24th, Brigade.

2nd, East Lancs.

July, 1915.

8th Division

121/6390

2nd East Lancs

Vol VIII

1-31-4-15

T9

WAR DIARY:

Army Form C. 2118

Instructions regarding War Diaries and Intelligence Summaries and contained in F.S. Regs., Part II. and the Staff Manual respectively. Title pages will be prepared in manuscript.

Hour, Date, Place	Summary of Events and Information	Remarks and references to Appendices
1st July 1915	Batt. relieved the Worcesters in I.P. 1.P. 1.Q. 1.R. and Bde: 1.B. 1.A. 1.X. "D" Coy occupying I.P. "B".1.Q. "D".1.R. "C" 1B with 2½ platoons in trenches in reserve. Bombers in Redts just N. of Post 1.B. Relief completed at 10-15 p.m. Lead Coy to move from Batt. at CROIX BLANCHE being 7½ Bde 8-40p.m. Remr: out at intervals of 10 minutes.	
2nd July — " —	Quiet night. Activity by enemy outside the trenches. Their archives from Lindberg. There are on the RUE PETILLON also 5 JP Des at 6 pm and 10 Mids 15 P? No connection this day.	3 lt Josswell 2 Lew Bde. 1: 2/8/15 +1: 2/8/15.
— " — 10 p.m.	12 rolls on the right to cover front passed over by us and sent in field dispit about 100 yards away. They were charged 16 pm	
3rd July — " —	Quiet night. At 2am enemy Lieutenant Bat: & several right Coys: Reds fired Werflichtens cartridges) 3/2 stars 20 minutes apart, they fought, Both sides quiet during the night. Our wiring parties out. On the left section guns on front to give gentle rifle fire. Fine day very hot. Reinforcements up to our Tool from I.P. 1.R and Bde 7-40 pm.	1 ut reinfored arrived 3/8/15.
— " — 10-15 p.m.	Quiet night. One burst of rifle fire from enemy about 1 am.	
4 July 1915	Coy employed from writing and racing entrenst to our trenches and digging communication trenches to	

WAR DIARY:

Army Form C. 2118

Instructions regarding War Diaries and Intelligence Summaries and contained in F.S. Regs., Part II. and the Staff Manual respectively. Title pages will be prepared in manuscript.

Hour, Date, Place	Summary of Events and Information	Remarks and references to Appendices
4th July 1915	To support trenches in rear. Enemy aeroplane busy morning & evening. Weather very hot.	Reinforcements 2 Officers. 2/Lieut TANNER & CROUCHLEY 3 Lewis Section joined.
5th July —	Quiet night. Battn employed on same work. Very little cloudy day no rain.	Reinforcement one officer 2/Lieut R.J. INGRAM-JOHNSON. Such reinforcement joining forces.
6th July —	Quiet night. Battn employed on same work. Found & buried body of 2/Lieut E. MASON 2/Worcester Regt. Same and 1 Sgt. Boy.	
— 5 p.m.	Casualties to date this tour :- 3 killed 1 wounded. Lieut Col. GROGAN 1/Worcester Regt came down at 9 am to arrange relief for tonight. Battn relieved by 1/1st Worcester Regt. Relief completed by 10-45 p.m. Marched to Billets (Divisional Reserve) at SAILLY. Battn all billeted by 1 am. Dark night with some heavy rain.	
7th July 1915	BILLETS Battn found working party of 4 Officers and 300 men for trenches digging behind our lines, parades 8-30 p.m. to 8 a.m. Interval 3 am. Billets day much rain.	
8th —	Great R.O.B & H Services Lieutenants D.E.M. Kirkham to be No. 10412 Pte Dudison, 6837 Pte Pearson, 9846 Pte Sythe and 10525 "McNamara" Fatigue party 6 Officers & 300 men on similar work to V. Townshill. night 8-30 p.m. to 3 am fine day.	

WAR DIARY:

Army Form C.2118

Instructions regarding War Diaries and Intelligence Summaries and contained in F.S. Regs., Part II. and the Staff Manual respectively. Title pages will be prepared in manuscript.

Hour, Date, Place	Summary of Events and Information	Remarks and references to Appendices
8th July 1916.	Heard 2/Lt INGRAM JOHNSON, Gurkhas Light Infy, attached to Batn, seriously wounded whilst on duty, their Fatigue Party.	1 Wounded
9th July —	Day dull and some rain. Fatigue party of 5 Officers and 200 men again on digging from 8-30 p.m. to 3 a.m. 2/Lieut R.J.T. INGRAM JOHNSON died of his wounds in 25th Field Ambulance. Digging party of 5 officers and 200 men again out from 10 p.m.	1 Wounded.
10th — —		
11th July "Sunday"	Fine day. Gurkha Burial. Expenses incurred Rs.— M.O.R. Digging party, 5 officers & 200 men again joined by the 10th Div as arranged by the Bn.	Captain B.C.M. WESTERN returned from Sirhind. Hospl. Re-assumed Cd of Bn.
12th July —	Fine day. Batn relieved the Yorkshire Lt I.P.I.A.I.R. and Patts 1 A & 4 (B & Y I X) in the trenches. Relief complete by 10-15 p.m. A.C + 9 Coys in front line. B Coy in reserve.	2 Wounded Reinforcement 2 Officers 17 ORs Lieut J.S. LEWIS, 2/Lieut S. JONES & E.J. BARROW.
13th July —	Quiet night. No casualties. Quiet day.	
14th July —	Quiet night. Quiet day. Twenty five some 20 shells from field gun in neighbourhood of Ov.Jobs, one which passed through the roof of Farm Buildings used as N.C.Os attached. Orderly Room Commencing about 7 p.m. Obsy work now to be recommenced. Hole to be repaired at 10.30 p.m. owing to the rain.	Returned A. One Officer & 2 ORs Lieut J.S. LEWIS 7 Killed 3 Wounded
15th July —	Enemy have entered Major Wm. Johnson reports working parties usually 7 Rifle reserves Rly Pkt Blank from about 500 yards in front of I.R.	2 Wounded 1 Wounded 9/16

Army Form C. 2118

WAR DIARY:

Instructions regarding War Diaries and Intelligence Summaries and contained in F.S. Regs., Part II. and the Staff Manual respectively. Title pages will be prepared in manuscript.

Hour, Date, Place	Summary of Events and Information	Remarks and References to Appendices
16th July A.S.	After this morning Brig-Gen' Oolly visited Bath. Bn.	
10.45 a.m	Cricketers arrived. Working Parties as usual. Very dark night. 13 Rifles received by Col Palmer.	2/Lieuts TANNER & CROUGHLEY 3rd Rd Regt arrived & reported for duty & posted to Batteries.
17th July	Stormy weather, with high wind. Working parties as usual. 2 men after noon received by Col Palmer.	Capt C.L.C. RATHBONE 3rd R.B. arrived. 2 Lieut R.H. PENNY
18th July -- (Sunday)	Fine day. Church service in Ravine.	3/R.B. and 2nd Lieut B.S. PRICE arrived & reported for duty. 10 O.R.s sent to rejoin Coy & report here.
,, 10 p.m	Party instructed in Trenches by H.Q. on the Right and marched to Redoubt at ROUGE DE BOUT and GUESNOY RD	
19th July	Fine warm day. Usual Fatigues. Raiders coming? Working parties at night 200 men, 3 Officers, nothing unusual.	
20th July	Fine day. Usual Parades. Grenadier Parades at Guns School. Cricketers using Foot Ground, practice of "Bomb" Parties at night. 4 Officers, 200 men.	Lieut P.B.M. POWELL, 3rd R.B. Regt arrived. OR arriving at Battn. Reinforcements H.Q. Battn for duty.
21st July	No dark threats parades. Grenadiers at Bomb School. Working party of 4 Officers & Officers 4700 Men.	
22nd July	This morning Flight rain and strong cloudy. Parade as before Bath. & Fatigues. Digging party at night 4 Officers 400 Men. Day not unlike.	
23rd July	Raining day. Church Service Usual Bn. Guard Duty. Practice with Rifle. Pay 20. 6 Officers & 50 Men attended at the P.B. Coy D.H.A. Rd. ... rec' letters to meet by hand. Mr Ormerod chemical expert. 2.30 p.m Coy Grenadier Salter at Brigade Bomb School.	Reinforcement from Base. 2/Lieut W.L. WILLIAMS ,, B. KEABLE ,, J.B. BULL ,, E.A. ELLEN

Army Form C. 2118.

WAR DIARY:

Instructions regarding War Diaries and Intelligence Summaries and contained in F.S. Regs., Part II. and the Staff Manual respectively. Title pages will be prepared in manuscript.

Hour, Date, Place	Summary of Events and Information	Remarks and references to Appendices
23rd July 1915. 5 p.m.	Brown Scheme (Infantry) relieves B Coy 1st at Bn the Revd HARGREAVES. Supping camp. 8 Officers 200 men Bearers	Two men very badly poisoned by gas. Nights return to our billet.
24th July —	Line with some showers. Morning parades as usual.	
— " 8.30 p.m.	Battn relieved Bacons R/ in 1.P.1.B. 1.R. Line and Perch 1.R. 1.B. 1.R. Relief complete 9.45 p.m. Evening very quiet & up to 5 a.m. Enemy shown on enemys infantry points in P.1 Machine Guns 10.30 p.m. Burst shrapnel over men ROUGE DEBOUT at Their own by 2/Northampton Regt. in Sunday Post 22.22.	
25th July (Sunday)	(Continuing) 2 gun shots in officers post Enemy shelled Ormington Post & PETILLON (V.E. CORNER) at 10.30 a.m. 9.12.30 p.m. Much damage but no casualties. Men on shelter line & Coms no call. Enemy put down 1 B.M.J.F.84 4.45 p.m. Two workers parties from the Queens twice carrier over. Some enemy came from 2.5 & 3.50 pr. carts in the support line. Patrol some at night relieved information sent to shelter & Coms. Tm line	1 killed 1 wounded
26th July —	Set day. Enemy shelled I.R. and SUICIDE CORNER and V.E. CORNER R.E. laying our Guy Ruts trenches. Our men retired whilst 1 A gather paid in Trenches. mounted station line during night. Working parties on wire in supporting Line during day. Quiet with exception of light enemy.	2 Officers wounded 2nd Lieut E NEVILL H.B. Peastland 8.44 and 2 B 10 30 p.m. Sgt T. Fuller Thos Wind, Capt. or Ad Camp or Bufford 2nd Lieut. BKE ABLE and M. Wright 2 men wounded MOT Night 2 men wounded — not danger.
27th July —	Brg. Gen. J. Oakley inspected troops in brought line 8.30 to 10.30 a.m. The Revd W. Southern visited men 12-30 p.m. Enemy shelled Duchess N.I Sh. about 2 p.m. 9 later V.C CORNER	

Army Form C. 2118.

WAR DIARY:

Instructions regarding War Diaries and Intelligence Summaries and contained in F.S. Regs., Part II. and the Staff Manual respectively. Title pages will be prepared in manuscript.

Hour, Date, Place	Summary of Events and Information	Remarks and references to Appendices
27th July 98.	No unusual occurance. A few rounds of bombs during morning. Nights 27/28 S.E. bombard observed by enemy commenced 9.30pm Hyde Park near Bng – Gpt Boxley Temporary Coy Q.M.S.W.	
28/7/18 4pm	Desultory rifle fire on our right about 11-30 pm last night. Also scale gun fire about 20 rounds. One nap Quiet day. At 6.1 J.S. bombard commenced. T Battn. At 9.30pm. Enemy shelled Bettar N.O.R. vicinity East Transport Lines. Left wady two men seriously hit.	The bomber Lt. to B.N.K GOODALL + Pt.C. ALLEN during 9th July were wounded on the Bluess and buried in Cemetery 1.8 Front ln Sunken Road nightly. An unnamed Pte.
29/7/18 Sunday	Quiet night. Bat off. fatigue 75 S.R.S.O Coy under Lt. O.W Hall left at 9.30pm. Usual wiring Transport Reported 8.45pm. Our Bat left up to several Coyn forward Lt. Transport Sap front vicinity Cryptic Bungalow.	Pte. Dudby temporary near Pt.q Sap Pt. N.O.R. also wounded & missing, Trench 9/L/18.
30/7/18 4pm	Quiet 9pm. Bde attack near reserves that been with 4yd 16th reports. De taken over by 11/Cameronians lighted on 30th/July. C.O. & officers of this Batt meeted Batt about 10.30am making spare in Welly Street seen (B. Settler) Our Casualty 3-30pm shells burst into Lt J.S. Coy again visible. No cas. This day consisted throughout in enact, but more enemy than usual especially at night. Numerous prisms not being actually near Ypres. Scarce on one of these from I.R. Patrols from J.R. for a majority of Equipment from the front of T.S.	2 wounded: / Sunshine 31/J Pte Palmer + QM Sgt wounded Sgt Berry, Pte Dilker and Pte Suttel Brought in body of Lieut C.G. WORTON killed 9/May, whose was buried in Cemetery 1.8, Pte Skelton was told day of that Regiment were reconst. wounded.

Army Form C. 2118

WAR DIARY:

Instructions regarding War Diaries and Intelligence Summaries and contained in F.S. Regs., Part II. and the Staff Manual respectively. Title pages will be prepared in manuscript.

Hour, Date, Place	Summary of Events and Information	Remarks and references to Appendices
31st July 1916	Fine, hot day. Commdr. returned. Bn. was relieved in trenches at 9 p.m by the 1/Bedfords. Reorganisation of HQrs taken over was to O.C. 8/Northants Regt. Bn was moved to billets by companies. A & B Coy to CROIX BLANCHE and Pont 26. C & D Coy to billets in RUE DU QUESNES. P. Coy finding garrison in pts 27 & 22. Relief complete 9.15 p.m. Bn. billeted 11 p.m.	One Platoon of "A" Coy in support of machine gun at pont 26. A Coy supplying at pont 22 & D Coy platoon at pont 21.

8th, Division.

24th, Brigade.

2nd, East Lancs.

August, 1915.

T 10

121/6753

Miss Foster

8th K Warren

2nd Post Raised.
Vol IX
August / 15

Army Form C. 2118.

WAR DIARY:

Instructions regarding War Diaries and Intelligence Summaries and contained in F.S. Regs., Part II. and the Staff Manual respectively. Title pages will be prepared in manuscript.

Hour, Date, Place	Summary of Events and Information	Remarks and References to Appendices
3rd August 1915.	Lce/Sgt Irwin KRR to Trenches with Instructions for Sgt informing inlying pickets. 8.45pm. Darky parties 250 ELR and 200 KRR. Rev. Horguvars held stores 6pm at CROIX BLANCHE.	
4th August 1915.	Morning parades on usual lot at 7 am. Mr Irwin lectured on M.G. Range by Capt Porter Asst MG offr. Both relieved patrols from Pt & Black Watch in trenches 8.30pm from CROIX BLANCHE. Rev. of Worcesters complete 10pm. Black Watch 10.45pm. Headquarters at 2o 3rd Nd O9 near DEAD DOGS FARM. No casualties. D Coy 10th KRR accompanied 10th to trenches and were detailed along the line for individual instruction. One platoon of each Coy OC & Adj 10th KRR accompanied party to the trenches. Quiet night. Late information 1 wounded. 11 June 3 1915	Irwin from BRUNKARD'S WALK (Condomaire Farm) in I.S.C. BOUTILLERIE Ree in H.Q. "A" "B" "C" "D" Coys in front line from the night. 4 Marshall guns ELR in trenches & one Machine Gun in Post F.3. One Lewis M Gun 10th KRR on Coy left flank. 1 Wounded. It Lieut J Hart
5th August --	Conditions normal. 12 Machine Gunners inspected to join 1st M.ELR by special request. Lieut Gen Bulfin & Brig Genl Jack visited trenches 8 am — 11.15 a.m. D Coy KRR relieved by A Coy & ½ B Dr instruction on platoons. Patrol from B Coy attempted to investigate hostile trip flare apparatus to be used by enemy, but were unsuccessful.	Lieut Jabez M Grun in F.3 Transferred to Trenches further right across our right trenches reported to F.3 over night. K.R.R Machine gunner relieved every 24 hours. 1 Wounded

Army Form C. 2118.

WAR DIARY:

Instructions regarding War Diaries and Intelligence Summaries and contained in F.S. Regs., Part II. and the Staff Manual respectively. Title pages will be prepared in manuscript.

Hour, Date, Place	Summary of Events and Information	Remarks and References to Appendices
8th August 1915 (Sunday)	Working parties in the Communic Avenues, Bryan Dry Walk, Herron Avenue all day. B Coy K.R.R. and M Gunners relieved 6 p.m. The Batn was relieved in trenches 4.45 p.m. by 7th Dr Middlesex Rgt on 3.S. 4.P. 4.Q. and by 2nd Seaforth Rgt on 2.S. 3.P. 3.Q. 3.R. at 10.30 p.m. Batn. marched to billets at 2 pounds B.9.C. Se MAUR and Bret Pierre. Arrived 12 MN. No Casualties.	On arrival men B.9.C. St Maur Coys Ran A.T.B in Rue BATAILLE. Coys at PORT a CLOUS.
9th August 1915.	Parade under Coy arrangements for cleaning up etc. Batn bathed at Gailly Baths from 2 p.m.	
10th —"— —"—	Parade at 7 a.m. & 10.30 a.m. under Coy & under A.T.B myr at Musketry 2-6.30 p.m. Captain Morton & fifty-five NCOs new drivers & joining Corps of Miners. Some stayed Limit Lie at Pulteney 3rd Corps. Govenors invited billets at Batn. 3 p.m.	A.T.B myr The new CO. HM
11th —"— —"—	Parade at 7 a.m., 10.30 a.m. & 2.30 p.m. as usual. 2/Lieut G.E Marsh arrived on eppt from 12th Lancers. Digging parties 9 a.m 100 men & 9.30 p.m. 200 men. Fine hot day	

Army Form C. 2118.

WAR DIARY:

Instructions regarding War Diaries and Intelligence Summaries are contained in F.S. Regs., Part II. and the Staff Manual respectively. Title pages will be prepared in manuscript.

Hour, Date, Place	Summary of Events and Information	Remarks and References to Appendices
16th August 1915.	Parade at 10·30 a.m. as usual. Officers marched past on their new ages. The Bands of the G.O. Ship 176 were received. Trigger work done by Patrols on R. and G. Coys. Honours & Mentions. Batten (Lieut C. Coy) Reading on near B. & a Coys Billets and marched to occupy ELBOW FARM, SMITH'S VILLA & FERRETS.	
" 7.40 p.m	C Coy marched separately from CROIX de ROME to SMITH'S VILLA.	
" 8 p.m	Billets at B & C. St MAUR hanouse over to Royal Bombs. Rest except Gm Sgt On which were taken over by Sergy R. Ottery	
" 10 p.m	After reporting Coys in Posts out morning, Daylight Orders were received to march to Billets as nominus remainder of Bae and Parade through to formed Sections. Batten marched Billets. a Coy at ABEL Post & Billets in	
" 12 M.N.	RUE DE QUESNE. D Coy (Remainder Coy) at call of OS (Daventh) in ELBOW FARM and SMITH'S VILLA. Billets mean. For HQ B in Rue de Quesne. Fine Starlight night. Wet morning with heavy Thunderstorm.	Billets Satisfactory for 2nd RB O.R. Rooms, which except at Ferrets, and not very clean. Water source not good.
17th August 1915,	A Coy at FLEURBAIX. Rifle Range 8 am to 10·30 a.m. Other Coys Parades at 10·30 am & 2·30 p.m as required. Digging party 200 by night at WYE FARM.	Watermills, 1 Leapistrix

Army Form C. 2118.

WAR DIARY:

Instructions regarding War Diaries and Intelligence Summaries and contained in F.S. Regs., Part II. and the Staff Manual respectively. Title pages will be prepared in manuscript.

Hour, Date, Place	Summary of Events and Information	Remarks and References to Appendices
21st August 1915	Fine day, work on four Communication Trenches in front of our rd. line alongside [sic] position, about 15 shells special BOUTILLERIE village at 11 a.m. no damage, working party 50 men under Lieut Libch sent to work under R.E.	1 Wounded - 3 Aug 15 Appx Return were brought up supply to BOUTILLERIE front & copies thence by Runners to Trenches
22nd August — (Sunday)	Fine day, R.C. Service was held firing the received. 20 Germans coming opposite were fired in rapidly 4-30 p.m There was an outstanding duel over our lines. Later two of our aeroplanes returned the Germans over their lines. One of our aeroplanes fought & seen to collapse, fell in German lines. Our M.Gun at O.C. opened heavy fire on 2 Germans aeroplanes, but then Officer of my Division wounded at 15.10. Two German Trench guns returned mostly but and Lieut Tarn & one M Gun Kaafir were there were slightly wounded.	
6-45 pm	German working party three stormy nights and Snow in. Usual working party 50 men from A Coy moved for R.E. Renaissance at W. Su. Allemee [Allemée] taken. Much strong work in front of a Coys front Our improved front Dugout suitable for weather.	
23rd August	Fine day. An increased amount of artillery across 2 Sept 15 Appx from the German lines during the night	1 Wounded - 2 Sept 15 Appx

WAR DIARY:

Army Form C. 2118.

Instructions regarding War Diaries and Intelligence Summaries and contained in F.S. Regs., Part II. and the Staff Manual respectively. Title pages will be prepared in manuscript.

Hour, Date, Place	Summary of Events and Information	Remarks and References to Appendices
6th August 1915	Very hot. Sniping still considerable, but condition of trenches improved. Some work done by small parties on Maori Avenue etc. +c. DEAD DOGS & CONVENT our "C" Coy, & 2 "B" Coy 10 KRR relieved A Coy & 2 B Coy 1st E. "C" Coy & 2 "B" Coy 10 KRR relieved A Coy & 2 B Coy 1st Devons as platoons. At 9-30 p.m. Capt Western, CSM Richmond, Sgt Darcy & Cpt Wilkinson attempted to reach enemy trenches but were heard and fired on by enemy. At 11-30 p.m. they made another attempt guided by Sergt Bright and reached and carefully examined enemy trench, bringing back one F, O, C & 3rd Bn. & 9th 24th Res sent their thanks to this patrol on their useful work.	2 Wounded (accidental) Kenyport, King 2 Lieut Q Hot.
7th August —	Dull day but nothing fine. Enemys trench mortary seen relieved during night, as they were very quiet. Our sniping up from different places. The platoons of KRR were relieved by D Co KRR.	1 Sent to Hos
— 3 p.m.	Our artillery shelled our destroyed Maoria cottage (number 869 on map) believed to contain snipers. Some outburst of rifle & MG gun fire after dark were shelling during day but not as our trenches except between Convents.	
8th August 1915	Quiet night. Usual morning sniping. Fine day. Some sniping but less during than before.	1 Wounded, 1 Lieut to Hot

WAR DIARY:

Army Form C. 2118.

Instructions regarding War Diaries and Intelligence Summaries and contained in F.S. Regs., Part II. and the Staff Manual respectively. Title pages will be prepared in manuscript.

HOUR, DATE, PLACE	SUMMARY OF EVENTS AND INFORMATION	REMARKS AND REFERENCES TO APPENDICES
24th August 1915	R.E. Officer arrived with 4 men to arrange for alteration of trenches to new pattern. Working parties in front of bunch disguising ditch & improving lines of parapet.	
— 11 p.m. to 12 M.N.	Enemy fired several times at their working parties but to no avail. During the night enemy fired a number of cannon about 100 yds forward from 8a trench". Officers present we heard to inspire our men by saying "Reserve is broken all over Russia, Transylvania progress in German hands. First 15,00,000 we is our [?]... army. French-Russians we have enough to win".	1 standard lost to 4th.
25th August —	R.E. Officer arranged with Offcer of French regiment to reinforce part of parapet and accordingly 8 men chosen to this work taken the 40 sandbags the 20 feet ridge at Bara from the plate. Parapet 5 m 20 feet thick at Bara During the afternoon Regt. Chaplain CH.F. sur the R.C. Chaplain visited the lines. May just to duty vacated HQ 5 p.m.	
— 4 p.m.	Enemy fired a number of shrapnel shells towards CROIX MARECHAL Headquarters, evidently in no uncertain manner at Pr HQrs. Much machine gun fire going on by C Coy while in our lines being the hour. Many casualties were caused and a large amount of their artillery fire and 20 as to the artillery gave a room in the forest.	

WAR DIARY:

Army Form C. 2118.

Instructions regarding War Diaries and Intelligence Summaries and contained in F.S. Regs., Part II. and the Staff Manual respectively. Title pages will be prepared in manuscript.

Hour, Date, Place	Summary of Events and Information	Remarks and References to Appendices
25th August 1915	Sgnt Col Pickle took over temporary command of 24th Bn vice Brig-Genl Oxley (on leave to England.)	
26th "	Fine warm day. Ripping & the trenches restored. Enemy fired about 15 shells round BOUTILLERIE FARM. No damage. Battn was relieved in trenches by 1/12th Reg't about 8.30 p.m. Relief complete about 9.15 p.m. Capt Guerrier inexplicably killed & taken over from Westminster Rgt. All reported in billets about 10.45 p.m. No casualties.	2 Lieut to Hosp! Casualties in trenches from 16-25th August. Killed 1 off and 2 o.r. Wounded 5 o.r. Slightly
27th " "	Inspections paid us by 10 off. Working Party 2 Officers & 100 men. Stores for Rooks checked over & completed. Fine hot day. 91 guns used FLEURBAIX Route.	3 men to Hosp!
28th " "	Paraded in Billets as usual. Working party 2 Officers & 100 men under R.E. Lt. D.C. P.H. Snr inspected Carr Draft. (42 N.C.O & men) Battn bathed at SAILLY baths. Rifle range. B Coy 7-10.30 a.m. A Coy 10.30 a.m. to 2 p.m. Working Party in evening 2 Officers & 100 men	
29th " " (Sunday)	Fine morning but removed to heavy rain in afternoon. Evening-Storm. Church Parade for all Denominations Working Party 9 a.m-2 p.m. Evening working party	4 Lieut to Hosp!

WAR DIARY:

Army Form C. 2118.

Instructions regarding War Diaries and Intelligence Summaries and contained in F.S. Regs., Part II. and the Staff Manual respectively. Title pages will be prepared in manuscript.

Hour, Date, Place	Summary of Events and Information	Remarks and References to Appendices
29th August (Sunday)	Several working parties in evening cancelled owing to wet weather. Special instructions required in consequence of capture of prisoner in previous three who states practicability of gas attack.	
30th " 1915	Recon: on enemy 7am, 10.30am & 2.30pm. Working party 4 officers & 200 men. Digging fire, generally been allow & strong. Battery rec'd several rounds except Hd/L Coy from 7am to 10 min past [?] of DC Trenches on account of dispersion of men by Germans. Stood to dawn.	2/Lieut R N Eyre joined from 3rd Bn. 4 sent to Hosp.
31st August "	Recon: on enemy. Fire continuing but dull and cold evening. Digging parties ordinary & expiring as usual. Heavy shrapnel firing therefore to right during afternoon. B Coy HQ On 2 2 6 platoons went to from B Coy HQ to Rue de Quesnoy trench. Morale [?] Post to Rue du from Jan H On G near BH R.A. Inter Coy Grenadier competition held in field near Bn Hd Qr. (Result Ch. 2. B. 13.)	Blue dot always Prush. 65. By reverse from strength - 50

8th, Division.

24th, Brigade.

2nd, East Lancs.

September, 1915.

8th, Division.

24th, Brigade.

24/8

121/7707

8th Historum

2nd East Lancs.
Vol X
Sep 15

T.11

This diary also gives practically
no indication as to where it was
fighting on 25/9/15 — this point
may be elucidated from the
8th Divn diary — H
28/10/15

Army Form C. 2118.

WAR DIARY:

Instructions regarding War Diaries and Intelligence Summaries and contained in F.S. Regs., Part II. and the Staff Manual respectively. Title pages will be prepared in manuscript.

Hour, Date, Place	Summary of Events and Information	Remarks and References to Appendices
4th September 1915	Very wet in early morning. Fine after & by 10 Late on evening. Church Parade at 10-30 a.m. Inspection of A & B Coy at Arms Drill at 2 p.m.	Inter Coy Football Competition started. Two sick to Hospital
5th September (Sunday)	Church parade 9-30 a.m. D/S Dr Field. Conference of C.O's at 10a. D/S Dr as with Brig Genl Stephens. Comd g 25th Infty Bde noon present.	Six sick to Hospital
6th September 1915	Inter-Coy Competition in Physical Exercises at 7-15 a.m. Result :- C.B.A.D. Orderly Room at 8-15 a.m. Conference of Officers at 8.30 a.m. Officers waited Cwno. to the Brig Major Leask Byles to arrange next for Tuesday.	Four sick to Hospital
" 2 pm	Inter-Coy Arms Drill Competition. Result :- D.A. with C.B. equal. Operation Orders 25th Bde & Operation Orders 62 from 51st Division received. Relief in trenches postponed from Tuesday & later doubt. Working parties provided	
7th September " "	Bright morning. Warmer. Coy Parade at 7 a.m. 10-30 a.m. & 2 p.m. March working parties. Trenchdigging Parties generally had a march of 5 to 6 miles each way, & which wages conveyance able to carry them. They had a long day's work.	Three sick to Hospital
8th September " "	Fine. Bath Parade on South bank of R. on T.Y.S. Cross Country Race run at same time on North bank. Teams of 26 per Coy.	Two sick to Hospital

Army Form C. 2118

WAR DIARY:

Instructions regarding War Diaries and Intelligence Summaries and contained in F.S. Regs., Part II. and the Staff Manual respectively. Title pages will be prepared in manuscript.

Hour, Date, Place	Summary of Events and Information	Remarks and References to Appendices
11th September (continued)	Captain A. Macpherman in command. Lectures the attack. Lieuten. Quart. Campbell Harris Flgmts sent to No 4 Division FORAY POST.	
12th September (Sunday) 1915.	Church Parade on Football field at 10 am. & General 9.30 am. O.C. & 24 n.c.o.s attended. Reinstatement Parade at 2 pm. The men who were wounded The Meerum engagement. Brennan. across That Boffe, were return to Sunday in ordinary tour of 15 days taken from Capt of WELL FARM station to SOUTH. ERIE Road both inclusive.	1 Warrant at Dismounted 1 sick at Hospital
13th September — "	Both bathed in SAILLY baths from 7. to 11 am. S.O.S.B.P. raised 5.37 am. Germans of the way firing Previously. There lost "S.O.S" from offering of Starting on all myline Covered by 5.45 am. Heavy Artillery fire over Boyt of SAILLY and rain of rifle ammunition from B & C ST MAUR. L.R.D 8 ?? Brown explosives cells of the South.	Officers reported of Out Seconson housing Forum with a more between Trenches 1 Sick to Hospital
14th September — "	Both Parades for maneuvre at 7 am. Dismissed in Emergency drawn. House Parade 10.30 am & 2 pm. 2 Col draff & 15 men of 5th F Ser Coy on Range. 6 to 11 am Lunch Breakfast on Range. 7 am to Ballr. Working Party of 200 with provisions.	L.rs sick to Hospital
15th September — "	Both maneuvre Parade at 7 am. Practice supply of Order, Cavalrie, etc. First Bt. Conduct attended Conference at Gen. Hd. Qrs. 9-15 am.	Three Sick to Hospital

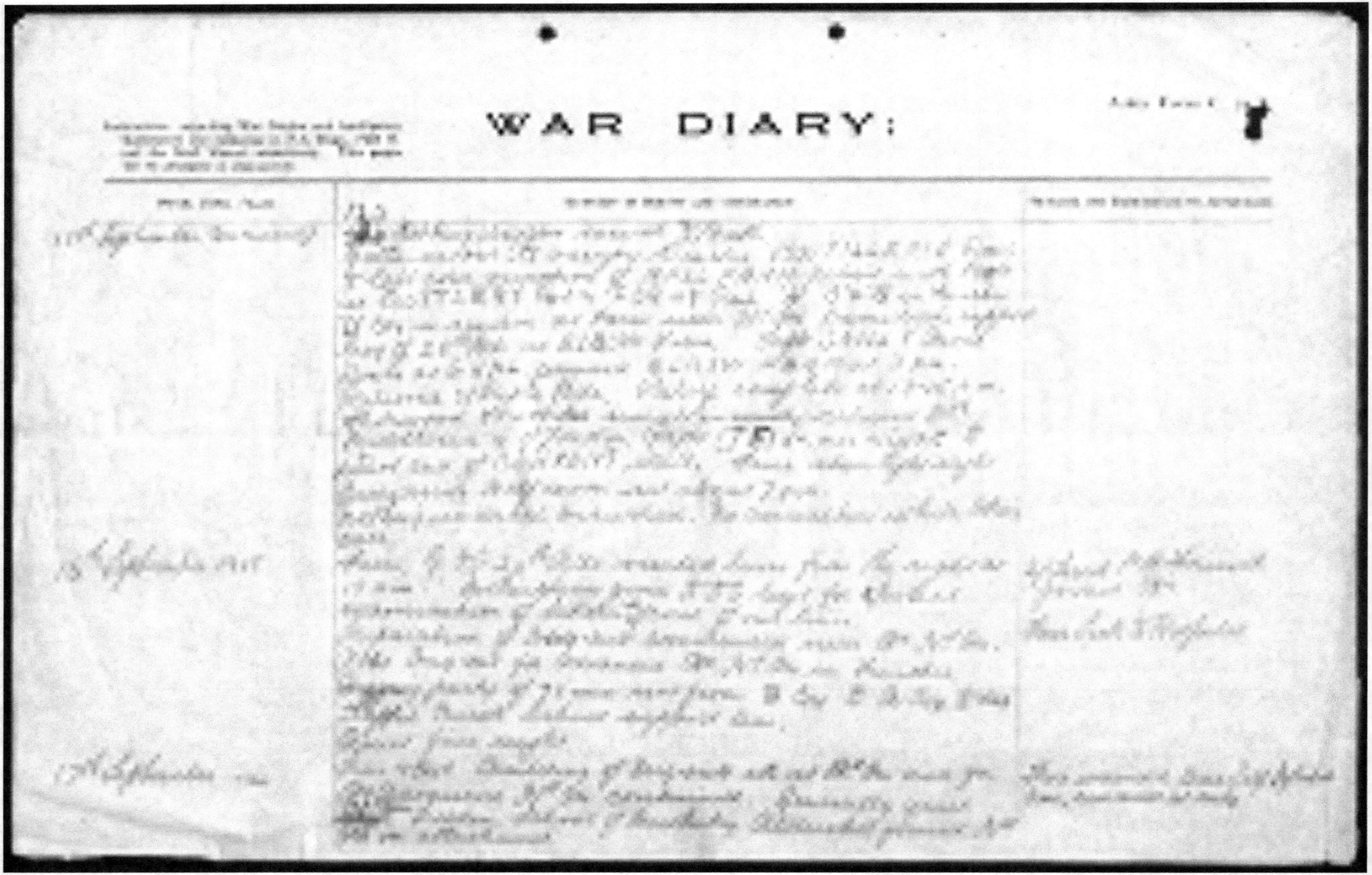
WAR DIARY:

WAR DIARY:

Army Form C.

Instructions regarding War Diaries and Intelligence Summaries and contained in F.S. Regs., Part II. and the Staff Manual respectively. Title pages will be prepared in manuscript.

Hour, Date, Place	Summary of Events and Information	Remarks and References to Appendices
17th September (continued)	that both opened with 8 Pdrs, Guns, also 2 enemy mobiles to detachment. D Coy provide 100 men to continue traffic control road. O.C. A Coy (Capt Pocerras) at night. The G.H.Q. 24th Bde vacated post of ruin.	
16th September 1915	4 a.m. Incomplete bombs and a long morning of the enemy trench considered mortar, any of bells nothing in exchange. Iron hurried over to Lieut Col Rennell & Lewis in BOUTILLERIE farm. Detonated etc by bombers under 2/Lieut Rogers and placed in the (very enemy) redoubt during the 6th & 7th Divs H.Q. 24 Bde interrogated, French & Lewis held by entrenched Gurkha TIN BARN AVENUE & BOUTILLERIE Road & line & H.T. day. D Coy fatigue gave trenches to prepare "stretcher case" track from MARBLE ARCH to TIN BARN AVENUE. Conference of C.O. 24th Bde at 2.30 p.m. N.9 D at 4 p.m. The intake in front of B Coy where it had previously been exposed on trench lines subsequently out by enemy, was re-examined & damage was found to be one of bullets except in certain passages which had been cut by 25th Bde. Careful examination of which made. A German Report was transferred not received. Two copies of the Gazette Ardennes were transferred back by Lieut Crosby of the patrol. Both bore inscriptions from the Germans to English denouncing atrocities & extravagances of another —	One killed. One wounded.

WAR DIARY:

Hour, Date, Place	Summary of Events and Information	Remarks and References to Appendices
20th September (Continued)	Trenches on ridge skirmishing about 6.30 p.m. Relief complete about 7.15 p.m. Hostile rifle + machine gun fire stopped to right to take over trenches held by 25th Bn. 7 Bn hostile + further supply of ammunition received from the Bn refilled at BOUTILLERIE Farm. Dug-outs for broken figures at same place further Dug-outs commenced at detachment of 28th Battle Reserves. HQ Bn Dug-Out complete during the night. Also 8 coy received Trenches. All roads worked hard up to 12.30 a.m. Small trench bridges along from BOTTLERY Rd to WATLING Street surveyed by Gunner & Pnr ____ Lieut _____ French Motors & R.E. Officers Patrol arrived from BOUTILLERIE Farm to stop rifle fire during the night by bonnets? Bn Pioneers? All wounded further Begun the night the Germans were heard to call out "When are you coming over, we are waiting for you." Besides knowing of snipers were heard on left of By under our fire behind N 61 & N 642 straight direction of close line WELL FARM Several my single machine gunfire was kept up at certain points throughout by our guns.	
21st September 1915.	4.19 a.m. G.P.F.A. Battery behind our line first single shot of gun about 4.8 a.m. hour. Security from enfilade the round from about 5 a.m. but not yet fully opened up. Bombardment by 6"," 8", rifle, heavy firing continued all day.	Four wounded. One wounded at duty. Four deep surprise.

WAR DIARY:

Army Form C. 2118

HOUR, DATE, PLACE	SUMMARY OF EVENTS AND INFORMATION	REMARKS AND REFERENCES TO APPENDICES
22nd September (continued)	Shrapnel against BATTERY CORNER by heart Lt Edwards Platoon, & Cpl Parapet was hit at four times but there was no serious casualties. During these six shots at times, but only nearly by day by night. Enemy fired 6 small bursts which fell (5 yds) from Shrine about 9 p.m. Sgt Jas. Hopkins (25 Btty) and Bty Qm Oxley wounded. On H.Q. Enemy parapet work opposite WELL FARM emplacement before. Received our Rifle Gun Spa... explosions all day & nights at intervals on both Parapet and emplacement. Trenches and flares where were had been put. Enemy made several attempts during night to press slough but was driven back at once. Upon successful made a Carrier Reconnaissance of the enemy's work in front of Gun Trenches by night opposite WELL FARM, towards CORNER Fort. He found it apparently not strong, but during his examination. It seems another search lots of cover, his examination it seems another search, the abyss was carried routinely, but depths first.	
23rd September 1916	Heavy bombardment of German trenches continued from 6.30 A.m. All the morning & increased in afternoon. They little retaliation till after noon when about very 15 Pounds H.E. shrapnel were fired at front trench, especially WELL FARM & Chapelle with Courtaulier from Southerly direction. Both rapt Luigi line Direct hits but no damage whatever.	Five Wounded One. They evacuated at duty. Two were to Hospital.

WAR DIARY:

Army Form C. 2118

Instructions regarding War Diaries and Intelligence Summaries and contained in F.S. Regs., Part II. and the Staff Manual respectively. Title pages will be prepared in manuscript.

Hour, Date, Place	Summary of Events and Information	Remarks and References to Appendices
23rd September (continued)	Shells also dropped near BOTTLEY Post. From 2 pm onwards fire increased, a large number of Heavy 4.2" & 5.9" Howitzer shells from front and gulleys near CHORD Line & between support reserve trenches. Also many 15 pounders. One shell fell among a number of rifles, but otherwise damage was not very serious. About 5 p.m. several shells fell in & round BOUTILLERIE Farm occupied by 2/ front PARIS & 3/11 St. Bourbons. No serious damage. No serious damage by our guns to enemy's shrapnel arrangements. Opposite 65 & B Coys. But Bays & 7/ft" in the lumps of concrete were seen in the air. The wire in front of "CORNER Post appeared to be demolished. During the day working parties from D Coy. deepened "Gunners Walk" and the Graffs trench in rear of support trench. At 4.25 pm. There was an intense bombardment for 10 minutes or to prior to assault. The weather was fine till about 6 pm. when heavy rain set in continued off & on during the night. 8.25/5 pm. There was again enemy's intense bombardment for 15 minutes then very stiff fire all down our line. The enemy at 3 whitish rockets being fired as y signal attack. The night was exceptionally quiet as regards enemy's fire. Our guns fired throughout at intervals on communications trenches & enemies trenches	

WAR DIARY:

Army Form C. 2118.

Instructions regarding War Diaries and Intelligence Summaries and contained in F.S. Regs., Part II. and the Staff Manual respectively. Title pages will be prepared in manuscript.

Hour, Date, Place	Summary of Events and Information	Remarks and References to Appendices
23rd September (continued)	and rifle machine gun fire was kept up at intervals throughout any chance of wire or notable being made. Wire field guns were trying to cut the front trenches during the night.	
24th September 1915	Rain ?? at intervals during night. All communication trenches etc very muddy & difficult. At 4.25 a.m. there was an intense bombardment occupied in view by very heavy rifle fire from our line from westward in all around the line in front of trenches. During it very strong ?? ?? were there ???. There was ?? ?? from the enemy about 4.55 a.m. ?? ?? from these positions or switch positions at length throughout but otherwise the enemy made no advance on our front. Hand did not begin to get really light till about 5.10 a.m. Our rifle fire from over 10 pounders ?? in B Coy firing at ?? yesterday one. Our heavy artillery bombardment was entirely recommenced at 7 a.m. This was not much kept on to 10 a.m. when enemy retaliated with 5"9" & other guns, mostly at our forward trenches & area. One 5"9" struck & Maxim Gun emplacement killing two ??? ??? (Pte. Bryant) & wounding three others (Pte. Maslym Gun. Otherwise our casualties were very small. Heavy shelling continued practically all day & appears ?????. Considerable damage being done to the ???.	During the day, 28 R.C. Queen of the 70th were permitted to leave the trenches and were replaced by the Bishop of Montreal O.A.C.S.T.M.A.U.R. the 70th when left from trenches by the Br Trenches ???. ?? ??? Pervis promoted (One from M.C. Fish ???) at duty) One injured

WAR DIARY:

Army Form C. 2118.

Hour, Date, Place	Summary of Events and Information	Remarks and References to Appendices
24th September (continued) 11. p.m.	The Bn was then distributed as follows:- "C" Coy holding H.Q. H.R. That of H.S. "B" Coy that of H.S. 5. P. & 5.Q. Two Lothian Farm POWELL FARM Special. B.& G. One "A" Coy on the supports line behind B & G. Dui centre at old P.O.Bn under Lieut. Calvert. Three Machine Guns under Lieut. Tuck, and P.O.Bn Bomber under 2/Lieut Brown in front line. Passage from C in C re reserve recommended to all ranks.	
25th September 1916 4-25 a.m.	A murky dull daybreak, wind South West. Our bombardment of the enemy's trenches commenced reprising by 1 O.B. & C Coy & Wilhelm Given their Series of cheering & cries of Goodluck. From the front line from Caithill another rumble of joyful sang the cry from Lieut. Also trench mortars & Stokes Guns fired smoke. Smoke.	Lieut. J.E. Killeen 3rd South Wales retained was killed Other Ranks. Five killed -- 11 -- 23 Wounded One Died of Wounds 27/9/16
" 4-30 a.m.	Reported by 2/Lieut. Brown the enemy trench were known was unfortun- ate & all smoke had to be discontinued.	
" 5.56 a.m.	The smoke ceased as 5.56 a.m. was not employed as the wind continued unfavourable.	
" 7.15 a.m.	Our Machine Guns went forward to Special Rifle Pits who had taken Goleman Trench. Low Lane Cot. The Guns up.	

WAR DIARY:

Army Form C. 2118.

Hour, Date, Place	Summary of Events and Information	Remarks and References to Appendices
26 September (Continuing) BOUTILLERIE	A/Lt. Ogonton to shelter. Lieut Boyd Thomson gun for saving the ground the day. By 9 P.M. the enemy's enterprise against the attack. Orders received from 24 Bde that Battn would be relieved in the trenches by 9 P.M. but as report of BCLambert in rear of parapet regd. to report by regl all Seargeants, rations &c to be collected. This order was cancelled & gun ordered to remain in the trenches. The fire accepted even then on interest:— C. Coy. 4, A. 4. R. keg of 4. S. B Coy Hay 4. S. 5 P. a picket being held by A. C. 21. a pairing of 5 P. L.Q. 9 Cy in Reserve at farm near Rifine Bn H.Q. Four Machine Guns in front line, 2 out of the 3 sent out of action having been replaced by Vickers Gun having been sent off to replace the gun permanently disabled. H.Q. Br. Brooks at BOUTILLERIE Farm.	
— 7·15 p.m.	Received N.Gr Closed H/O returned to regul H.Q.Bn Lieut Col S.D. Lambert resumed command of the Battn.	

WAR DIARY:

Army Form C. 2118.

HOUR, DATE, PLACE	SUMMARY OF EVENTS AND INFORMATION	REMARKS AND REFERENCES TO APPENDICES
26th September (Continued)	Officers present with the Battn. during the operations:- Major G.E.M. Hill Captain G.W.O. Protyn, Actg Adjt. Lieut W.T. Rutherford Orderly Officer to Hon. Col. J.S. Lambert 2/Lieut Jenkinson, Liaison Officer to Lieut Col F.J. Lambert 2/Lieut H.G. Morris Y. R. M.G. Brigden Lieut S.E.C. Lewis, Machine Gun Officer "A" Coy:- Capt. G.B. Newcombe Lieut M.C. Finch (slightly wounded, at duty) 2/Lieut J.A. Marshall 2/Lieut B.L.R. Cope "B" Coy Lieut P.B.M. Powell 2/Lieut J.W. Bell 2/Lieut J.E. Killick (killed in action 27/9/15) 2/Lieut O.E. Vienna	

WAR DIARY:

Army Form C. 2118.

Instructions regarding War Diaries and Intelligence Summaries and contained in F.S. Regs., Part II. and the Staff Manual respectively. Title pages will be prepared in manuscript.

Hour, Date, Place	Summary of Events and Information	Remarks and References to Appendices
	"E" Coy:- Captain C.D. Martin Lieut. A.W. Long 2/Lieut E.J. Pegler 2/Lieut E.A. Glen "D" Coy Captain T.C.M. Draken Lieut. R.Y. Parker Lieut. R.W. Keyser Transport officers:- Lt. & Mr J. Shaw 2/Lieut. F. Lewis-Jones. Medical Officer:- Captain D.D. Craig, R.A.M.C	

WAR DIARY:

Army Form C. 2118.

Instructions regarding War Diaries and Intelligence Summaries and contained in F.S. Regs., Part II. and the Staff Manual respectively. Title pages will be prepared in manuscript.

Summary of Events and Information

Strength of Battalion

Available to Trenches	24th		25th		26th	
	Offrs	ORks	Offrs	ORks	Offrs	ORks
Fighting line including Machine Gunners	20	721	19	737	18	714
Signallers	-	19	-	20	-	20
Stretcher Bearers	-	21	-	21	-	21
Regt'l H.Q. Brs	4	76	4	75	4	70
Total	24	836	23	853	22	825
U/transportation	1	72	2	72	2	72
Div'l Train	-	4	-	4	-	4
— Fatigue Coy	-	20	-	20	-	20
Clearing of Battn. show	-	5	-	6	-	5
Keane	-	4	-	-	-	-
Absent with Regt' leave	-	1	-	2	-	2
On Orderlies	-	3	-	3	-	8
Attached T.R.E.	-	34	-	10	-	10
Total	1	143	2	116	2	116
Strength of Battn.	25	979	25	969	24	941

Army Form C. 2118.

WAR DIARY:

Instructions regarding War Diaries and Intelligence Summaries and contained in F.S. Regs., Part II. and the Staff Manual respectively. Title pages will be prepared in manuscript.

Hour, Date, Place	Summary of Events and Information	Remarks and References to Appendices
29th September (Ordinance)	Working party of 500 found in the evening for bringing new cut. wire. Coy 9 minenwerfer night for them.	
30th September 1915.	Bright morning. Enemy Field Guns dull & extra Coast Still. About 2 p.m. when our came out & shy shower commenced. Our snipers (6) + 30 arrived but were relieved by snipers of the 9th Linc. Bn. arrived at 5.15 p.m. marched to relieve the Warwicks Regt in Trenches. A Coy in WELL FARM Salient, C & D Coy in new cut into trench to DEAD TREE. B Coy holding CITY POST + JAY POST + WYE FARM. On H.Q. Coy & Bombers Police Prisoners at WYE FARM On Liaison in support at TEMPLE. Relief complete at 7.30 p.m. A good deal of sniping going on. During the night Germans fired machine gun in our lines by enemy opposite WELL FARM. No casualties from Bullets &. Quieten during the evening. Whizzbang Batteries were covered by us during the night. Peaceful again. No rain in the evening. O.C.'s communication trenches were barely passable.	In Trenches. One wounded at duty. Two sick & Hospital. Total sick to Hospital during month 53. Total injured from Hospital during month 41.

8th, Division.

24th, Brigade.

2nd, East Lancs.

October, 1915.

8th Hussars

2/ Rose Lancs.

Oct '15

Vol XI

12/7493

to 69+13ar 20.10.15.

T12

WAR DIARY:

Army Form C. 2

Instructions regarding War Diaries and Intelligence Summaries and contained in F.S. Regs., Part II. and the Staff Manual respectively. Title pages will be prepared in manuscript.

HOUR, DATE, PLACE	SUMMARY OF EVENTS AND INFORMATION	REMARKS AND REFERENCES TO APPENDICES
1st October 1915	Cold bright morning. Turned cloudy but remained fine practically throughout the day. The communication trenches were previously hardly passable. To-day spent much time in draining out sinking trenches & by evening they were in passable condition the new trench was still very heavy going. It was strong practically finished on a programme left only for the relief by a fresh division. Hostile snipers intermittent who kept our men carefully aloof. No men injured without any trench mortaring. Front CORNER FORT - elsewhere quiet. Our Arty. engaged with 30" RFA 6 the from CORNER FORT during the night. Large enemy party of 200 working men seen in white cricket trench under cover of OB & E.L. Rainton was just moving detachment & there was no attempt. Batty opened 8pm at MARBLE ARCH much activity. 8.17 p.m. noticed of the line hours went in rain under fire.	Sergt & 6 Rgt 41 O'Roch applied for exhaustion & gone all victim of 7 Rgt 8 wounded (2 sick of enemy) 1 sick to hospital
2nd October 1915	4 OC p.m. Surrounded Trenches with 9 OC 21.6 Rgt. Platoons along new cut trench. Work of Cleaning & drying trenches were continued during the day & also clearance of dugouts, drains, holes etc. There was a strong westerly wind during Preceding night. Day was Pleasant opening with little rain during fore-noon 26 H.E. 4:2. Round 9"" OP Obs. and the fall of trenches followed from by a number of shrapnel 15 Pounders ... ... all the 4:2 ... brought except one which burst my Father the Gun	2 Sick to Hospital

WAR DIARY:

Instructions regarding War Diaries and Intelligence Summaries and contained in F.S. Regs., Part II. and the Staff Manual respectively. Title pages will be prepared in manuscript.

Army Form C. 2118

HOUR, DATE, PLACE	SUMMARY OF EVENTS AND INFORMATION	REMARKS AND REFERENCES TO APPENDICES
2nd October. 1915. (Ctns)	The transport done eight & one draft (eighty) left our depot. All the morning the men were relieved by the york Regt except for one platoon on the B.of D. Coy & the CITY BnY which was taken over by B.of D Middlesex Regt. Bn HQ left camp for the RPz at 3 pm. Reached railhead about 10.15 pm. Billeted in RUE DE BRUGES and RUE QUESNOY with Bn HQ in room 29 of Rue Rue Post. Everything went uniform could be heard during during much trouble no injury.	At 3 pm RUE DE BRUGES & RUE QUESNOY
3rd October --"--	Staff inspected by G.O. 10 a.m. by Medical Officers 12 noon. Fine day but cold. Horse lines (of D) in field opposite Bn HQ. Rest H.Q's arms Coy & Sergts 12 noon. Room for dispersal. Bn. Coys in Billets during day.	A good draft in good condition and on all in. Weather easier during the day. 1 sent to hospital.
4th October --"--	Batn. parade (ceremonial) 7.30 a.m. on mission form at intervals. During T am muster batl. Coys. Lieut. One Coln. Baton Bathed at S.A.T. Y Baths. Batl. relieved for company-stores-in transport lines-72 men & 24 under Lieuts Boilerworked arrived 1Octr 205 DUBOIS in addition to 17 already employed with 18th By at BOIS GRENIER. Obey 19.00 0. 10 for preparing billets at HIEPPE. Road to roof Transport Stations.	1 sent to hospital.
5th October --"--	Met all day to outdoor parades practice. Drawing party 200 sent to CROIX DE RNOME for Batn Regt every afternoon. 3 sent to hospital. on Bann on A Boys billets. Roads in a very muddy state.	3 sent to hospital
6th October --"--	Very early in Ret & etc 9 at none only commanders of the day. Lieut Col Rumbold attended Divert Conference at SAILLY. G.O.C 6th Div (Maj Gen Keeler) inspected Bn & Private upon billets at 3 p.m. and congratulated all ranks on the behaviour during	8 sent to hospital

WAR DIARY:

Army Form C. 2118

Instructions regarding War Diaries and Intelligence Summaries and contained in F.S. Regs., Part II. and the Staff Manual respectively. Title pages will be prepared in manuscript.

Hour, Date, Place	Summary of Events and Information	Remarks and References to Appendices
6th October (Con)	Starting Recruit Operation, Stocking Parties 200 at BOIS GRENIER etc. Marched down in Range.	
7th October 1915.	Fine sunny morning but cold. A & B Coy 460ft rifle Range during morning. Coy parade 7am. 10.30am & 1.45pm. Roads still very muddy. Football match. Officers v Sergt Kirkbury Rifled 150 yds. Range. 3 offrs & 25 men attended from Hd Qrs. Field Hospital included by 2nd Lieutenant and Capt. Heavy firing from L.F BASSÉE 5 Mins or any. F BASSÉE	1 wounded 3 sick to Hospital
8th October —	Fortifier early morning but fine day. Whole coys out working. Returned 7am & 11.45pm. 7.30 am. Coys inspected with Bde. & Govmr report. 8am Coys inspected. Fatigue Chaps LF were for Bn Lungs. an Repair of front 7 front Revell E,D,B,A. Also a trip as for 7. each man carrying 440 yds. 11am. fmy hurt Try of Wire. Also D 2:30pm. L/mal. Try of Wire. B C,D,B. A solitary shy Syzzgun Sister was opened by a grenade which they found.	the trans lines very peaceable with the ✕ ✕ senses report. 3 F.E. GRRSEE when we wounded. 4 sick to Hospital
9th October —	Parades as inclusive Truman. Fine day but dull. Working parties of 200 from trenches. OB Coy wanted Sunday with Galper Hill on river Lillie or Lunney. G. Rugby football match. B, Coy. vs. SPATLY during the afternoon. Mr Officer 2/Lieu. A. Officer BAgus R.E received in a arm for the letter. Bng Gnl Oakly Camm 24 Inf/Bde. visited Bde HQ and inspected Barin days left at 11am.	1 sick to Hospital

WAR DIARY:

Army Form C. 2118

Hour, Date, Place	Summary of Events and Information	Remarks and References to Appendices
10th October 1915 (Sunday)	Line arrangements. Church service by Field near B[attalio]n H[ea]dq[uarte]rs at 9 a.m. Extraordinary silence in C Coy, relief at 11.10 a.m. Court of Enquiry at Comm[andan]t Robert re loss of a rifle from a sergeant Coy. 3rd Batt[alio]n being President. Death returns of Middlesex & 1/7 Middlesex re-numbering to-day from 1/1 WATLING STREET (Convent) (when welcome huns) to 1/111 non-commissioned(?) 9 mounted 510 rank and file. R no 5/4. men N 6/1. Relieved by half of 11th Royal Fusiliers in pouring rain to an enormous depth inundation marched CROIX MARECHA about 6:45 p.m. very moderate. Reached Rly Crossing about 7.30 p.m. Planet took up etc etc. Rly Crossing B[attalio]n H[ea]dq[uarte]rs on RUE Guard on LA TRANQUILLITE Headquarters, Stores by, Coys in Fields. JONATHAN and others C' Coy in reserve. 20 casualties. Comparatively quiet. A, D. B from the night. Quiet night.	1 sick to Hospital
11th October — do —	Quiet night. Fine day but inclined to rain from early morning. Bon y[?] ambulance arranged from BOUTILLERIE Farm (where had been by) during day then Brit[ish] & French tried by new (trans) to carry from QUINRITE. New places used by Ambulance were found full of wounded Ammunition, Bandages, Equipment &c. &c. left in Fr[ench] Huts quiet men in on notable(?) fete. A store of Grenades which had not been drawn into was found & discard. M[edical] h[or]s[e] Graves moved throughout. was cleared by the M[edical] O[fficer]s moving during the time sent to staff again put in order. R.E. Officer C.O. 10th ?? BOUTILLERIE and CONVENT put in order. water supplies & chlorinated near ramparts reserve and ???	1 sick to Hospital

Army Form C. 2118

WAR DIARY:

Hour, Date, Place	Summary of Events and Information	Remarks and References to Appendices
11th October (Con)	2nd regiment reinforcing on right. From 9.30 a.m. to 12 noon the 1/5 Black Watch holding trench to right of the farm were heavily shelled by enemy artillery. Capt Bracket commanding D Co. shot dead. Evacuation CHOT HILTON. Some of the shells fell in area occupied by Battn. During afternoon an aeroplane fight was observed in which Lieut Boutellier to R.F.C. brought down an enemy German aeroplane during the day of the first flight. The German aeroplane fell in RUE BATAILLE near billets occupied by B Coy in 9/20 ⟨?⟩. Lt Boutellier might a good deal of trouble was done by Germans on the new Bouquet avenue. C Coy retired BOUTILLERIE under enemy fire and ground there & Bouquet that had been demolished by shells fire recently. The night was quiet but there was some rain. Trenches and good deal of trouble rifle fire about 4.30 – 5.30 a.m. which passed our Q.M.S. on farm the right.	
12 October 1915.	P.Q. of 5/Lp B.W. was wounded trouble sent to Boy. For Dely during evening. On line from the right and supported Engines. Lines were on convent. Very quiet day. About 11.30 a.m. & 12.15 p.m. a group at 3.30 p.m. in response to rumour from our TURKS POINT giving third premises & past the 4 BOUTILLERIE and the CONVENT. No damage suffered. Close and no casualties. Our shells also struck BOTLEY Avenue 9 near D Capt headquarters. This period work continued after dark on new Bouquet also ⟨?⟩	1 Rank & Hopkins

Army Form C. 2118.

WAR DIARY:

Instructions regarding War Diaries and Intelligence Summaries and contained in F.S. Regs., Part II. and the Staff Manual respectively. Title pages will be prepared in manuscript.

HOUR, DATE, PLACE	SUMMARY OF EVENTS AND INFORMATION	REMARKS AND REFERENCES TO APPENDICES
12th October (Con)	water supply to Y BOTTERY anxious. The water supply generally been causing some difficulty. The right supply CONVENT for the Troops — BOTTILLERIE to those with take it was a doubt but storing right with some result in early morning	
13th October 1915.	Dull foggy in early morning with slight rain. Enemy very quiet all day anything gun Gun Reveval & continued pitched. Coys infused working on new parapets during night and all day. If rained until twenty about 11.0 a.m. but cleared later. Afternoon evening moonlight. No incident drawn attention of 1st Army against HOHENZOLLERN Fort. HULLUCH & the 20th Bde in new right entrance and a front on relief M.30.A. and Lombards. Artillery out order & bombardment commencing 12.30./7pm till about 1.10 p.m. Firing died down about 2.30 pm. Our RA responded faster at about 6 p.m. onwards. Twenty fiving event by French South. Brd attacked must seem the HOHENZOLLERN — all had been expected and 1st Army ammunition all gone on. Another attempt TRANQUILIFE. 5.30 Road guards, in front collected by Bombs anxious Reas Bryan was suffered to Brigade to distribution of Grenades and the lines in accordance with the new scheme. Further confirmation of water supply arrangements was made & reported 5 p.m. Brig Gen Oxley Troops arrived until 6.40 pm where heavy rifle fire opened, from right hand towards As the wind blown Enemy sniper minor accidents.	1 Killed 2 Sick to Hospital

WAR DIARY:

Army Form C. 2118

Hour, Date, Place	Summary of Events and Information	Remarks and References to Appendices
13th October (Cnx)	9.55 p.m. S.O.S.1.308 was called off from BRIDOUX Fort. Firing died down about 10.15 p.m. During some seven hours enemy front had been busily engaged under the enemy sniping, wires standing & arti fire at transport lines.	
14th October 1915	Dull, foggy morning, work one time during the day. Little enemy firing, either rifle or arty. Coys on the front line continued to carry out the work on revetment, floors of dugouts, parapet, revive Coy (C) worked at improvement of the water supply in BOUTILLERIE. Battn relieved on Friday by the 1st [?] Canadian reletf. Complete by 6.55 p.m. HdQrs "GERRY HOUSE" C Coy at Madame Ennens old in RUE DEQUESNE; A Coy at CROIX MARECHAL, B Coy at CROIX BLANCHE D Coy in the RUE BASSIERES.	1 took to Hospital
15th October —	Dull, foggy morning. C Coy had one fr rifle range at ROUGE DE BOUT, Coy Paraders. Lieut Col J.S. Lombard ordered to proceed at once to GHQrs to report to A.G.	1 Killed 1 Wounded. 2 took to Hospital
— " — 3 p.m.	Major G.B. McNell assumed command of Battn. Working parties of 50 in the morning & 150 at night.	
16th October 1915.	Dull, foggy day. One man of the working party killed last night. Paraders fired on rifle range from 7am to 9 a.m. Coy Paraders 7am, 10.30 am & 1.45 p.m. 2/ Lieut Livingstone left for England on receipt of cable from G. Halford to report to War Office instructing on [?]	1 Wounded (Livin Bird) 17/10/15 2 took to Hospital

WAR DIARY:

Army Form C. 2118.

HOUR, DATE, PLACE	SUMMARY OF EVENTS AND INFORMATION	REMARKS AND REFERENCES TO APPENDICES
16th October (cont)	Ten general working parties. Captain F.S. Rivington arranged system of 24 Hr Communal Standing using the Coy. A.G. Rees Lieut. Working parties of 50 on the railway line 100 at night	
17th October 1915.	Church parade at 10 a.m. for A & B Coys at CROIX BLANCHE and 11 am for remainder at No. Coy H.Q. Moved at 5pm to Billets at 8.9.C ST MAUR and RUE BATAILLE (A, B & C in RUE BATAILLE. N° A in 8.9.C ST MAUR. N° B in 8.9.C St. Maur). Foggy day but fine. Evening station. Our men relieved. Arranged working party tasks night.	3 from Hospital of the 5th Bn. 2 reinforcements from Base Details.
18th October —	Battn. Sappers orders of 23rd Bde. (?) for subsequent operns. Issued to O.C. R.E. (Commanded by Brigadier F.S. Anderson). Early morning 10th M.E.L.R. the Battn is being attached in Reliefs. That the Battn's of the new army hourly from the experience gained in the road hourly, F.C. Byrick was seen. Entered to Reliefs Covy FORT ROMPU. Capt. Tulloch at Hutt's FTB on S. of the Road. C.T.B. N Lieut McLery Capt. Stace at 3.30 p.m. all in by 4 p.m. Gen. Bentham others Staff Captain (Capt Reade) visited the T.M. at 5.7 p.m.	10 Res O.R. Hospital.
19th October —	2 Lieut Reyns proceeded to the Bde Bomb School. Line trench day Cept. Rees' Robington Community 23rd Gen. visited the lines also Gen. Billy 24th Bde. Coy Parades. O.C. Coy invited Cmdt allotted Phine Recens. 23rd Gen. Defence scheme.	2 Lieut to Hospital.

Army Form C. 2118

WAR DIARY:

Instructions regarding War Diaries and Intelligence Summaries and contained in F.S. Regs., Part II. and the Staff Manual respectively. Title pages will be prepared in manuscript.

Hour, Date, Place	Summary of Events and Information	Remarks and References to Appendices
20th October 1915	Dull fine day - 25th Battn arrived at Bulklin Place M.A.R.E and joined the 59th Bde (4th Canadian Division). Route Off 4.35 pm and arrived Bulklin at 6.40 pm. Bay. J & B two coys 2nd in Command Please note ly Billets housed us to M/West Ridings and Fives Battn Taken over.	1 copy N.P. to Innsbrunners Lists 5 Hospital 5 Other ranks cross to Hospital
21st October ---	Dull day morning. C & D Coys proceeded to trenches occupied in relief of 9th ??? for instruction keying orderly to Rest Battn. C & D Coy w/and ??? Yorks ??? ??? French to night in accordance with orders of 4th Battn. C & D Coys perished at 5 pm. C & D Coys w/Sevt Yorks arrived in trench at 8.30 pm. A working Party of two Officers & 150 other ranks paraded at 5.40 pm. Cas. paraded killed during the day, to return at 9 pm.	2 Leave to Rydisties
22nd October ---	A fine day. Gen. Goody Thorpe Inspect quarters of Hedrs. N. Coy. the amalgamation of the two Battns. took place after 10.30 am. C and 9 Coys now consist of 2 Platoons of 6.4R & 2 Platoons Y/5th Yorks. The two Coys M/Went Yorks went to Bro-Battn. Working Party of 2 ??? & 3 Officers. The Officers of the M/West Yorks who joined our Captain Booth, O.C. E Coy, Capt Mitchell. O.C. F Coy, Lieut Bethington Briggs E Coy, Captain Armstrong C.W Coy, Lieut Hazlett E Coy, 2/Lieut Davison F Coy, 2/Lieut Douglas E Coy, 2/Lieut ??? F Coy	2 Warrant 3 Leave to Hydisties

Army Form C. 2118.

WAR DIARY:

Instructions regarding War Diaries and Intelligence Summaries and contained in F.S. Regs., Part II. and the Staff Manual respectively. Title pages will be prepared in manuscript.

Hour, Date, Place	Summary of Events and Information	Remarks and References to Appendices
23rd October 1915.	Orders received unexpectedly to take over trenches tonight from 8th Yorkshire Regt. O.C. approaches trenches in the morning. Also C.O. Brigade 5.15 p.m. Relief completed at 7.30 p.m. No casualties. Our occupying such as follows:- A Coy. J.15/1. B Coy. J.15/2. C Coy. J.16/1. & Coy. J.21/4. A fine day, etc.	2 Lieut. [?] Hughes
24th October —	Quiet night, very little firing, no casualties. Fine day. Quiet all day, a few machine gun fire about 5.30 p.m. generally trying to surprise. Will sent a day [?] arm returns about 10 p.m. 1/14 to J.52. 15 La Chapelle One horse in water cart wounded on [illegible] road mine J.1/a.2 [illegible] d'Armentières about 9.30 p.m. No casualties.	7 Cork to hospital
25th October —	Very quiet night. Heavy rain which continued up to 7 p.m. after that same only intermittent. Have Lewis night on front parapet and course. G.O.C. 69th Bde visited lines about 12.15 p.m. C & B Coys reported the Bosche & C & B Coys [illegible] about 9 a.m. reported their arm Bosche. Relief except Bn. by 6 or 30 p.m. New shells arm of which shrunk front parapet of A Coy.	
26th October —	Fine day. Quiet night. Distribution of trench correct and in accordance with Bde Defence Scheme, very rough night. 4th Bn scout. 4.0.0. 69th Bde Maj. Rolls Trupp granted Lieut Bn Steere trouble over obtaining food. Lieut A.W. Ireland reports from scout Conf. 2 hour duty. Quiet Day.	2 Lieut T. Hughes

Army Form C. 2118

WAR DIARY:

Instructions regarding War Diaries and Intelligence Summaries and contained in F.S. Regs., Part II. and the Staff Manual respectively. Title pages will be prepared in manuscript.

Hour, Date, Place	Summary of Events and Information	Remarks and References to Appendices
27th October 1916.	Still very wet weather. Quiet night. Work on parapet continued weather interfering a great deal. Capt Craig R.A.M.C. rejoined from leave and Capt B Landy R.A.M.C. (T) rejoined 2/4 Field Ambulance.	2 Cas to Hospital
28th October —	Quiet night. Heavy rain. Major Kerberg marked sick. Gen Bonham also Capt Babington F.O.O. R.F.A. during tour. Gnr Biggs C/104 R.F.A. Gnr Sharp " " " " " "	1 Case to Hospital
	Battn relieved in front by 8/Yorks whom we relieved in the BOIS GRENIER line. Accommodation for all ranks very poor in centre lines. Bgd. and staff dugouts muddy. 2 front nuclei of coy gas alarm, consequently muddy & cramped. Reld complete by 7.30 p.m.	
29th October —	Still day but no rain. Relieved by 2/Northants Reld complete by 9.30 p.m. Billets FORT ROMPU	1 Cas to Hospital 2 Cas to Hospital
30th October —	Billets FORT ROMPU Capt distributed on Bgd, Brewhouse, Farmhouse & FORT ROMPU. Wpn. Gen Darcy & Major Kerberg inspected under the lines. Fine day.	1) Hampshires– Hys Brown to S.L. 2) Kerns with Ly Smith 3) Kerns Mr Browne S.T.O.S.H.
31st October	Cold wet day with several rain. Church parade at 10 a.m. Wiring party of 200 at 5.30 p.m. Sniping and gun fire on flanks on Bn. Lewis on which turn our Brance in either state.	2 Cas to Hospital

Total rejoined from Hospital, leave, course – 36

On the Field in France
17 – x – 15.

To
The Officer Commanding.
2nd Battn. The East Lancashire Regiment.

On behalf of myself and all officers and other ranks of the Battalion under my Command I wish to convey to you and all officers and other ranks of the 2nd Bn. The East Lancashire Regiment our most heartfelt gratitude for all the many courtesies and kindnesses which have been shown to us while we have been serving together in the 24th Infantry Brigade and for the forebearance extended to us on so many occasions.

The helpful advice which has been so often readily afforded us will never be forgotten and the lively friendship and comradeship which has sprung up amongst us all may I trust never die down.

Jno Blair-Imrie
Lieut Col
Comdg 5th Bn The Black Watch

NOT FOR VISITORS.

Private Diary.

Lt Col Nicholson,

2nd, East Lancs.

Private Diary

Lt. Col. Nicholson

2 E Lancs.

1915

NOT FOR
VISITORS

Private Diary

Lt. Col. Nicholson

2 E Lines

NOT FOR
VISITORS

Lieut Colonel C.L. Nicholson, Commanding 2/East Lancs Regt.
24th Infantry Brigade, 8th Division, IV Corps.

18th November 1914.

It rained almost continuously the first two days and froze on the third day. There were scores of Hun snipers behind our lines and one night, outside H.Q. I emptied my revolver into what I afterwards discovered was a Cow. The Cow was unhurt. On the night of the 18/19th the West Yorkshire and 2 Companies Devonshire of the 23rd Brigade relieved all 6 Companies. Phillips Commanding West Yorks relieved me and dined at H.Qrs. while relief was going on. Dinner was interrupted by a Hun shrapnel which burst in the courtyard and we quitted. Relief was complete about midnight, and we got back to billets near Pont du Hem about 2 a.m.

19th November 1914.

Casualties during the tour Other Ranks 5 Killed, 23 wounded. The result of the wet spell in trenches followed by frost was apparent this morning. Over 50 men had to have their boots cut off them and were carried to the nearest Field Ambulance. To make matters worse our Doctor - a drunken little beast - said the men were frost bitten and could think of nothing better to do than put their feet in hot water, with the result that several men lost toes and one or two a foot. This was our first experience of "Trench Foot".

18th December 1914.

At Brigade H.Qrs I found Pinney Commanding 23rd Brigade and was told that 2 Bns of his Brigade, Devons and West Yorks were to attack a portion of the German line in order to straighten our line at the junction of B and C lines. Our role was reserve to these 2 Bns. under the orders of G.O.C. 23rd Brigade. The attack was made at 5 P.M. after a short but heavy preparation of 18 pdr. time shrapnel and apparently succeeded. No news came for some time and it was not until 11:30 p.m. that I was told to rejoin my Battalion. Another 2 Coys up in close support behind the Battns which had been engaged and take the remaining 2 Coys to a farm further north along the Rue de Bacquerot also behind the engaged Regiments. These moves were completed about 2 a.m. I then went up to the trench line from which the attack had taken place and found Travers (Devon Regt) and Phillips (W.Yorks Regt) in a dugout both very angry. Apparently the Devons who actually carried out the attack only got orders, with no preliminary(xx) warning, about ½ an hour before zero hour and the West Yorks about the same time. The Devons got the trench but were driven out by a counter attack from front of it. The W.Yorks retook it and relieved the whole of the Devons, but were themselves bombed out of most of it later on, about dawn, in the morning. Both battalions had many casualties - especially the W. Yorks in Officers.

20th December, 1914.

Note.   A Lines was the right section of the 8th Div front. The line ran along the western road ditch of the Estaires-Labassee road, almost at right angles to B Lines. There was a small out post about the centre of the line across one of the roads leading into Neuve Chapelle and another longer salient known as Port Arthur at the extreme right of the line the whole of which lay to the east of the Estaires - La Bassee Road, another road into Neuve Chapelle from Richebourge - L'Avoue ran through the southern end of this salient. Port Arthur was wooded contained two or three ruined houses and a partially destroyed brewery facing East and South at the southern end of the salient. This Brewery was put into a state of defence after Xmas and gave us a certain amount of command over the Ham trenches- less that 50 yards away- and also formed a good supporting point on that flank and covered a gap which existed between our right and the left of the Indian Corps on our right. The garrison of Port Arthur consisted of from 8 to 6 platoons. After the water rose i.e. just after Xmas a good deal of the trench line of Port Arthur had to be abandoned and it was impossible to get into it by daylight, except by wading, waist deep in water through flooded trenches. To get to the extreme right of the line from the Brewery by daylight one had to crawl on one's belly across Suicide Corner (so called owing to the proximity of Snipers House the upper windows of which commanded the whole area) and then wade through water up to the arm pits. The usual procedure visiting trenches was to leave H.Q. about 3 a.m. walk on the top of the ground to the extreme right of Port Arthur and get back to the Brewery just before it was light enough for the Hun snipers. Thence it was possible to walk round the remainder of the salient and back into the main line. The left of the line was not at first continuous with B lines but the gap was eventually joined up by a half trench half breastwork line.

Battalion H.Qrs. were in a farm house at the corner of the Rue du Berceau whence a road ran straight to the left of the trench line about 1500^X away. About half way along the road a ditch ran from it to the right of the line, which when we first took over the line was used as a communication trench. The water however rose in this trench to such an extent that it was (~~impassible~~) impassable and the only way up was by the road except across deep muddy fields. All reliefs took place by the road or by the fields if not too wet. Although part of the road was in full view of the enemy's line the Hun rarely took an notice of parties of 3 or 4 or less moving on it. When we first went into the line we had no telephonic communication with Coys at all and all communication was by runner. About the middle of January we got a line to one Coy H.Q. in the line and all messages had to be passed from that Coy by runner. It was not until well on into February that we got our full telephone equipment.

Sanitation in the trench line was difficult as anything out of the actual trench was under fire and all trenches had more or less water in them. Burial of the dead was also a difficulty. At first men killed in the trench line, were buried in Orchards behind their own sections, later on all (~~xxxxxxxx~~) bodies were brought down to Bn. H.Q. and buried in the orchard behind the farm, Leckham Townsend and Larkin our own subalterns and 3 others attached to us were buried there and 3 or 4 of the Sherwood Foresters. I saw the place in Nov, 18, after the armistice - it had been heavily shelled and only the cross over Townsend's grave remained.

All through January and February the men suffered very much from wet and cold, constantly wet up to the knees, but we had comparatively little trench foot thanks to regular parades before going into the line for whale oil treatment. In these days we always went into trenches fully equiped and full packs. This was not realy necessary

but the

situation as known to Bn H.Qrs. was to uncertain to leave any equipment out of the line.

During this period Moloney, Fletcher and Inniter were all posted to the 1st Bn in the line 4th Div. at Ploeystreet. Robinson as an attached Officer took over the Mac Gun section increased to 4 guns from Moloney.

25th December 1914.

Soon after daylight the Hun displayed Xmas trees in his trenches and shouted "Merry Xmas East Lancs" This was pretty smart considering that it was our first tour in this line.

The Brigadier Carter and Robinson C.R.E. 8th Div. came up to the line with me in the afternoon to try and diagnose the water situation. They did'nt get much beyond making futile suggestions and fixing a pump which was drained out 24 hours later. There had been perfect peace on both sides all day and while in Port Arthur with the Brigadier I saw a lot of our men hobnobbing with the Hun in No man's Land. I went out to see what was going on and found Fryer one of our attached subalterns talking fluent German to a German N.C.O. I gathered that they wanted leave to bury the dead of which there were a good many lying in No Man's Land. After vain endeavours to get hold of the a German Officer I sent the German N.C.O. with a message to the Bn Commander that he could have an hour and a half and that we would bury all the dead lying close to our line and they could do the same with theirs, this was accepted and subsequently extended for another hour, in the course of which we buried all the dead and Landus went out from the Adv Post in the 3rd Sector and recovered the body of Dilwater, Shwr. Fr. who had been killed about a month before.

Diary of Lt. Col. C.L. Nicholson
Comdg. 2 East Lancs. 24th Inf. Bde.

3rd January 1915.

On the 23rd our artillery shelled enemy trenches for about an hour. This was a most unusual occurance as Art. Ammunition was very short about 12 rounds a Batty. a day.

8.

8th March 1915.
to
9th March 1915. During these days various rumours which had been in the air for some time regarding an attack on ~~Neuve~~ Neuve Chappele took place.

24th Brigade had been relieved in A and B lines to take over C and D, E and F lines relieving the rest of the 8th Div which was taken out for training. It was not until the 8th that this scheme was altered, 24th Brigade warned also in the attack and C and D taken over by Northamptonshire Yeo, and 4/Camerons. In the meantime the whole area was very filled up with guns of all sorts, Horse and Field Artillery were registering line and every transport driver behind the line was talking about the attack. It is a curious thing that the attack when it did come off on the 10th; was undoubtedly a surprise to the Boche. ~~fxxxx~~ Some rumour must have got to them for on one occasion they shouted across and asked when we were going to attack.

On the morning of the 9th I went to a conference at Brigade H.Q. at which Carter told me that 24th Brigade was to be reserve Brigade 8th Div. and that as I was senior Col in the Brigade we were to be near ~~Brigade of~~ Battalion of line so that I should be handy if anything happened to him. Subsequently he changed his mind and put us in as leading Battalion reserve Brigade. At this conference we were given the maps and the general plan of the offensive was explained to us - as it turned out a very ambitious one.

Davies Commanding 8th Div came to Bn H.Qrs during the afternoon and told me what troops were engaged and others discussed. Just before we moved from La Planque. Dalais B.G.G.S. 4th Corps came in with 4th Corps Special order. Copies of this order were subsequently taken by the Boche and gave them a handle to hang a good deal of Bombust on.

We left the La Planque area about 7:30 p.m. and I marched to Rougecroise area.

We went into close billets. I then went back to Red Burn where Brig H.Q. was established. There we discussed and finally got orders on numerous details on dress, equipment etc. which ought to have been issued long before.

I got back to Bn. H.Qrs between 10 and 11 p.m. and issued Bn.orders as soon as I could.

th March 1915.

Coy Commanders came to H.Q. about 6 a.m. and I explained orders and situation to them. Mewes Ciae who was 2nd Capt of B Coy turned up with an enormous boil between his shoulders and I had to send him back to the transport lines and get up Western - who was very badly wounded on the 12th. Our bombardment began at 7:35 a.m. and lasted for 25 minutes at a very rapid rate.

25th Brigade on the right and 23rd on the left advanced at 8 a.m. the former captured Neuve Chappelle line 1st objective but the latter got held up by uncut wire. At 9 a.m. we got orders to move up to trecnehs vacated by the left of the 25th Brigade in the Rue Tillelory. On the way up Bn. H.Q. came under   long range rifle fire and my servant Douglas, one of the best men I ever came across was badly hit. He died 2 days later. By 10:30 a.m. we had 2 Coys in the Rue Tillelory Breast-works and H.Q. and 2 more in assembly trenches just in rear of the trenches. I reported myself to Loury-Cole Commanding 25th Brigade about 11 a.m. he sent for me and told me to move 2 Coys up to support his left. Simultaneously I got an order from the 24th Brigade to close the gap between 23rd and 25th Brigades. One movement fulfilled both orders.

The two rear Coys A and C moved forward from the orchard and the N.E. edge of Neuve Chappelle and established themselves there in the old British trench (Oct 14th) facing Bois du Briey.

The two remaining Coys B and D moved up to a position about 800X in rear of the two leading Coys.

The West Yorkshire and remains of the Camerons (23rd Br) came up on our left and we were much crowded up between them and the R. Irish Rifles of the 25th Brigade.

I established Bn. H.Q. in the road leading North from Neuve Chappelle between the front and rear Coy. whence Arnott and I went round the forward 2 Coys and them digging them-

11.

selves in and protecting their left flank which as we were constantly ahead of the W Yorks on our left, was in the air

There was very little hostile shell fire but a good deal of rifle and M.Gun Fire. The Bois de Briay which faced us appeared to be occupied also some trenches on our left front but I thought if we could have got our own artillery to lift we could have advanced. The Rifle Brigade of the 25th Brig. were I believe then to go on to the Bois du Briay and if that Br. and ours had been able to go forward they could have got the Bois and we could have got the trenches and houses in the Moulin du Riche road and the next two days fighting practically resolved itself into a struggle in these two ....
About noon I was hit in the back by a bullet which went through my side and broke my forearm. I lay in the road until about 3 p.m. after being bandaged by Arnott and Duckworthy (R.S.M) and had my arm put into a splint by Craig our Doctor. It was an unpleasant position as the M.G. fire down the road was pretty continous and our own guns were firing very short over us. Some of the shells going into our 3 front Coys.
The stretcher bearers fetched me out about 3 p.m. just before we we got orders to assemble the Battn with a view to a further advance. I was put into a motor ambulance on the Rue tillelory close to Adv.Br. H.Q. when I saw Carter and was taken to the 25th Fd. Ambulance in Estaires passing the 5th Cav Brig. on the way - Greys, 12th Lancers and 20th Hussars who were on their way up to go through.

At Estraiers Heley whom I knew in L.A. put me to rights and set my arm properly. Thence I went to Meroille C.C.S. While there one of Sir. D. H's A.D.C's announced in the square that the days operations had been entirely successful - a gross if ....exageration. From Meroille I stated in a hospital train about 8 p.m. and eventually arrived, after a most uncomfortable jouney at No. 2 British Red Cross Hospital at Rouen.

<u>Note on Neuve Chapelle.</u>

Note on Neuve Chapelle.

The subsequent course of the action, so far as the 2/ East Lancs is concerned is as follows :-

About 4 p.m. 10th A and C Coys were withdrawn to Brigade Reserve in the Rue Tilleroy the remaining 2 Coys were placed as a support to the Sherwood Foresters on the right of the Brigade which made a slight advance.

7 a.m. 11th The Brigade resumed the advance on La Clicqueterie on a front of about 1000 yards with the right directed just N of the Bois du Biez. This advance was stopped almost as once by fire from the Bois du Biez and the houses on the ..... Road and the Regt less 1 Coy in Brigade reserve dug in in 2nd line where they remained throughout the 11th.

During the night of the 11/12 fresh position of assembly were taken up with a view to an attack on the 12th. About 6 a.m. the Hun attacked in considerable strength. The right of the Brigade was pushed back(inXX) for a short distance but quickly recovered itself and the whole Brigade advanced about 100 yards to a German trench. This line was consolidated and preparations made for a night attack. This attack was cancelled.

23rd Brigade relieved 24th early on the 13th and the E. Lancs withdrew to the Rouge Croix area. Casualties 10th 13th
Killed 4 Officers   46 Other Ranks.
Wounded 6   "   147 "   "

The Officers were Sanders, Gaelagher, Wolseley and . ? on the 14th while D Coy was turning in at Rouge Croix a shell burst in the middle of it and killed 34 O.R. and wounded 1 Officer and 37 O.R. of whom the Officer Robinson (attchd) and 11 O.R. died of wounds.
Total casualties Killed 5 Officers 81 O.R. wounded 6 Officers 173 Other Ranks.

23RD. DIVISION
24TH INFY BDE

8 DIV

2ND BN EAST LANCS REGT
NOV 1915 – JUN 1916

24/23

2/3. Lancs Rgr.

Nov¹ / vol XII

10/7663

T₁₃

[illegible initials/signatures]

WAR DIARY:

Army Form C. 2118.

Instructions regarding War Diaries and Intelligence Summaries and contained in F.S. Regs., Part II. and the Staff Manual respectively. Title pages will be prepared in manuscript.

Hour, Date, Place	Summary of Events and Information	Remarks and References to Appendices
1st November 1915.	Very wet. Coys. interred with all equipment. Orders refused to relieve 9th Coys. in trenches.	One sick to Hospital
2nd November 1915.	Very wet morning. Barred all day. Relieved 9th Yorks in left sect. of trenches. Relief completed by 7 p.m. Supporting coys. came forward to the line so Batt. Headquarters in a fair way for accommodation all dug-out, looking and fully comfortable.	3 sick to Hospital. 1 wounded (self inflicted)
3rd November 1915	A quiet night. Enemy persistently sends in a very hot attack, they were made for enemy positions higher only. Parapets and parados collapsing. They go on repairs to the line then everything disarranged. Visits of the operations not fairly communicated to general Bulfin on visiting the lines. General Bulfin and G.O.C. "C" Battery, R.F.A. 10th R. Brigade to executive.	2 sick to Hospital 1 injured.
4th November 1915.	A quiet light. Fine day, with sunshine. Much work done to the lines - draining and repairing fallen parapets and parados.	1 sick to Hospital
5th November 1915.	Quiet night. Some little machine gun and rifle fire. Baths open. Busy on same effort. Div. Gen. the Hon. White with a little rain. Gen. Kerran visits the lines and expresses his appreciation of the work done in the lines by the Battalion. Much rifle and machine gun fire between 6.30 p.m. and 6.15 p.m. in two diff. places. The distance of one Battalion front away. Quite quiet along our front.	Anniversary of our leaving England.

WAR DIARY:

Army Form C. 2118.

Instructions regarding War Diaries and Intelligence Summaries and contained in F.S. Regs., Part II. and the Staff Manual respectively. Title pages will be prepared in manuscript.

Hour, Date, Place	Summary of Events and Information	Remarks and References to Appendices
6th November, 1915.	Quiet night – Battalion relieved by General Sir Douglas Haig, Commanding First Army with the Legion of Honour. Capt. CROIX-DE-CHEVALIER at Merville. General Rey-Lieutenant in the trenches – very misty – overnight. Northampton Battalion occupying trenches on right of Battalion. On our left 5th Wiltshires. Headquarters of Army on our left rear.	5 sick to hospital
7th November, 1915.	Quiet night. Very foggy but this relieving Battalion of the piece of the Wiltshire trenches by OC Forces and took over Rifle Companies & the BOIS GRENIER sector in front of CHAPELLE-D'ARMENTIÈRES. Headquarters in Brewers Brigade's Head Quarters. I.14.a.8.7.	Appointments: Lieut. to Ride Specialist – Ammunition Report to honour of Military General O.R. to Battalion in his present East Lancashire Regiment Arts. & cox 1915. Entertainment Hol 20.53. Sick to Hospital (7.8) 7 men sick
8th November, 1915.	Quiet night – Battalion turned out during the day. 6 officers to Commander's General Wilmington accompanied by Brigadier General Bertram and Captain Fraser visits the lines.	2 sick to hospital
9th November, 1915.	Quiet night. Still day. Working up for training. Enemy likely lines after the explosion wounding one James OK Loud Stafford's Pioneer Battalion, who formed me a working party. Battalion Headquarters moved up into dug-out in the Orchard, which went scrubs commonly owing to raining, which drove the men to come in. Working party of 100 help in the morning and fifty evening.	2 sick to hospital 1 injured

Army Form C. 2118.

WAR DIARY:

Instructions regarding War Diaries and Intelligence Summaries and contained in F.S. Regs., Part II. and the Staff Manual respectively. Title pages will be prepared in manuscript.

Hour, Date, Place	Summary of Events and Information	Remarks and References to Appendices
10th November 1915.	Quiet night. Some heavy rain during the night. Morning fine. Afternoon bright with showers. Enemy fired heavy shelling all day by 4.2" our guns and the trench mortars, the battery guns mostly at the BOIS GRENIER Line and searches to & from our batteries. Little or no damage was done. Lines: We looked in the front line, some trenches I.20.4., I.15.1., I.15.2., I.16.* Relief completed by 6.15 p.m. Battns on our right 9th Yorks on our left 12th West Yorks. Lines much damaged by rain.	3 sick to Hospital Wounded. ※ Trenches - Sheet 36. N.W., Sheet IV 1/5000
11th November 1915.	Quiet night incident our right where the Battn holding that position, the line fires a good deal. Night was rang fine. Day fairly fine until 12 noon when it clouded over. Both General Barington and General B. Rigby visited the lines by the morning. Much shelling from our side, but none on our lines from the enemy a most evening - no casualties.	1 sick to Hospital Wounded.
12th November 1915.	Quiet night. Work of repair continues - Wet day. Very little enemy firing	1 sick to Hospital Wounded.

WAR DIARY

Army Form C. 2118.

Hour, Date, Place	Summary of Events and Information	Remarks and References to Appendices
13th November, 1915	A quiet night with bursts of machine gun and rifle fire. Gen Cavendish explored Chateau du Bois in morning, was very muddy and warmer in the afternoon. Less rain falling. Working parties resumed continuing to stagger and widen accumulators & communications report all efforts at drainage of camp area the ditches behind the huts are Hotchkiss as it is impossible to carry away the water. Trench strength:- Officers 14. Other Ranks 634. Signallers 1. " 8 Stretcher Bearers " 2. " 1 At H.Q. Gr. Officers 3. " 43 Total in trenches " 17. " 716 Battalion Strength Officers 24. O.R. 937.	1 Wounded
14th November 1915	Quiet night. Very heavy rain and much wind. Trenches and communications in a very bad state. Much water and mud everywhere. One casualty last night. High winds and heavy showers.	1 Wounded

Army Form C. 2118.

WAR DIARY:

Instructions regarding War Diaries and Intelligence Summaries and contained in F.S. Regs., Part II, and the Staff Manual respectively. Title pages will be prepared in manuscript.

Hour, Date, Place	Summary of Events and Information	Remarks and References to Appendices
14th November 1915 (continued)	Relieved by the Lorbs. Relief complete by 6.30 p.m. Proceeded to billets at HAZEBROUCK. Hit hit at by 9.40 p.m. Two killed in Rue Neuve Marie suffered severe hours and by some unknown cause arriving at the end of a quiet night. The march to billets from Fleurbaix took over seven (7) hours.	Rejoined 24th (B.G.)
15th November 1915.	In billets. A fine day. CHS party day. Cleaning up & refitting. (13) kept in the trenches. Brigade orderly waited the lines in the afternoon.	3 died in hospital
16th November 1915.	Marched to billets near LA ROLANDERIE. 12th Bn Durham Light Infantry, 3 sick, 10 hospital Bay his 2th came from their billets on arrival, in which calves a good sgt of infantry 15th Bn Brigade Reserve, 3rd Battalions here in Keep in newly finished accommodations May 6 a.m. Day much too fine.	
17th November 1915.	In billets. Moved parade 7.30. 10.30 am and 5 Keys. 2 a.m. Inne filling lub afill of 5 Keys platoons, the fitful wash malnis in the transport tine making strenuous for the battalion. Arrived station of mind and half 1st Battalion No orders.	1 sick to hospital
18th November 1915.	A fine CHS night. Enemy artillery front much shelling of green and sifts about 5 to 11 mg— (Grove)	1 sick to hospital

WAR DIARY:

Army Form C. 2118.

Instructions regarding War Diaries and Intelligence Summaries are contained in F.S. Regs., Part II. and the Staff Manual respectively. Title pages will be prepared in manuscript.

Hour, Date, Place	Summary of Events and Information	Remarks and References to Appendices
18th November 1915. (continued)	Enemy sent back a fair number, but no one was flared/injured. Working Party of 2 officers and 120 men per night spent night repairing front trenches front-ceiling.	
19th November 1915.	Lots of rifle grenades killed large skull. Pt. near "D" Coy. Shells at junction RUE DES AUQUETS & RUE DELETTRES. No casualties. Usual amount still in day.	1 Cos. to Hospital
20th November 1915.	Lots of rifle bull. "D" Coy's Billets again shelled. One passing through room of one of the officers. No casualty. Bombs & Rifle Grenades in vicinity of 1st & 2nd lines. I.32. "B" Coy fire held. I.26.b. "C" Coy, "B" Coy in support. Knee & platoons in BOIS GRENIER. Hive on either side of Rifle Avenue at like northern end. One platoon "S" line. Headquarters "The Vault" near I.A. FLAMENGRIE Farm. Relief complete 6.25 p.m. A very cold night. Quiet.	5 sick to Hospital 1 wounded
21st November 1915.	Arrival, Inspecting of equipment by General Mclee, visited the lines (AMAH), Head quarters and tour line seen Infantry Agents. One Casualty in Bomb Battery South Stafford Regt... Battalion on our left. 1st Munster Fusiliers on our right. All permits move for tomorrow when we	2 sick to Hospital

Army Form C. 2118.

WAR DIARY:

Instructions regarding War Diaries and Intelligence Summaries and contained in F.S. Regs., Part II. and the Staff Manual respectively. Title pages will be prepared in manuscript.

Hour, Date, Place	Summary of Events and Information	Remarks and References to Appendices
21st November, 1915.	The Battalion takes over trenches from 11th Warwicks. Trenches and the Hibgery line will soon be a good deal for our trenches are in a very bad state and very wet. A full C.O's day.	
22nd November, 1915.	Battalion in trenches. Wet and cold. The following officers joined the Battalion from the Base:- 2nd Lts. W. I. 3/4, I. 3/4, I. 3/3 and W.M. I. 3/4 and I. 3/5. Directed and lights shown from the Brittana — this Pottern with lent surrounding the BRIDOUX salient. The case was not in working order. 2 Lts. A, B & G use two machine guns in 1st Trench A, B & G Platoon. EMMA Corner and BRIDOUX (also 2 extra Pattern in 115 Vine (Hudson Bay) on support of Retrn. ONe lot of Worcesters to support if required on our left. CROWBAOT WoodReally complete by 3pm. Energy shelled very in active at 3.45 p.m. by by walks long from 11.45 night. 2nd Bedfords Occupy reserve trenches in our right. to shelling. Very cold night. Enemy not very active, sniped specially the right. BRIDOUX SALIENT very wet. Brigadier visited the line. Very much sniped and more from Bn. K.R.R. on our right. Col. Bryant, E.D.R. Division.	5 Sick Hospital
23rd November, 1915.		1 Sick Hospital. 1 Wounded
24th November, 1915.	Dull day. Rifles with Prins. Rifles. 5 of 1st Warr. 2 Wounded Cros. Regt. Relief trench 6.40 pm. 1 killed R.V.E.	

WAR DIARY

Army Form C. 2118.

Hour, Date, Place	Summary of Events and Information	Remarks and References to Appendices
24th November 1915 (continued) 25th November 1915.	RUE DELETREE. By 7.30pm. heavy shells also Mhr 4.30pm. RUE-DES-CHARLES. In billets. Enemy shelled our entrenched huts yesterday very heavily, following this sniped heavily. Both 2nd Battn (officers) Battns & A Company C.S.M. wounded, 5 O.R. killed, 5 O.R. wounded, 1 fine day. Having 16 minutes they killed. Stood arms during the night. Fresh Brigadier General Curly visited the lines during the morning. At 3pm he started for a week's rest on France. Circumstances stand 10.5 in the bn/commanding for the month. Every place and man who has gone beyond to fifteen. (5) minutes to 4. At 5:25pm the Brigs. ordered the Battalion to dismiss. 9 sightest strength of Battalion Officers 733 other ranks. Three officers (Capt A---on, Lieut Sears, Lieut Jones) spent the day with Germans, the Brigade, watched trenches, positions and control of fires.	2 Lt. Hospital
26th November 1915.	Sharp frost during the night. 6:15 two fine days. Lieut Col VM Sill having proceeded on leave Capt. 26th Martin assumed temporary command of the Battalion. Early morning artillery changed from 7.30am to 6.30am. At 3.30 pm Lieut aeroplane flew over our area. Heavily fired at by our anti-aircraft guns, from one of four billets	3 Lck. Hospital

WAR DIARY

Army Form C. 2118.

Hour, Date, Place	Summary of Events and Information	Remarks and References to Appendices
27th November 1915. (continued)	Two bombs were dropped from aeroplane but falling near Brigade Headquarters. No damage was done. French situation: 28 Officers, 922 other ranks. Our Officers (Lieut. Fitch and Lieut. Smith) inspection reports the batteries in the Brigade taking over 5 aghd. On horseback were carried out the	
28th November 1915. (Sunday)	Very heavy frost during the night. Bright sunny morning. Church parades by all detachments. Between 10.15am and 11am ten (10) shells (5.9) fell in the vicinity of LA TOULETTE (H 23 c). The fire was most accurate but two registered high two on the road but two registered the Battery. There only casualties to Canadian the Battery. Relieved the 1st Worcester Regiment in the trenches. Relief complete 6.30pm. Companies took up pre-arranged lines:- "D" Coy, "A" Coy, "B" Coy, "C" Coy. Remainder of I.31/2 and I.31/3, "A"Coy in I.31/2; "B" Coy, "C" Coy, Remainder of I.31/4 and I.31/5, "A"Coy in Brigade billets, "D" Coy, New Divisions of WHITE CITY. Enemy's machine guns Lilas ride fort, too completes our Artillery bombarded the DISTILLERIE and 2nd rations opposite FLAMENGARIE farm. No retaliation but our own troops Artillery opened at the invitation of General Stokes C.R.A. visits the lines. He wished to put up more continual pulling between the artillery and infantry and also to establish free communication between F.O.O and Companies. Lieut Ellery left for Brigade Bomb School Course. Officers wounded (not officially)	and Hospital 1 Lieut. Hospital
29th November 1915		

WAR DIARY:

Army Form C. 2118.

HOUR, DATE, PLACE	SUMMARY OF EVENTS AND INFORMATION	REMARKS AND REFERENCES TO APPENDICES
29th November 1915 (continued)	Training course at Dunnequer – Wet day, rain turned towards evening. Dark night.	
30th November, 1915.	Very wet night. Heavy shower of rain and sleet shortly before reveillen. From 2 a.m. it rained more or less continuously until about 12 noon. SALIENT very wet. Water above the knees in some places. Brigadier General Oxley accompanied by his Brigade Major, visited trenches last night 12 night. Our Artillery bombarded behind the German lines at 8 p.m. No retaliation. Our little bombing party blew four of the north line a little before "C" Coy & four Baden Powell and Potter (G) W.O.H. Ky. 4 men left for the Corps' course at the Divisional Bomb School.	1 sick, hospital. [illegible] returns from [illegible] during the month 29.

2/E. Lancs Rgt.
Dec
vol. XIII

Sheet 1

Army Form C. 2118.

WAR DIARY:
2nd East Lancashire Regt

Instructions regarding War Diaries and Intelligence Summaries and contained in F.S. Regs., Part II. and the Staff Manual respectively. Title pages will be prepared in manuscript.

Hour, Date, Place	Summary of Events and Information	Remarks and References to Appendices
1st December, 1915.	Fine, starlight night, but rain came on about 5 a.m. Very fine day. – Slight shelling. About 6 p.m. hostile machine guns swept our avenues and lines of approach for men of a ration party slightly wounded. A great deal of work was done draining and pumping dry trenches and building up parapets, banks and traverses. Patrols went out, but encountered none of the enemy.	3 Wounded 2 sick to Hospital
2nd December, 1915.	Fine Morning. Enemy shelled a barn in front of "B" Coy. HQrs at I.31.3, I.31.4. Four shells (5.9') bursts of explote. that three burst in our parapet. One man his of wound. (Lbcpl Whittam) and later his leg blown off, and he thus was wounded in the eye and arm. Later "A" 6 "B" were wounded on BREWERY Rd. The Brigadier visited the trenches at 11.30 a.m. and remained until 1.15 p.m. He expressed great pleasure at the amount of work done by the Battalion during the last four (4) days, especially on returning the trench water in the salient. BREWERY and neighbouring shells about 2.30 p.m. with 5.9' and 15 p.m. Seventy-five shells – to casualties. Eleven allied aeroplanes crossed our line at 4.30 p.m. on an air raid. Relieved by 1st Worcester Regt. Relief complete 7.30 p.m. took over killed from 1st Worcesters. C. Butler	✻ Buried by Capt Western at 4.15 p.m. at White City. 4 Wounded (2 arm & one 2 pm)

WAR DIARY:

2nd East Lancashire Regt.

Army Form C. 2118.

Sheet 2

Hour, Date, Place	Summary of Events and Information	Remarks and References to Appendices
2nd December 1915. (continued)	"C" Battalion "C" Coy at COMMAND POST and HdQtrs. "A" Coy at LA TOULETTE. Ems. "B" and "D" Coys in RUE DELETTREE. H.Q. Coy on same front H.17.d.1.0.	
3rd December 1915.	Wet morning and continued all day. Usual inspection parades. Brigadier visited the Transport Lines.	
4th December 1915.	Wet night and steady rain in morning. Physical drill and 10.30 am parade impossible. Inspections and lectures in huts and farms. Three officers spent the day with the Battery group in this area. Glared up in afternoon and parades. Capt Stokyn Libery processes. Cmdg. Lieut Richmond took tuition of A/Adjt. Comdy. Officer visited the Transport Lines at 3.30pm. They were very muddy and wet. The horses being mad, and well turned out. Paras to other Regiments.	1 sick 5 Hospital. ※ Capt Parker, Lieut Long, Lieut Guth.
5th December 1915.	A fine morning. Three (3) officers visited Battery group. to check horse service as follows:— Communion 8am at Soldiers Blot, 9am strong as possible. 10 am Bullus. 10:30am Church Parade "G" Coys killed. 10:30am (Cantuary Riy'S). "D" and "HQ" Coy at trained hut. Billet. Punches.	※ Beauplepe, Pickens and ypu.

Army Form C. 2118.

Sheet 3.

WAR DIARY:

2nd Berkshire Regt.

Hour, Date, Place	Summary of Events and Information	Remarks and References to Appendices
5th December, 1915 (continued)	for those who lay in. Strict church. Voluntary service at 5 p.m. Officers' Club. Other training. Stores had naval parade. Shots & airplane flew over our area about 4 p.m. and was engaged by an Allied aircraft gun and forced to retreat. No shells fell in our area.	Reinforcements 2 officers and 6 other ranks.
6th December, 1915.	A wet day. Marched at 4.15 p.m. and took over billets from 11th West Yorks at HALLOBEAU. Parties were sent at 8.30 a.m. and 10.30 a.m. Lieut. Col. G.F.M. Still having returned from leave resumed Command of the Battalion. Lieut. ffrenner (Wks)	3 sick to Hospital.
7th December, 1915	Day fine up to 4 p.m. then much rain. General parade at 8.30, 10.30 a.m. and 2 p.m. General Burlington visited the lines during the morning. Billets in huts in field, which are ankle deep in mud and water.	
8th December, 1915.	Usual parade. The day was very fine. Working party of 160 men and proportion of N.C.O.s from 9 to 4 p.m. Two (2) officers with this party. 3 N.C.O.s and 80 men also sent to assist Divisional Ammunition Column in making winter standings for their horses. 250 men had baths.	

Army Form C. 2118.

WAR DIARY:
2nd Bedfordshire Regt.

Hour, Date, Place	Summary of Events and Information	Remarks and References to Appendices
9th December 1915.	A very wet day. Lieut. Col. Onslow, 1st Wr. cester Regt. (temporarily commanding the Brigade) visited the Battn. Enemy shells ERQUINGHEM. Kemmel between 11am and 3pm. A lecture on gas which was to have been given to all officers had to be postponed on this account. Nine officers and 100 men work "N.C.O." in preparation on fatigue from 4.30pm to 12 MN; also 3 N.C.O.s and 30 men assisting D.A.C. column as fatigue parties unloading entrenching work & like stores. Weather.	
10th December 1915	Very wet day. Found parties. Training very difficult owing to the weather. Split two redoubts the gates impassable. Lamp, writing parties are taken. Reinforcement of 16 other ranks arrived all men who has previously served in France.	
11th December 1915	Weather still very bad. trans new are *2 killed & started Revrs L.V.S. flares. Day Commdrs visited the trenches the Battn will occupy on the 14th inst. Working party of 100 men and two officers at 9 am – fatigue 150 and 3 officers at 8.30 pm.	

Army Form C. 2118.

Sheet 5

WAR DIARY:
2nd East Lancashire Regt

Instructions regarding War Diaries and Intelligence Summaries and contained in F.S. Regs., Part II. and the Staff Manual respectively. Title pages will be prepared in manuscript.

Hour, Date, Place	Summary of Events and Information	Remarks and References to Appendices
11th December, 1915	8 N.C.O's and 27 recruits arrive as R.R.C. with their transport lines.	
12th December 1915 (Sunday)	Weather slightly better, but river continues to rise and ERQUINGHEM Bridge is in almost impassable on the north side. Church Parades for all Denominations.	
13th December, 1915	A fight cets day. Parades as usual, got some night work. Water subsiding in River Lys but very gradually. Machine Guns sent to the Bois Grenier line in order that they may take place in daylight. Both reliefs the 13th N.J. in trenches	1 died in Hospital
14th December, 1915	I 21/2, I 21/3, I 21/4, I 19/1, I 19/2, I 16/1, I 16/2 Armentières and Jones Farm style left of Brigade relieving the 1st East Kent, 11/th K. Fusiliers, Markers at 2.30 pm Relief complete 6.45 pm. During the bridge at ERQUINGHEM being impassable in account of the flood, the march was considerably longer than usual. whole have been "A" Coy two platoons occupied right of the line, "B" Coy in support. "B" Coy the platoon "B" Coy, the left of the "D.S.M." platoon two platoon in reserve. the left of the four machine	1 died in Hospital

Army Form C. 2118.

WAR DIARY:
East Lancashire Regt.

HOUR, DATE, PLACE	SUMMARY OF EVENTS AND INFORMATION	REMARKS AND REFERENCES TO APPENDICES
14th December, 1915 (continued)	Machine guns in the front line. Two manned by Battn Officers, but sent by 1st Worcester in the Bn in reserve. "B" & "C" Coys the Bn's Lewis guns in reserve. "B" & "C" Coys was the above in the nerve in the Bns Reserve. Wire fine. Battn on left & M. Artillery. Battn on right lost the most support. They fay ago and that clouds are toward evening, and there was some rain.	
15th December, 1915	The night passed very quietly, some shelling on the extreme right of the line about 10 am. The barrage. Our Lewis guns knocked an the enemy trenches opposite the Brigade on our left supported by morning. Enemy reported in ARMENTIERES.	
16th December, 1915	At [?] hour, during the night the regt was made by the Brigade on the right (63rd Brigade) 3rd Army on the German trenches. The Imperial Light Infantry led the attack, capturing 12 Germans and killing forty. Our guns fires very heavy before and after the regt which took (place at 9am). Tonight 15/16th. Some 150 enemy shells went fired at the lines held by the Battn little damage was done. Two men were slightly wounded. The Bay was still 15 pm. — The day was fine with some	2 wounded.

WAR DIARY:
East Lancashire Regt

Army Form C. 2118.

Sheet 7

Instructions regarding War Diaries and Intelligence Summaries and contained in F.S. Regs, Part II. and the Staff Manual respectively. Title pages will be prepared in manuscript.

Hour, Date, Place	Summary of Events and Information	Remarks and References to Appendices
16th December 1915 (continued)	Some rain in the evening. General spying on machine guns, about 9 a.m. Several lights also started some at 10 a.m.	
17th December 1915	Quiet night and day. Work throughout the two trenches carried out in the first parapet and wire. Much trenching was done. The enemy were not very active, with their rifles, or machine guns and for the last ten days have done little shelling. F.O.O. Lt. Craigh A.190. R.F.A.	3 sick to hospital
18th December 1915	Quiet night but enemy's rifle fire was rather keen and little rifles. Relieved by Worcesters Regt. Relief complete 6.30 p.m. Between RUE MARLE & CHAPELLE D' ARMENTIERES we lay in a reserve position at CHAPELLE D' ARMENTIERES. The day was quiet, our guns more active than those of the enemy. Dark fine, some rain.	2 sick to hospital 1 wounded
19th December 1915	Very fine day. Enemy shells CHAPELLE D'ARMENTIERES at 7.30 a.m. Steadily falls up in the garden of the house in which the officers are billeted. No damage done. Guns very active during the morning. 50 N.C.Os and men on fatigue into R.E. from 6.45 a.m. till dark.	1 wounded 2 sick

WAR DIARY:
Warwickshire Regt.

Army Form C. 2118.

Hour, Date, Place	Summary of Events and Information	Remarks and References to Appendices
20th December 1915	All day snipers and machine gun fire swept through the huts. Large numbers on fatigue. General Babington having previous to this, several days ourselves considered that Division, and ruin brittle enough. 11 Worcester Regt of the Brigade Row fell into 9 p.m. no shell had except one D Coy billets.	unusually dull & tropical
21st December 1915	A wet night and day very misty. quiet.	
22nd December 1915	A wet day. Relieves the 11 Worcester Regt in the trenches taking over the line no on 19th December. The relief was completed by 5.50 p.m. Parties at 4 p.m. The day was very quiet, much mist.	1 died & hospital
23rd December 1915	A good night. Day June in the morning had evening mist, heavy rain about 4 p.m. Rifle fire slight but a good deal of shelling carried out in this places by 15 pr Shells. Our own bearings: Battn in our left the Lincolns, 63rd Bde., 21st Divn: on our right 11 Sherwood Foresters 24th Bde. 23rd Divn. F.O.O. Lieut Leighton R.F.A. C.194.	

Army Form C. 2118.

WAR DIARY:
Enshancelue Regt.

Instructions regarding War Diaries and Intelligence Summaries and contained in F.S. Regs., Part II. and the Staff Manual respectively. Title pages will be prepared in manuscript.

Hour, Date, Place	Summary of Events and Information	Remarks and References to Appendices
24th December 1915	A quiet night. Heavy shower of rain throughout the night. General Kenny commanding 23rd Bdn, and Colonel Boyes, commanding 24th Infy Bde, visited the line. Enemy very quiet. Our guns shelled our lines length in reply to our gun fire. "A" & "D" Coy Chapel but still very little engage. "A" & "D" Coy Chapel and "B" & "C" Coy (Rue Chapel) were practically unstop anything.	
25th December 1915 (Christmas Day)	Enemy were trending our way and has a good deal more than were firing the night. Our machine gun replies. A rifle fire was very much ranged. Snipers very active, and were firing from my continues rain very little shelling on Battn line; though our guns shelled enemy trenches reports and telescopy, about 11 am enemy replies on Baston on our night. — 11 there had thunder.	
26th December 1915	Quiet night. Much rain. Bryan rain was the fringe in WINE AVENUE some considerable setting by full after during the morning. Relieved by 8th Yorks for 12 hours Relief completed 6.30 pm. Battn. RUE MARLE with advanced Coy (A) in CHAPELLE D'ARMENTIERES.	Reinforcements of 25th Oth. Ranks

Army Form C. 2118.

Sheet 10.

WAR DIARY:
2nd East Lancashire Regt

Hour, Date, Place	Summary of Events and Information	Remarks and References to Appendices
27th December, 1915	Rain during the night. Working party of 50 under R.E. Sgt. by truck siding firing up the sidings. Very fine with some showers.	
28th December, 1915	A fine day. Billets shelled, took in RUE MARLE "C" Coy and CHAPELLE D'ARMENTIERES, "A" Coy, no casualties. Usual working party of 50 under R.E. Usual parades. Voluntary service for all denominations. Lieut. Colonel Bryan commanding the Brigade, inspects the Lewis gun fg. by 24 MGs, gave a lecture to officers by Colonel Strahan commanding 23rd Divisional Artillery on artillery commanding duties in trenches. Working parties carry out twenty stores into trenches of 5 officers, 20 of N.C.O's and 210 men — details 6.30 pm to 12 pm.	Two sick to Hospital
29th December, 1915	Battalion moved into Brigade Reserve at JOH Rompu. H.T. Q. 9.44, Sheet 36. N.W. 1/20,000; taking over billets from the West Yorks and Landing over to the 10th West Yorks. Marched at 4.20 pm — sniper killed at 5.45pm. A fine day. Nails in which mine huts are situated.	Two sick to Hospital

Sheet-11

WAR DIARY:
2nd East Lancashire Regiment

Army Form C. 2118.

HOUR, DATE, PLACE	SUMMARY OF EVENTS AND INFORMATION	REMARKS AND REFERENCES TO APPENDICES
20th December 1915 (continued)	Situated in a very bad state – a few H [?] men – still not trench boards. Bay fires.	
30th December 1915	Regt HHrs – Usual parades, two groups very fit. Capt. Alsop and the Bde Major, Capt. Miller, inspected about 8.30 p.m. Pay day. Working parties of one officer and 70 other ranks and one officer and 50 other ranks.	One sick to hospital
31st December, 1915	Usual parades as far as grounds permits. Pay day until 3.30 p.m. when C mines kindly took over. Working parties of one officer and 50 other ranks, and one officer and 50 other ranks ran by day, and one by night. 300 N.C.O. and officers went to Divisional Baths – Regimental Baths in transport lines in use for first time. 16 men has baths and complete change of clothing.	3 sick to hospital. Total reprints [?] R.O. Reinforcements 28 other ranks.

W. Hill Lieut-Col
Commdg 2nd East Lancashire Regt

2 E. Lancs Regt
Jan
Vol XIV

A.F.C. 2118 (?)

WAR DIARY

1st Easslancashire Regiment   Sheet 1

Hour, Date and Place	Summary of Events and Information	Remarks and references to Appendices
1st January. 1916.	A dull day; with strong heavy wind and some rain. Battalion went for a Route March, 9.30 am to 12.30 pm. 300 N.C.O's and men went to the "Divnl" Baths. Two working parties of one officer and 50 other ranks were employed finding R.E. 30 men had Baths in the Transport Lines.	1 sick to Hospital
2nd January. 1916. (Sunday).	Church Service for all ingredients with communion service for C. of E. Run communication rooms. 12 noon and full heavily. 30 men of of the day. Working party of one officer and 50 other ranks under R.E.	1 sick to Hospital
3rd January. 1916.	Fine day. First gas attack message received at 3.15 pm. Battn: on parade by 3.45 pm. stood down at 4.15 pm. Usual parades were held. 300 men had Baths at the Divnl Baths. 30 at the Transport Lines. 150 men and 3 officers on working parties.	1 sick to Hospital
4th January. 1916	Fine until 4 pm; after that Snow, rain. Conference of commanding Officers at Bde Hd Qrs. 11H HHHH 3 to 4.30 pm - Battn Route March, 9.30 am to 1 pm. 100 other ranks and 3 officers on working party.	1 sick to Hospital
5th January. 1916.	A fine day. Usual parades. A Battalion Concert was	1 sick to Hospital

A.F.C. 2118 (P1)

WAR DIARY

1st East Lancashire Regiment

Sheet 2

Hour, Date and Place	Summary of Events and Information	Remarks and References to Appendices
5th January - (Contd)	was held in the soldiers' hut. RUE DORMOIRE at 8 pm. Working party of 3 officers and 100 other ranks employed under the R.E.	
6th January - 1916.	A dull day - with strong wind, but no rain. Commanding Officer and Coy. Commanders visited the trenches in the 13th Div, as Right Battalion will relieve the 13th Div, as Right Battn: (or "A" Battn:) in the Right Brigade area tomorrow. Orderly visited the Skillets.	3 sick to Hospital
7th January. 1916.	(Arrived at 3.20pm to relieve 13th D.L.I. (Lieut-Col Beauclerk) in the trenches I.31/1, 2, 3, 4 and 5, which includes BRIDOUX SALIENT positions just south of BOIS GRENIER. Relief complete without casualties at 6.50 pm. Line was held as follows:- "C" Coy, I.31/1; "D" Coy, I.31/2 & 3, (includes salient); "A" Coy. I.31/4 & 5; "B" Coy. One platoon, Hudson's Bay Post; platoon, Stanway Post; 2 sections Emma Post; two platoons - also two sections - WHITE CITY. Battn: Head Qrs at WHITE CITY. Day fine until 4.15pm. 3pm often very heavy rain fell until 4.15pm. The night was then fine.	5 sick to Hospital 1 injured
8th January. 1916	A quiet night. One 15 pdr. shell fell in Hd Qrs during	

A.F.C. 2119. (M.S)

WAR DIARY

2nd East Lancashire Regiment   Sheet 3

Hour, Date and Place	Summary of Events and Information	Remarks and References to Appendices
8th January (Contd)	During the night no damage; rifle fire was slight. 2 wounded (one arm one nose) trenches I.31/2 and 3 in a very bad state; parapets fallen in and Gun - much smoke and mud 2.5ft - trees in places. The remaining trenches in better condition. Lts Orr and Capt Milly visited the trenches. General Oxley and Capt Milly visited the trenches. One man saved by steel helmet; bullet struck front and glanced off without doing any damage.	2 wounded (one arm one nose) 5 sick to Hospital
9th January 1916.	During the night 24th Brigade - Co. operating with 20th Brig. (only immediate right of Batton), who were raiding the German trenches opposite by us. 2 to smoke bombs were given to the Battn, to discharge between 2.15 am and 2.40 am - these were to recur the enemy whilst relieving the Brigade were having guns. The bombs were discharged successfully but were much rifle (?) machine gun and still fire all quiet by 3.15 am. No casualties, except one machine gun struck by a piece of shell. Reavill of 20th Division Raid unknown. Day fine; some rain about 3 am.	Officer Rev. Anthony retained (as 10thy)
10th January 1916.	Quiet night with usual hostile machine and rifle fire. Chiefly directed against the road from BOIS GRENIER to Battn HQ. Bro. BRIDOUX SALIENT still in a bad state - water 2 feet to 3 feet up, but some improvement	1 wounded

A.F.C. 2118 (late)

WAR DIARY

1st Worcestershire Regiment Sheet

Hour, Date and Place	Summary of Events and Information	Remarks and References to Appendices
10th January (contd)	wind is keeping moist. There was very little shelling. The day was fine and mild.	
11th January, 1916. Rgt. RUE DELETTREE.	Relieved in trenches by 1st Worcestershire Regt. Relief complete by 6.50pm. Billets in huts of RUE DELETTREE. No casualties during the tour in trenches. Enemy during the day were quite than usual. Weather fine.	2 men wounded
12th January, 1916.	In billets. Usual inspection parades. No shelling. A fine day. One officer and 50 other ranks on working party, from 9.30 am to 4.30pm.	1 sick to hospital
13th January, 1916.	6 Officers – 400 NCOs and men went to the Bird Baths. 90 o.r. Battn. Baths. 2 officers and 100 other ranks on working party. Usual parades. Fine day with some showers.	1 sick to hospital
14th January, 1916.	A cold fine day. Usual parades and working parties. Very little enemy shelling. Much water in spite of the comparatively dry weather – very bad in the (huts) fields where the men huts are situated.	1 sick to hospital
15th January, 1916.	Relieved 1st Worcestershire Regt. in trenches I 31/1, 2, 3, 4 and 5. Left billets at 4.45pm – A."Coy. leading	

A.F.C. 2118 (P.4)

WAR DIARY

2nd East Lancashire Regiment   Sheet 5

Hour, Date and Place	Summary of Events and Information	Remarks and References to Appendices
15th January (cont)	Relief leading remainder at 5 minutes' interval. Relief complete by 6.50 pm. The line held as on previous occasion except that "A" and "B" will hold the salient in turn for 48 hours and "D" I. 31/1 and 2 and "B" I. 31/4 and 5. The day was cloudy with a little rain early but fine later, and towards the night quite clear with bright moon.	Sick & Hospital 1
16th January 1916.	A quiet night. Less rifle fire than usual. One machine gun opposite I. 31/4 was taken in evidence. A dull day with a little rain. About 1 pm to 2 pm many shells were fired into the vicinity with about seventy (70) (Bn. Hqs Qrs) and the BOIS GRENIER Rd. shells - mostly 15 pm, some of what went unexploded, no damage of any importance was done.	Sick & Hospital 1
17th January 1916.	A quiet night. Some rifle and machine gun fire. Few enemy shells fell in the neighbourhood. Kept of H.Q. Qrs during the day. Much water has been done on the front parapets which are still in a bad state - and requires the relief so in a very heavy wet state, and requires still	Sick & Hospital 1

WAR DIARY

2nd East Lancashire Regiment — Sheet 6

A.F.C. 2118 (b.)

Hour, Date and Place	Summary of Events and Information	Remarks and References to Appendices
17th January 1916 (contd)	Still a lot of work and much draining; the water is still from 4 to 5 inches deep. Day fine with cold wind.	1 wounded (at duty) 2 sick to Hospital
18th January '16	Light gun - Some machine gun fire on trenches. Work continued on the front trench. W/Adjt and Capts. and Lts. B.102, R.F.A. (Capt Iittlert commanding) in front of trench I.3.11. with 70 rounds and Capt Ittlert commanding, came in connection with a scheme by which it is hoped the enemy will believe the Battalion is about to raid their trenches, and so induced them to man their parapets, when guns and machine guns already laid on, will at once open fire. The enemy retaliated with some 96 shells in the neighbourhood of the Brewery, Queen St, and white City (Button St. Arc), no serious damage was done. A dull day with slight rain.	1 sick to Hospital
19th January, 1916	Endeavoured between 3.30 am and 5 am to make the enemy man his parapets in order that machine guns and shrapnel, previously laid on the trenches, might open fire.	

WAR DIARY

2nd Eastlancashire Regiment.

Sheet 7

Hour, Date and Place	Summary of Events and Information	Remarks and References to Appendices

19th January (Contd) fire on him at a given signal. No success was achieved — enemy made no reply to our trench mortars, rifle grenades and finally rifle fire. The night was too light with a very bright moon. Capt B.G. McQuestin was in command of the artillery grenade to this demonstration and carried them out with great care. Lieut Lowe and Richards were in command of the bombing party summoned. The party was very fine with bright sunshine. Relieved by the 1st Worcestershire Regt. who holds the Battalion took over the **RUE DELETTREE**, "C" Coy being the company in support of "A" Battn as command post. The Battns on the Right (XXX) and [XXXX] of the Battn during the tour in the trenches were Rifle Brigade and 2nd Middlsex Regt. 25th and 23rd Brigades respectively. The relief was complete by 6.20 pm and the Battalion in billets by 9.50pm.

20th January 1916. A fine day with some changes and showers. No shelling. Status in billets. Conditions — fields

WAR DIARY

2nd Earl of Manchester Regiment Sheet 5

A.F.C. 2118 (24)

Hour, Date and Place	Summary of Events and Information	Remarks and References to Appendices
20th January (cont)	-fields in which they are situated very muddy and wet — still no trench boards. General Oxley visited the fields.	
21st January. 1916.	Some rain during the night. Working parties also — 200 men went with Capt. Bath though working party of one officer and 50 other ranks under the R.E. Three officers spent the day with the R.A. for purposes of instruction.	1 sick to Hospital
22nd January. 1916.	A fine day. Usual parados left. Working party of usual strength under R.E. Enemy shelling vicinity of command posts at 11 am and 1.45 pm. With 10-15 pr. H.E. and at 2.45 from the fields near 5"- 8" orys fields received 6 - 5.9 inch shells. No damage was done in either occasion. Some work was done in command post, but little could be done to make dug-outs near fields for safety against enemy shelling as no materials were supplied in spite of numerous applications.	
23rd January 1916.	A fine day with much mist up to 10 am; afterwards bright sunshine — Moved into Arcrd	1 sick to Hospital

A.F.C. 2118 (P24)

WAR DIARY

2nd East Lancashire Regiment. Sheet 9.

Hour, Date and Place	Summary of Events and Information.	Remarks and References to Appendices.
23rd January. 1916.	Point Reavy with billets at Pond Farm. Taking over from the West Yorks. Owing to the Battn. billets in the RUE DELETTRE being with the exception of 'C' Coy. and Commanding Offr. marched at 5.30 p.m. and Battn. marched at 6.45 p.m. — 'C' Coy. at 8.15 p.m., reached billets.	
24th January. 1916.	Dull day with some rain, about 2 p.m. Usual parades. 2 Officers and 100 other ranks working party under R.E. Trenches rather too muddy than usual. Officers with few exceptions in huts. Lewis Gun Officer, 1 Sergt., 2 Corpls. and 25 privates struck off duty to join Brigade Machine Gun Coy. 2nd Lieut. Howe appointed.	2 Lieut. ? Hospital
25th January. 1916.	A cold frosty night followed by a bright sunny day. Usual parades, except that 10.30 a.m. was a Battn. parade, and all 1st Class Reservists present were given their badges by the Commanding Officer. 3 Officers and 160 other ranks were employed as a working party under the R.E. from 3 p.m. to 10 p.m. The Battn. played the 1st Sherwood Foresters at Football and were beaten by 6–0. Lieut. Howe appointed	

WAR DIARY

2nd East Lancashire Regiment — Sheet 10.

Hour Date and Place	Summary of Events and Information	Remarks and References to Appendices
25th January (cont.)	Appointed Machine Gun Officer of the Battalion. Four Lewis Guns received in place of four Maxims, taken over by Brigade Machine Gun Company. Map square of Fleurbaix B.26.d.4.1. Map 20,000. 36. N.W. Belgium and France.	
26th January 1916.	A milder night — Usual Parades. Two boys/sick to Hospital of 15th Royal Scots 34th Division, Billeted with the Battalion in the Sentry, Killed with Bruce, Commanding D Coy. Killed at the fine day, Working party of 8 other ranks and 1st officer.	
27th January 1916.	A dull day with slight showers. Usual/Sick to Hospital Parades + 9 men to Grant Backs. 26 officers Regt sent to left Battalion Billets for Brigade Reserve in rest of left area. Conferences of Commanding Officers at Brigade H.d. Qrs.	
28th January 1916.	Trench Strength. Total with Battn in trenches — 21 officers 697 other ranks. Transport Lines, attached in live 11 officers 203 other ranks. Total Strength 32 officers (including Medical Officer and 3 2nd Lieut. Little, Lambert, Porter not posted). 900 officers rank — a dull warm day. No rain — 4 officers and 210 other ranks working.	

A.F.C. 2118 (b/s)

WAR DIARY

2nd Easy Lancashire Regiment. Sheet 11.

Hour, Date and Place	Summary of Events and Information	Remarks and References to Appendices
28th January 1916 (contd)	working parties under R.E. - Usual parades. Commanding Officer inspected part of the Regimental transport.	XXXXX/XXXXX
29th January. 1916	A dull day, quiet and mild. Battn paraded for a route march at 10am returning to billets at 1pm. Commanding inspected the remainder of transport. Bombers were instructed in throwing of live bombs: 100 Mills in all were thrown. They paraded at 3pm.	2 sick to Hospital
30th January. 1916 (Sunday)	C.O. 23rd Division presented medal ribbons the following on parade at 10am. Captain M.G. Fitch, Military Cross. 6274 Sergt. R.M. Auck, R.M. Auck. with Military Cross. 6274 Sergt. Agnew. 1067 (the bottom) 110474 Corpl. R. Rigby. Distinguished Conduct medal. The day was fine with heavy mist and very cold. Commanding Officer, Company Officers visited the trenches which the Battn. will take over tomorrow from 13th N.F.	1 sick to Hospital. 1 Injured.
31st January. 1916	A fine cold day. Coy parades in the morning. 1 Officer (2/Lieut T.E. WIT- Battn. HERS) to Hospital sick	1 Officer (2/Lieut T.E. WIT-HERS) to Hospital sick

A.F.C. 2118 (M)

WAR DIARY

2nd East Lancashire Regiment

Sheet 12

Hour, Date and Place	Summary of Events and Information	Remarks and References to Appendices
31st January. 1916. (Contd)	Battn. relieved the 13th Kts.I.9 in the trenches from ading at 3.45 pm. Relief complete at 7.20pm. Coys. occupied the line as under:- "A" Coy. I. 21½ and 3; "B" Coy. BOIS GRENIER Line, east of Wine Avenue, I. 15½ and I.16. "B" Coy I. 3½ and I.15½. "C" To. Coys. each hug 3 sections in support in "S" Line. The 2nd Ari. Bombers were also there. One Lewis gun was with "B" Coy. three being in the front line, together with the maxim guns from the Brie M.G. Coys. the 1st Sherwood Foresters held the line on our right, and the Hants and Leicesters Regt. on our left. a fairly quiet relief.	Total to Hospital 55. Total injuries 16

W.I. Hill
Lieut. Colonel.
Commdg. 2 E. Lan. R.

WAR DIARY
or
INTELLIGENCE SUMMARY

Army Form C. 2118

Sheet 1

East Lancashire Regiment

Place	Date	Hour	Summary of Events and Information	Remarks and references to Appendices
	1st Feb. 1916	—	A quiet night. Fine day and dry. State of the trenches which have much improved since the Battalion's last tour, yet needing much work to be done in the front line. The parapets had been somewhat damaged especially in J.21.2. by the bombardment of the next night of 27/28 January, and suffered quiet days. There was no shelling by the enemy.	
	2nd Feb. 1916	—	An excellent patrol was carried out in front J.15/2 by Sjts. Ellin and Begson, and Sjt. Shakyr, B. Coy. Last night. The night was very cold and frosty. We continued in the line with 10th Liverpools attached to K. Battalion for instruction. One pl. 10th Liverpools attached to B. Coy and one platoon. One platoon to A. Coy. A fine sunny day. Very little hostile shelling of 6.6m. Lieut. Colonel Jones Williams commanding 3rd Welsh Fusiliers attached to Headquarters.	
	3rd Feb. 1916	—	A quiet night. Less cold. Night some rain. Continues in the trenches. General Berrington are occasionally with us from time to time during the morning. A fine day. Very light shelling. Some sniping.	
	4th Feb. 1916	—	A quiet day & night. Any stealthy grist were dwas raining heavily. By 5pm it had ceased. Relieved in the trenches by 1st Worcester Regt.— relieving not over until 8pm. Battalion in Brigade Reserve as supporting Battalion. One & 2 Coys in RUE MARIE. One Coy in CHAPELLE D'ARMENTIERES (A) and one in BOIS GRENIER Line (B). Also the 11th Lincoln Coy – 2 platoons in RUE MARIE and	T16

WAR DIARY

INTELLIGENCE SUMMARY Sheet 2

Ba**s**sa**n** Regiment

Place	Date	Hour	Summary of Events and Information	Remarks and references to Appendices
4th Feb. Sunday	1916		One platoon with "A" and "D" Coy.	
5th Feb.	1916		A very fine day. Inspection parade held by Coys. A working party of 1 officer and 50 men O.R. under the R.E. A draft of 16 O.R. arrived at 9.45 p.m.	2 to Hospital
6th Feb.	1916		Some rain during the night. Fine day with rain shower in afternoon. Church parade and toy gun platoon when they were not doing work. 7pm to 10pm. V. was found that the gas gong was to be redundant & they were under R.E. 2 officers and 100 O.R. working party under R.E. Two platoons relieved by 10th Lincolns attached regiment Reserve Jhh An in RUE MARLE from "A" and "D" Coys.	Reinforcement 16 O.R.
7th Feb.	1916		A high wind with heavy showers, a fine afternoon. The Coy of the 10th Lincoln rejoined the Battalion. Usual parade. 400 O.R. went to the Divisional Baths. Rain during the night.	
8th Feb.	1916		Relieved the 1st Worcesters in the trenches, taking over no 10 the previous reserve, except that "C" Coy is in Reserve, and "B" in their place in the front line. Relief complete by 7.30 p.m. Pr. Northamptons took over the Battalion's Billets. It rained very hard during the relief but cleared up later, after a good deal of rain fell during the night.	
9th Feb.	1916		A very quiet high. A fine day - much work in the trenches the only known of the morning. Not much improvement since the last time the Battalion was in.	1 Coy

WAR DIARY
INTELLIGENCE SUMMARY

Forel— 3rd Regiment

Place	Date	Hour	Summary of Events and Information	Remarks and references to Appendices
9th Feb. 1916 (Contd)			One Coy of the 24th Northumberland Fusiliers attacked by instruction, 2 platoons attacked B Coy, 1½ "A" and 1½ "C". The 3rd General (Coby) routed the Battalion Headquarters in the afternoon. The Battalion on our right, 1st Lancashire Fusiliers, on our left, 12th Northumberland Fusiliers.	Wounded to Hospital 3 to Hospital
10th Feb. 1916			The night was cold, with slight frost. The enemy's machine guns were rather more active than usual. General Babington visited the lines about 9.30 a.m. Much was done during the day on the parapets and pumps. Also the enemy shelled the lines about 10.15 a.m. and again rather heavily between 1.30 p.m. and 3 p.m. Some damage to parapets and wire—	2 to Hospital
11th Feb. 1916			The night was quiet, with the exception of a little activity on the part of the enemy's machine guns. The weather turned to a thaw. The enemy's snipers were steadily all day. The enemy's artillery were very active throughout the day shelling the approaches, lines, support lines and billets in ERQUINGHEM and BAC ST MAUR. Slight damage was done to our parapets. The Colonel Commanding the 25th Northumberland Fusiliers and some of his Officers to whom the Battalion mostly the tour during the morning. Relieved by 1st Northumberland Fusiliers took over billets in the RUE MARLE and ARMENTIERES. Relief complete by 7.30 p.m. and no casualties by 8.45 p.m.	12th Feb. 1916

Army Form C. 2118.

WAR DIARY: Sheet 4
2/7th Warwickshire Regiment

Hour, Date, Place	Summary of Events and Information	Remarks and References to Appendices
12th February 1916	A fine day. The Hun was shelling about 12 noon. One shell striking the chimney of the house next to Battn. Room. Another hit the Church & opposite H.d. Qrs. Strong direct hits nearly were also struck. There were no casualties. Working party of one officer and 50 O.R. went to R.E. Dump. Party had trouble with about 2000 rifle grenades which were working incessantly. The trenches they were working in very thinly.	4 to Hospital
13th February 1916.	A fine day. Enemy shelled the fields repeatedly from about 10.15 a.m. until 5 p.m. with short intervals. The Battalion was very busy in burying & evacuating casualties. The 2/7th Northumberland Fusiliers had material also H.d. Qrs. Dugout together who were billeted in Ars. when since the two Coys (A&B) near the H.d. Qrs. in the RUE MARIE Church parish had to be abandoned. The artillery in this also were more than usually active. We lost 2 killed by 2/7 Northumberland. Which were rescued by the 11R. War. Yorks. in RYE DORMOIRE.	1 to Hospital
14th February 1916.	Relieved in billets by 2/7th Northumberland Fugitive marched to billets in RYE DORMOIRE The day was not unlike a very high wind. That was no.	1 to Hospital

WAR DIARY: 2 Lt 5

East Lancashire Regiment

Army Form C. 2118.

Hour, Date, Place	Summary of Events and Information	Remarks and References to Appendices
14th February 1916 (contd)	No shelling during the day. Battalion to move in Divisional Reserve. Reached billets at 10.30 pm. The 1/4th Kings Own left us as the 2/7th Northumberland Fusiliers have kept the four coys in the trenches till day-light given which they had been relieved for instruction.	
15th February 1916.	A fine day with a strong W wind. The billets were muddy and my all Coys engaged in attempts to bring the fields in which the huts stand into offices and CR a reasonable state under the R.E. Carrington hoisted the C.O. the two Coys about 12 noon. Report duty at 5 pm. Lieut Colonel F.M. hoisted joined the Battalion from sick leave and assumed command of Battalion from 17th inst.	1 K Hospital
16th February 1916.	Strong very cold SW gale all day with squalls of rain especially during morning. Coys engaged in tugging full drains round huts and an transport lines. The work done was noted by A.A. & Q.M.G. 23rd Divn during afternoon. Owing the moisture and the strong wind the mud in the fields decreased. Capt & Adjt R.M. Amrest took over duties Adjutant.	3 K Hospital

WAR DIARY: 1/4th East Lancashire Regiment

Hour, Date, Place	Summary of Events and Information	Remarks and References to Appendices
16th February 1916. (contd)	Adjutant saw Capt Ellis Wakym who resumed command of "A" Coy vice Capt Fitch. About 10.45 p.m a Zeppelin was reported passing over trenches East of YPRES at 10.19 p.m.	
17th February 1916.	Fine, stormy, cold wind, but no rain. Ben. Ashly visited lines and inspected drain arrangements which were continuous during day. Improvement to 60 ft of MS Ben & No. At 3.45 pm Major Ertwood Burlington visited the lines about 8pm a "Bright Sparkler" in the Divisional Club run at Burlin Hse Coy at 7pm. A Zeppelin was reported at 12.15 a.m also passing and Brillant at 12.44 p.m.	1 to Hospital
18th February 1916.	Cold and wet all day after about 9 am. Arrangements were continuous up to 12 noon. Remainder of day spent in company inspections for march. Many Bags of Mail Bus arrived 1pm and stores Offs. Ostericio' Club.	3 to Hospital
19th February 1916.	Cold and wet. Slight morning parade no rain after the night. Strenuous efforts of Company Inspections and preparations for march. About 10pm a Zeppelin or their aircraft was heard and also reported from direction the passing over vicinity but	1 to Hospital

Army Form C. 2118.

WAR DIARY: 4th
Warwickshire Regiment

Instructions regarding War Diaries and Intelligence Summaries and contained in F.S. Regs., Part II. and the Staff Manual respectively. Title pages will be prepared in manuscript.

Hour, Date, Place	Summary of Events and Information	Remarks and References to Appendices
19th February 1916. (contd)	in spite of bright moonlight, it could not be seen from Lille.	
20th February 1916.	9th Bn. Bn. marched to VIEUX BERQUIN. The Battalion left RUE DORMOIRE plus marching in order by Coys at 5 minutes interval. Battalion followed 1st Worcester Regt & 1/8 Corps. Travelling kitchens together and blanket wagons in rear of Coys. Remainder of Transport in rear of the Battalion. Transports marched at 11.57.5 Am. Course very muddy but weather fine. Battalion rested side before entering village to enable men who reported sick to rejoin in ranks. ※ Arrived in RUE - ERQUINGHEM. Bridge, - LA MENEGATE - STEENWERCK - LE VERRIER - ST VIEUX BERQUIN. - Billets of Battalion centred in farms between LA COURONNE and VERTE RUE. - Cold and frosty night.	※ arrived about 4.30 pm
21st February 1916.	March continued to SERCUS. Heavy Bn. Left VIEUX BERQUIN 9.30 am. Battalion which was main road lined, marching from VERTE RUE 8.30 am in tows, and joining in rear of 1st Worcester in Fifteens. 100 yards between Battns. Order of march; Bn. HQ., D. A. B. C Coys. Ration	

Army Form C. 2118.

WAR DIARY: Sheet 8

5th Worcestershire Regiment

HOUR, DATE, PLACE	SUMMARY OF EVENTS AND INFORMATION	REMARKS AND REFERENCES TO APPENDICES
21st February 1916.	CRUI - LA MOTTE - PAPOTE - MORBECQUE - STEENBECQUE, where 1st Division finally arrived. Battalion finished march in rear of Brigade in pouring rain, en rear of Baggage waggons in rear of Battalion Transport Officer, who naturally was in poor condition. Arrived about 12.45 p.m. had just been on a fortnights preparation, took men billets. Inhabitants unanimously unwilling and difficult at first, possibly mis-billets scattered over several miles and mostly rather uncomfortable, chiefly owing to lack of places for drying and washing any covered utensils, cooking places or washing places for men. Cold, full inclined to snow at night. Heavy permanent frost gives in all day to thaw. Teams later that 103 Field Ambulance lost 200 yards of transport and had fallen & retaken.	BELLE

22nd Feb. 1916

WAR DIARY: 2nd Bn 9

East Lancashire Regiment

Army Form C. 2118.

HOUR, DATE, PLACE	SUMMARY OF EVENTS AND INFORMATION	REMARKS AND REFERENCES TO APPENDICES
22nd February 1916.	Inspection parade in billets. Enjoyed nearly all day till evening, but Snowing. Bright & very cold. Strong E wind. Snowing officers inspected.	
23rd February 1916.	Rank march about 5½ miles. 8.30 am. Henry snow on the ground and stiff frost at night. Arrived Nearly Raoien 10.30 am one 2 pm. Forming officers voice billets of H Coy F L contains. Brain received forward regt day to ESTAIRES. Transport moves from main billets under cover in SERCUS. Later when became permanent moved to ESTAIRES. Sharp frost at night after 11 pm. Lewis Hoggers reported temporarily from Bn Bomb school.	
24th February 1916. (Thickly)	Rank march in marching men about 7 mls at 9.30 am. Very cold morning, the about midday sun came out and sky was pleasant though still freezing in the shade. Arms drill parade during afternoon ground still covered with snow. Very cold evening and sharp frost.	
25th February 1916.	Rank march, about 5 miles in marching order at 9 am. Very cold day. Snow still laid on the 6.6 Hospital ground. Knocks & children	

A.F.C. 2118 (M)

WAR DIARY

2nd East Lancashire Regiment. Sheet 10

Hour, Date and Place	Summary of Events and Information	Remarks and References to Appendices
25th February contd	and for Battalion Baths and drying shed, commenced with what wind and corrugated iron was available. Very cold N.E. wind during afternoon and still towards evening. Candles for arms drill in afternoon.	
26th February, 1916.	Route march about 8½ miles in marching order. 8.45 am cold morning. About 2 inches snow fell during night. At about 9.30 am sun appeared and later it grew much warmer with resulting thaw. Arms drill parade at Coy Billets 2pm – 2.45pm. Divisional Headquarters moved to Berrington. Frost at night.	
27th February 1916. (Sunday)	Dull morning. Later, sun came out and thaw followed. Divine service in Billets near Servian Cross Roads. Roman Catholics at Church. Brigadier General Aylse attended, escort to C of E Service. Major General Barker visited the Battalion about 11.30 am and motored to Northampton Regiment. Dull afternoon with occasional attempts to snow, but no frost.	2 b Hospital
28th February 1916.	Slight frost in early morning, followed by thaw all day. Route march 5½ miles in marching order. 2 noon 8.45 am. Billets – 2pm arms drill. Musketry instruction at Coy Billets for early morning. Orders received. Instructions for Pontoon Bridge were turned into Battalion just before came afternoon. Dull & cold and damp all day.	3 b Hospital
29th February. 1916.	Fine day. All horses and transport marched under field umps. Brigade Transport Officer during crossing south	3 b Hospital

A.F.C. 2118. (M5)

WAR DIARY.
2nd East Lancashire Regiment. Sheet 11

Hour, Date and Place	Summary of Events and Information.	Remarks and References to Appendices
29th February (contd)	South of Lillers near Billy Houses. 8.30am. Battalion transport in charge of Gilman left Lillers 7.45am. Transport marched via AIRE – ST NILAIRE – PERNES to BRUAY. Country very hilly round BRUAY. Poor condition and country very heavy. After dark only moving by estimation of horses could not join the Battalion that night. Distance when 20 miles. Battalion left Lillers 9.45am and marched 5 miles to entrain at THIENNES, finish for entrainment by 21st and 2nd one Company 9th South Staffs. do and 2nd French mortar Batteries. Entrained in East group Brigade, Corps and 23rd Division with Staffs, which entrainment. 1pm. arrived THIENNES. 1pm arrived at THIENNES. 1pm arrived at BRUAY. About 9.15pm detrained and marched off as the French troops had marched into Lillers. Long delay in getting into Billets in consequence. The heavy surplus heavy of Battalion arrived at CATONNE, RICQUART, but transport detrained at VILLERS, RUE DESSERTIGNY and RUE DE LA MAIRIE. No British troops had previously occupied the area and Battalion arrangements were very defective. In that with transport arrangements started until about 10pm.	43rd Hospital during month 2 wounded and 1 injured. 22 men sent from hospital during month.

L.J. Sumter
Lieut Colonel
Commanding 2nd East Lancs R.

O.C.
East Lancashire Regt.

It is a great pleasure to forward the remarks of the Corps Commander and the G O C Division --

Please convey these remarks to those concerned & add my congratulations on their very excellent work —

R.S. Oxley
B.genl.
Comd. 24th Inf. Bde.

7/2/16

E.L.B.606.

> GENERAL STAFF
> 23RD DIVISION
> 2 - FEB. 1916
> Register No.

Head Quarters,
    24th Infantry Brigade.

   I attach report of the patrol referred to in my morning report. Map attached.

   The patrol consisted of the following:-

   2/Lieut.E.I.Barrow.   in charge
   2/Lieut.E.A.Ellen.
   No.11500. Sgt.Hosker.

   They carried out the work with the greatest determination and courage and although discovered by the enemy and fired on very early in the proceedings, finished the work they had set out to do, most thoroughly. A searchlight was turned on them.

   The patrol was to investigate the ditches at I.16.c.8.4., I.16.d.4.4. and the point near I.16.c.1.1. where a sniper was suspected.

                                sd. G.E.HILL. Lt.Colonel,
2nd February 1916.   Commanding 2nd East Lancashire Regt.

23rd Division   B M 654

Forwarded for information of the G.O.C.
I consider this reconnaissance most creditable to 2nd Lieut Barrow & those with him —

                              R.S. Oxley B. General
                              Comdg 24" Inf Bde

2/2/16.

Headquarters
3rd Corps.

Forwarded for information

J. M. Babington
Major General,
Commanding 23rd Division.

February 2nd 1916.

This is very good work for which
2/Lt Barrow and the men with
him should be highly commended.

W. P. Pulteney
Lieut General
Cmd'g 3rd Corps

4.2.16

H.Q.
24th Brigade

Forwarded for information & communication
to 2/Lt Barrow & Ellen; also to Sergeant
Hooker, &c (I should like to add my own
appreciation of the enterprise shewn by
this patrol.)

J. M. Babington
Major General,
Commanding 23rd Division.

February 7th 1916.

Army Form C. 2118

2/East Lancashire Regt

WAR DIARY
or
INTELLIGENCE SUMMARY
(Erase heading not required.)

Place	Date	Hour	Summary of Events and Information	Remarks and references to Appendices
Ourton 1st March 1916				
	March 2nd		Stay fine and at times sunny. Battn readjusted & transport arrangements changed. Coy parades at 10.30 a.m. & 2 p.m. Baggage collected from station. They stay with Bun at times but start up suddenly. 8 a.m. Coy instructed by Coy Commanders (Capt Dixon). Battn S/Mr Reeve 24 h Duty. Bn orderly room near Bois d'Olhain. 8 a.m. Off horses groomed near Bde H.Qrs. Turned up in heavy by Roster. After parade. Lieut Ockley held conference of C.Os, with regard to probable tube down. Day grew greying till about 3.15 when it turned cold & afterwards much colder. Coy paraded at 2 p.m. Remainder of surplus kit was brought up from the Railway Station. Most of the Transport were not filled thirstily standing in stores at foot of hill & were already nearer the Battn than at first filled for ease of room some had to be left as the mud made stamping beyond Bois d'Olhain.	
	March 3rd		Running & physical training Parade 8.30 a.m. Rain fell from about 8.45 am practically all day varied by snow. Cold & dreary day without any marked Bath parade had to be cancelled - Lectures on Rifle. Bayonet fighting and musketry 2 p.m. Two inter-company football matches attempted than before take Place, but rain came on heavily. Brig Gen Ockley marked For a Fit. Orders for move received.	
	March 4th		Heavy snow from dawn continuing all day. No parades possible except Lectures. Roy special arrangements north Chief Engineer of French mines, the Battn was bathed in the Mines shower bath from 10.30 a.m. to 2.30 p.m. Lecture by Coy Commander (4th Corps) to all officers held at Cinema Hall in BRUAY. 3 p.m. Frost at night.	

Army Form C. 2118

2/ East Lancashire Regt

WAR DIARY
or
INTELLIGENCE SUMMARY
(Erase heading not required.)

Place	Date	Hour	Summary of Events and Information	Remarks and references to Appendices
Billets (Sunday)	March 5th 1916		2/Sherwood Foresters moved to GRAND SERVINS & PETIT SERVINS prior to taking over trenches at NOTRE DAME DE LORETTE. All C.O.'s Smith-Bingham & Coy Comdrs of Bn went by Motor Bus to reconnoitre ground generally, & O.C. "C" Platt Gy, Motor Car, Motor Bus which is rumor & Gaff myers above 1 mile from Grand Servins. Consequently Officers had several miles to walk to night. N.D. de LORETTE spur, Cold day but fine with some sleet. Officers had to get back by morning lorries etc. The mists being at its thickest. Church parades as usual. Snap Sun Pit washer blankets collected at Mr Stores.	Running orders to base & hospital
Billets	March 6th	8.30 to 9 a.m. 12.30 p.m. to next day	Heavy snow from about 7 a.m. and also during night – Colder night. Coy parades 10.30 a.m. to 12 noon. Snow came but about everywhere. Country generally very wet & water lying everywhere. Orders general to next day was not received till 10.30 p.m.	
– " –	March 7th		Frosty morning but thaw awakegan. Brigade order issued (3) M.T.& hurry & everywhere. Otts & made a second journey, Brigade marches from Bruay 1 p.m. (lead) Sherwood Foresters, (then) of which Northamptons, Worcesters & East Lancashire, first line transport followed unit. Wagons were bypassed & commenced arriving about 11 a.m. and improved continually all day till about 11 p.m. at night. Brigade marches to GRAND & PETIT SERVINS. 2 field kitchens having been sent on with billeting parties 5 hours in front of Batter. Billets cantoned & poor & dirty. Had been used for one night by 69 Bde, but previously by only by French troops. Sanitation accommodation everywhere utterly poor. Only one man of the Batter fell out on the march, rest, but the march was not Constable owing to constant halts, due to meeting other troops	

Army Form C. 2118

2/E. Lancashire Regt

WAR DIARY
or
INTELLIGENCE SUMMARY
(Erase heading not required.)

Instructions regarding War Diaries and Intelligence Summaries are contained in F.S. Regs., Part II. and the Staff Manual respectively. Title Pages will be prepared in manuscript.

Place	Date	Hour	Summary of Events and Information	Remarks and references to Appendices
	March 7th to March 8th		Stopped en route to sleep with FRESNICOURT at which the transport of 121st Brigade were in difficulties.	
Billets			A cold sunny night. Readjustment of billets on departure of French Troops. Junr H. Ross's Billets were very dirty, verification for carelessness by O.C. absence. Report hospital. Conference at 6.35 p.m. It Col. J.S. Lambert having taken over command of the 69th Infy Bde, Major L.G.M. Hill assumed command of the Battn.	Reinforcements 1/3 O.R.
"	March 9th		A very cold frosty night. Coy Parades at 8.30 am, 10.30 am & 2 pm. Bde Commander & Coy Comdrs watched Coy trenches now occupied by the 8th Infs. which are to be taken over by the Battn tomorrow night. A fine day. Thawing. The trenches are in a very poor state. Parapets hardly exist and the support lines are practically useless. They appear to be very little rifle fire - though there gives bombing is pretty general.	3 Sick to Hosp.
"	March 10th		A very cold sunny night. Parades at 8.30 am & 10.30 am. Relieved 8th Yorks in the trenches. Paraded at 6 pm. Relief complete by 2.30 am. Distance 6 miles. Communication trench 1½ miles, one way available for two Battns; very difficult and tiring relief. Y/Mancorken on right of Battn & S/Northamptons left. A cold day. Thawing.	4 Sick 5 to Hosp.
Trenches	March 11th		A quiet night. Enemy in front of Battn not aggressive, no rifle fire at all, some shelling. German listening posts 15 yards away Coy Herr visit plainly visible. German trenches very bad, wet & muddy. A dull day. Thawing. Genl Osley visited the lines. Regt & 2nd in command of 13th DCLI worked Battn HQrs. in order to see the lines. Carrying of rations & R.E. stores very long and difficult.	

1875. Wt. W593/826 1,000,000 4/15 J.B.C. & A. A.D.S.S./Forms/C.2118.

WAR DIARY or INTELLIGENCE SUMMARY

Army Form C. 2118

2/ East Lancashire Regt

(Erase heading not required.)

Place	Date	Hour	Summary of Events and Information	Remarks and references to Appendices
Trenches	12th March		A quiet night, except about 4.30 a.m. when there was heavy gun fire on the Right of the Brigade. (Worcesters) reported about 5.15 a.m. they shelly Jellicus hit 2/8th front line through a sap 15 f.s. sw. near Bn H.Qrs. No H.E. fire however as yet most insignificant. Some attempt was to snipe M.G. firing but the shortage of our expended small arms matter difficult. Drainage attended to. 2nd Lieut A. Topp & C.S.M. Archibald joined unit. A fine warm day.	Lieut Topp 29th & S.Sgt A Topp & CSM Archibald joined 2/Lieut Ashcroft Afton attached 2 officers R.O.R. Smith 5 O.R. C.A. 5th.
— ,, —	March 13th		Relief completed by 7th Seaforth Hrs. A very quiet night. Work continued in the trenches, but overhead shell looking screen erected. The Batt. was reviewed on the Trenches on after noon day. Passed several aerial torpedoes into left of B Coy line between 1 pm & 3 pm and several aerial two seven air slightly, there was also some wounding 2 Lieut H. Wilson & two other ranks. A very fine warm day. Genl Bosley noticed the Batn H.Qrs about 12 noon. Trenches still very muddy.	2/Lt R. Wilson wounded 5" Trench mortar Sd 147794
— ,, —	March 14th		A very quiet night. Much work carrying up duck boards and supporting the line. The Enemy's torpedoes of gillers very noisy withing throughout the day, also there were two chambers. The No. 19th London Coy & Ter. Coy Counties wanted the Trenches, also Engr. Thwaites Coving the Brigade. The day was very fine and again.	R. Wilson 5" Trench mortar Sd 147794
— ,, —	March 15th		A good night. Much work done in the lines. Enemy Artillery and aerial torpedoes active throughout the day. Our Artillery & Trench Mortar replied, Still five two kept so rainy as the two preceding days. Relieved in the Trenches by the 19th London Regt. Relief delayed two hours by heavy shelling of CARENCY. The relief was completed by 11.30 pm and the Batn. in Builth at GRAND & PETIT SERVINS by 3.15 a.m.	H.Q. C.E. Russell 3 O/Rs Cash Hospital

1875 Wt. W593/826 1,000,000 4/15 J.B.C. & A. A.D.S.S./Forms/C. 2118.

Army Form C. 2118

2/ East Lancashire Regt

WAR DIARY
or
INTELLIGENCE SUMMARY
(Erase heading not required.)

Instructions regarding War Diaries and Intelligence Summaries are contained in F.S. Regs., Part II. and the Staff Manual respectively. Title Pages will be prepared in manuscript.

Place	Date	Hour	Summary of Events and Information	Remarks and references to Appendices
Trenches	March 15th		The Brigade during this Tour had 3 Bns. in the front line with one in support. The 2/10 wkshire were on the right, & the 2/8th on the left, & the Bn. in support, & of Hertfordshire & 2/ Sherwood Foresters, the Bns. being in the front line & support alternately.	2 Fews. H Wounded (Mounted orderly)
Billets	March 16th		Bn marched independently at 1 p.m from Trench Lines to OURTON where they were billeted by 5 p.m. Lt. Col. G.O.S. H. Capt. Sir Henry Willcox saw the Battn. march past him on the road and expressed his satisfaction at the appearance of the men. The day was cold and over-cast with a slight shower about 3 p.m.	1 O.R. Sick to Hosp.
" "	March 17th		Day spent by Battn in cleaning up the Billets clothing & equipment. Billets on the whole, comfortable. Lieut. Oxley visited Bn H.Q.s during the morning. The day was fine.	2 Fews. NCOs & 2 proceeded to the Staff Iron School.
" "	March 18th		The whole of the Battn. proceeded to BRUAY for baths in the morning, but the afternoon Gen'l Sir Douglas Haig C. in C. visited the Billets. The day was very fine in the morning, but there came rain in the afternoon. Capt B.C.M Western proceeded to PERNES to take charge of the Div. training school for young Officers, the remaining Bn of the Brigade are billeted in the Neighbourhood.	
" " Sunday	March 19th		A fine warm day. Parade service for all denominations. Billeting parties & 2/Lt. L. Duffy started to take over billets. 2/Lieut. Hopper & one NCO sent on Attachy. billets at HERSIN. Leave re-opened, 2 Offs & 23 O.R. proceeded on leave to England at 11 p.m.	2 O.R. Sick & Hospital
Billets	March 20th		Battn marched to Heroin Couday at 12.40 p.m and reaching billets at 4 p.m on the march of the Battn. were in a very dusty state. The 7 Bush L. Infy, the 2nd Bush L. Infy, and the 24th R. Fusiliers. The following Baths were passed. 2/W.R. Inf.	8 O.R. Sick to Hospital

1375 Wt. W593/826 1,000,000 4/15 J.B.C. & A. A.D.S.S./Forms/C. 2118.

Army Form C. 2118

WAR DIARY
or
INTELLIGENCE SUMMARY
(Erase heading not required.)

2/East Lancashire Regt

Instructions regarding War Diaries and Intelligence Summaries are contained in F.S. Regs., Part II. and the Staff Manual respectively. Title Pages will be prepared in manuscript.

Place	Date	Hour	Summary of Events and Information	Remarks and references to Appendices
	March 20th En-		A warm dull day. Roads very dusty, much Crumpton on the square. Three Coy Courses moved by Motor Bus to Pt SAINS. R.2.6. Sheet 36 B. to Reconnoitre the new area.	Reinforcements 30 O.R.
	March 21st		"A" & "B" Coys. Lewis Gun Section & B./M./Gun searched M at 1pm at intervals of 100 yds between Platoons to BOUVIGNY BOYEFFLES in relief of 1/R.R.R. from whom billets were taken over. "C" & "D" Coys at 4.45 p.m. from to hut in BOIS de NOULETTE, the latter to dig out in B.19.9.6. (Sic). The Batty is in Div Reserve. Billets and dugouts most uncomfortable mostly dirty. The 24th Infy Bde relieved the 99th Infy Bde in the SOUCHEZ area, and the 23rd Infy Bde the 2nd Bde. The day was cold and dull with some rain. Gen'l Oxley & Gen'l Babington both visited Bn HQrs at HERSIN during the morning. A draft of 25.O.R. joined at HERSIN at 1.15 p.m.	
Cuincy M.A.P. Sheet 36.B. S.E. 1/20,000 Sq. R.19.C.	March 22nd		A dull night with some rain. Minor parades at H.Qrs, C & D Coys the afternoon Bn "B" Coy. who practically cannot move about by to do very much especially "B" Coy who drilled in the company? Line day. County Officer inspected Billets of H.Qrs & Lewis Guns Section in the morning & C & D Coys in the afternoon. "C" Coy moved into H.Qrs after dark on relief by a Coy of the 9th Bn St Staffs (Pioneer Battn) The day was fine and cold with short fine intervals. Working party of 1 Off & 60 O.R. at 5.4.5 p.m.	Bde 23/3/16 See to H.Qr.
Billets	March 23rd		A fine day but dull and cold, some sleet early in the morning. Minor parades at H.Qrs. C.O. inspected billets of "A" "B" & "C" Coys. Working party 3 Offs & 220 O.R. from 6 p.m. to 7 a.m. in the front line.	See to H.Qr.

1875. Wt. W593/826 1,000,000 4/15 J.B.C. & A. A.D.S.S./Forms/C. 2118.

WAR DIARY or INTELLIGENCE SUMMARY

Army Form C. 2118

2/East Lancashire Regt

(Erase heading not required.)

Instructions regarding War Diaries and Intelligence Summaries are contained in F.S. Regs., Part II. and the Staff Manual respectively. Title Pages will be prepared in manuscript.

Place	Date	Hour	Summary of Events and Information	Remarks and references to Appendices
Billets	March 24th 1916		A very cold night with heavy fall of snow, snow 5 inches deep in the ground. Usual parades. Coy officers visited the trenches as far as H.Q. on R.J. Wortspur. It is not possible to move up to the front line by day. Snowing until 11 a.m. After fine with very cold wind. Working parties of 3 offrs & 250 men.	
—"—	March 25th		Another cold night with heavy snow followed by a sunny day. Relieved the 1 Worcesters in the SOUCHEZ Sector (Souchez I). Very poor trenches, no communication between NE Coy. and any other part of the line. By day, no movement. The relief was a poor one and took considerable until 10 a.m. two officers returning by the same communication trench.	6 OR Book to Nov?
Trenches	March 26th		A quiet night. Enemy sent up many Very lights but there was practically no rifle fire. Some shelling during the day but no damage. Heavy rain during the night. Little work done. Guns can only be visited by night. Approaches are all bad and no protection if the lines are found up. Ration parties, water & carrying parties very heavy. Baths in the Byes. 22 at Jouenus. On the left 1 Sherwood Foresters.	2 OR Book Stores?
—"—	March 27th		A very wet night, in rifle fire, but some shelling, not much work done, owing to the weather & difficulty of bringing up materials. Work cannot be done by day as movement/Couran? Shelling and sniping our lines being much interfered.	2 OR Promise 2 OR Book 5 Stores
—"—	March 28th		A very dark wet night with heavy showers. A quiet day with some shelling. Gun's body smelt up from the morning. Enemy rifle fire not heavy.	1 BB Bk of Right Pinot City 2 OR guard
—"—	March 29th		A very dark wet night. Enemy guns busied up somewhat & may; number of RE. stores posted again. Almost impossible to do any work owing to darkness and rain.	1 OR Book ?

WAR DIARY
or
INTELLIGENCE SUMMARY

Army Form C. 2118

2/East Lancashire Regt

Place	Date	Hour	Summary of Events and Information	Remarks and references to Appendices
Trenches	March 29th		Relieved in Trenches by 1/6 Manchester Regt. Relief Complete by 9.45 p.m. Battn. in billets at BOIS DES NOULETTE (Labourette) by 11 a.m.	1 wounded
Billets	March 30th		A very fine day but cold. Coys spent the day cleaning up. 4 Officers & 100 OR. attended a Flammenwerfer demonstration at SAINS EN GOHELLE in the morning. "B" Coy at the Div. Baths in AIX NOULETTE. regimentally, and "B" Coy at the Div. Baths in AIX NOULETTE. 2 Officers & 130 OR. on digging fatigue from 6.30 pm to 1 a.m.	7. Wheeler to Field Hospital
" "	March 31st		A very fine day. Name Coy Paraders, C & D Coys at the baths. Games & Dei & lectures to Batln. Baths. Headqt & Brigade Guards. 24 Rifle under Bn. N.C.Os during the morning. Similar number of Officers & OR. on digging fatigue.	1 man to Hosp. New leave 5 Officers leaving France. 56 total appointed from hospital 31

W.H. Tripp

O.C. 2/East Lancashire Regt

WAR DIARY
or
INTELLIGENCE SUMMARY

Army Form C. 2118

Place	Date	Hour	Summary of Events and Information	Remarks and references to Appendices
	1st April 1916.		A very fine day. Usual parades and other work. Men digging and carrying fatigues. Lt Capt Sempill M.O. having proceeded off sick. Capt. Smith assumed temporary command of the Battalion. Capt. Kirkpatrick taking over the duties of acting Adjutant.	
	2nd April 1916.		A fine warm day. Battalion relieved 1st Worcesters Regt in the trenches in SOUCHEZ (?) leaving billets at 6.45 p.m. Whilst the relief was in progress the enemy opened a short but intense bombardment on the ground between skirmish trench and the front line, followed by ten similar bombardments on "Kholonaks" trench and the ARRAS Rd — the majority of the battalion was on the ARRAS Rd at the time, but except me truly a few casualties. Germans used small H.E. shells only, and no shrapnel. Relief was complete at 11.5 p.m.	
	3rd April 1916.		Fine and very warm. Enemy guns quiet during the day, but from 7 p.m. to 12 midnight shelled intermittently with H.E. Shrapnel the SOUCHEZ Valley and the position near SOUCHEZ Station, hill by "C" Coy in support. No damage worth mention. Practically no rifle or machine gun fire. Wrote sixteen (?) communication between H.Q. Trench and the front line by day. Trenches improved. Formation posts constructed. Dug trench through Mid-Battalion from the right by rungs and changed dug-outs formed out. Battalion was also strained with the 7th Middleses Regt, Killing NOTRE DAME DE LORETTE.	
	4th April 1916.		Cold and cloudy. Enemy shelled the right front Coy (D) with H.E's about 1.40 p.m. and "C" Coy at SOUCHEZ intermittently during the afternoon. No damage done. Enemy was very quiet during the night. Work on trenches and dug-outs continued and wire put out in front of "D" Coy.	
	5th April 1916.			

Army Form C. 2118

WAR DIARY
or
INTELLIGENCE SUMMARY Sheet 2
(Erase heading not required.)

E. Lyon R

Instructions regarding War Diaries and Intelligence Summaries are contained in F.S. Regs., Part II and the Staff Manual respectively. Title Pages will be prepared in manuscript.

Place	Date	Hour	Summary of Events and Information	Remarks and references to Appendices
	5th April 1916.		Cold and cloudy. Enemy shelled the Right from 6.0 a.m. until 6.15 a.m. from 7.30 to 8.15 a.m. At 9.30 a.m. they opened with artillery fire in the same place, continuing until 10.15 a.m. In all about 40 H.E. 5.9 torpedoes were fired, considerable damage being done. Five trench shelters were practically destroyed in parts, three men were killed and 5 wounded. Retaliation from our artillery was asked for, and obtained at 10.45 a.m. Enemy were again quiet during the night, with the exception of some sniping, which fired regularly at portion of the trench which had been damaged. Work in trenches and on the damaged parapet was carried on after dark - more wire was put out in front of R bay.	15 pm 3 killed. 15 pm wounded. 40 H.E. torpedoes
	6th April 1916		Cold and cloudy. Between 7.0 and 7.30 a.m. the enemy shelled the Right Front Coys with 16 pm - no damage. Between 1.30 and 2.30 p.m. the enemy fired about eighty (80) 5.9" H.E. shells at the parapet of the Right Front Coys obtaining many direct hits, which destroyed about ten yards of the trench. Between 8 and 11 pm about twenty 5.9" H.E. shells were fired at Kinmel's Trench - no damage done. Battalion relieved by the 1st Worcestershire Regt. the relief being completed by 12.40 a.m. Battalion in billets in Armoricial Reserve at BOUVIGNY (Boisoy in BOIS SIX) by 3.40 a.m. Battalion in billets.	enemy shelled / 16 pm wounded.
	7th April 1916		Fatigue at 7.15 pm - A suff. off. 6 fatigue in billets. Some officers and 100 others went on dipping Battalion in billets -	
	8th April 1916		Battalion in billets. Fine but cold. Usual parades and a fairly cold similar number of officers and men in digging fatigue.	
	9th April 1916		Battalion in billets. At 9 a.m. orders were received for Company to hospital to take precautions in the event of shell fire, as our artillery would carry.	

Army Form C. 2118

WAR DIARY
or
INTELLIGENCE SUMMARY

(Erase heading not required.)

E Lan R   Shw 3

Place	Date	Hour	Summary of Events and Information	Remarks and references to Appendices
	9th April contd.		Carry out a bombardment of the enemy's fortified work known as the PIMPLE, West of GIVENCHY (S.G.D), commencing at 4.30 p.m. At 1 p.m. this was cancelled owing to a mist preventing observation. Enemy who never bothered the relief of the 1st Worcestershire Regt in the trenches, until the 12th. Usual digging parties were sent out.	
	10th April, 1916.		A fine day. Battalion in billets. Usual parade in the morning. Artillery carried out the bombardment postponed from the previous day commencing at 4.30 p.m. There was no retaliation in the neighbourhood of BOUVIGNY. Usual digging parties were sent out at night.	
	11th April, 1916.		Battalion in billets - Cold wet day. Practice Cap respirators with 2 Hospital D.P. helmets during the morning, by all Coys and the Battalion. Usual digging parties at night.	
	12th April, 1916.		Very wet day. Battalion relieved the 1st Worcestershire Regt, in SOUCHEZ I, during billets at 8.30 pm. Relief was complete at 11.45 p.m. Enemy was very quiet during the relief.	
	13th April, 1916.		A fine day. Showery in the evening. At 9 a.m four 4.2" shells were fired into SOUCHEZ village, and between 10.45 am and 11.15 am the ARRAS Rd was shelled with H.E. Otherwise the enemy was very quiet. A good deal of work was done on the communication trenches. It is now possible to reach the left support by daylight and the Right front Coy can be reached without difficulty. Support trench has been very badly damaged by 4.2 trench mortars. Two platoons	

Army Form C. 2118

WAR DIARY
or
INTELLIGENCE SUMMARY

(Erase heading not required.)

Sheet 4

E. Fyn R.

Instructions regarding War Diaries and Intelligence Summaries are contained in F.S. Regs., Part II. and the Staff Manual respectively. Title Pages will be prepared in manuscript.

Place	Date	Hour	Summary of Events and Information	Remarks and references to Appendices
	13th April (cont'd)		Gun platoons are withdrawing during the day and put in Company B. Hospital at night. Bnj. Skt. Battalion on the Right, was the 22nd Infy. Regt. 47th Division. French was also relieving with the 23rd Zouaves.	
NOTRE DAME DE LORETTE	14th April 1916.		Cold and showery. General Barkington, Commanding 23rd Division, visited the trench at 9.30 am. Enemy was very quiet. There being practically no rifle fire against the section held by the Battalion and no artillery fire or machine gun fire. At 11.50 pm S.O.S. "GAS TEST" received. Precautions were carried out and all working arrangements appeared to be adequate.	
	15th April 1916.		A quiet night. During the day the enemy shortened the line trenches. Weather was fine. Major Campbell assumed from leave and resumed command of the Battalion.	1st Hospital
	16th April 1916.		A quiet night. Enemy shells the front line trenches heavily between 7.30 and 9.30 am, doing considerable damage; and again between 6.30 and 8.30 pm, doing some damage. Our retaliation was very ineffective. Day showery.	1 killed 2 wounded
	17th April 1916.		Heavy quiet on the Battalion front but heavy rifle and gun fire on our immediate right (CARENCY SECTOR) held by the 47th Division) between 12 MN. and 1 am. There were some very heavy showers of rain with a high wind. During the afternoon the enemy shelled the front line trenches heavily doing considerable damage. Our retaliation was very ineffective. Battalion relieved by the 22nd R. Imwalin. Relief complete by 12 M.N., and Battalion in billets in FOSSE 10, ⅔ of a mile N.N.W. of AIX NOULETTE, by 4 am. The night	2 killed 2 wounded 1st Hospital

1875. Wt. W593/826 1,000,000 4/15 J.B.C. & A. A.D.S.S./Forms/C.2118.

WAR DIARY

Army Form C. 2118

Place	Date	Hour	Summary of Events and Information	Remarks and references to Appendices
	17th April. (contd)		The night was very wild with very heavy storms of cold rain. Capt R.A.S. Ward, with a draft of 25 other ranks, joined Battalion during the day, and remained at the Transport Lines during the train the 18th. Sickness troops were on the Right. Left with the 19th Division on the Right.	
	18th April. 1916		Battalion moved from FOSSE 10 at 11.30 am to billets to BRUAY. Coys marched at intervals of 100 yards, account of the traffic. Battalion was in billets by 3pm. The weather was showery with heavy rain & wind. Lewis Mellush and 30 other ranks joined the Battalion at BRUAY.	
	19th April. 1916.		A very wet day. Coys all busy with inspection of clothing/equipment, etc. Billets very fair.	hospital
	20th April 1916		A showery day with bright intervals. Parades 7.30 am, 10.30 am and 2pm. 125 other ranks and 2 officers on digging fatigue, from 8 am to 4pm. General Oxley visited the billets at 11 am. "B", "C" & "D" Coys and H.Qrs had baths at the mine from 1 to 5 pm.	hospital
	21st April 1916 (Good Friday)		A very fine morning, but wet afternoon and evening. Parades as yesterday, also working parties. Voluntary Church Service was held in the morning.	
	22nd April. 1916.		A very wet day. Parades much interfered with - Coy Officers lectures to the men. Divisional working parties were found by the Battalion. "A" Coy went to the baths at the mine at 3pm.	hospital
	23rd April. 1916		A fine day, with bright sunshine and some wind. Church parade for	

WAR DIARY or INTELLIGENCE SUMMARY

Army Form C. 2118

Place: E. Lan R. Sheet 6.

Date	Hour	Summary of Events and Information	Remarks and references to Appendices
23rd April 1916. (Sunday)		For all denominations. Two foot-ball matches were played in the Coy league. A fine warm day.	Hospital
24th April 1916.		Usual Coy Parades at 7.30 am. Battalion parade at 10.30 am. Gas demonstration at 2.30 pm for the whole Battalion. Lewis Gun section made up for rifle range and very satisfactory in action. Coy football match in the afternoon. Conference of C.O.s at B'n HQrs at 4.30 pm.	1 Hospital
25th April 1916.		A very warm fine day. Usual parades. General Rawlinson, G.O.C. 23rd Division, accompanied by Divisional Staff. Commanding 24th Bde., saw "A" and "D" Coys on parade at 11 am. One officer and 50 other ranks watching firing from 4 pm to 6 pm. Two parties of 20 other ranks employed in the town on fatigue, one in the morning and the other in the afternoon. Coy football match.	3 Hospital
26th April 1916		The Battalion marched from Bryas at 9 am, for the manœuvre area, taking over billets from 2nd W. Yorks, 8th Bde at LAIRES. Dinners were served in the men just outside village of FIEFS, where a halt of ½ hour was arranged. The point was eleven miles from Bruiley. The total distance being just over seventeen (17) miles. The day was excessively hot and the roads were dusty. Going to the heavy. Traffic on General Munro Commanding the First Army saw the Battalion on the march. The Battalion routes loaves at 5.30 pm.	2 Hospital
27th April 1916.		A very fine day. Hot again excessively hot. Inspection of billets by 2 Hospital commanding Officer. Dinners at Breakfast. Coy training from 1.15 pm to 5 pm	

WAR DIARY
INTELLIGENCE SUMMARY

Army Form C. 2118

Place	Date	Hour	Summary of Events and Information	Remarks and references to Appendices
	27th April 1916. (Cont)	5pm	to 5pm in the trenches area.	
	28th April 1916.		A very fine warm day. Boys digging continued in the trenches area. Battalion put into front line at 5pm. Arriving of this made 3 platoons of B Coy were near by the Regd Barn in reserve. Lieut S.E. Withy rejoined the Battalion in sick quarters. The trenches were as follows: ref. map. 5A HAZEBROUCK — CROCQ, REELINGHEM, RUPIGNY, BOMY, PETIGNY.	2 Hospital
	29th April 1916.		A very fine day with a cool northeast wind. Battalion training from 9am to 3pm. Ammunition being prepared in Battalion & Companies. One Coy was on guard & Battalion returning from parade.	
	30th April 1916.		A very fine day. Battalion training for the coming Brigade Battles. The Battalion Band performing for Divisional General and the Brigadier in the Ruine grounds.	Commanding

WAR DIARY
INTELLIGENCE SUMMARY

2E Kames Regt.
KR18

Place	Date	Hour	Summary of Events and Information	Remarks and references to Appendices
	1st May 1916	—	A very fine day. Brigade Field day from 8 – 5:45 pm. General commanding 1st Army. saw the troops at work. Lieut Colonel Cavendish DSO Commanding the 7th Bn came over to see the Regiment	
	2nd May 1916	—	Cloudy day. Brigade with a Kinderston and other Battn Training from 9 am to 2 pm. Bus picture at 5:15 pm. The 7th Battn is at RELY. Move to HERSIN postponed from tomorrow to 5th inst.	
	3rd May 1916	—	A cloudy morning but fine sunny afternoon. Battn Training from 9am to 5pm. Games on the ground. The Battn 2nd XI team went over to RELY & played the 7th Battn and won the game by 3 goals to 2.	
	4th May 1916	—	A fine sunny warm day. Battn Training from 9 am to 2 pm back to No. Arrive to return to billets.	
	5th May 1916	—	Battalion marched from LAIRES at 7:40am – Billeting Party under Lieut RN Kiper along four fine journe at 8:30 am by motor bus at PERNES. the Battalion entrained for HERSIN – the former place was reached by at 11am	Distance

WAR DIARY
INTELLIGENCE SUMMARY

Army Form C. 2118.

Place	Date	Hour	Summary of Events and Information	Remarks and references to Appendices
	5th May 1916. (continued)		Distance of the march was 17 kilometres. The day was very hot and close. The Battn proved the 68th Bn in the march and the dust was very trying. Four men only fell out, all of whom arrived in time for Reveille 2nd Train, which left half-an-hour after the first. The C.O. and Lewis Gun Officers f[ou]nd Jour [enine] remained in PERNES when a lecture given by Major Baker Carr on the tactical handling of Lewis machine Guns. We arrived at HERSIN at 2.5 pm. 1 Coy plus 2 platoons of B coy marched to PETIT SERVINS, to work under 138th Coy R.E. in the 3rd Div. The remainder of the Battalion billeted in HERSIN.	
	6th May 1916.		A still day with cold wind. Coy parades – 3 officers & NCOs and 175 other ranks went on working party under front line trenches from 6.30 pm to 3 am.	
	7th May 1916.		A wet & chilly with showers of rain Church parade for all denominations – a similar working Coy party to duty yesterday.	

Army Form C. 2118.

WAR DIARY
or
INTELLIGENCE SUMMARY.
(Erase heading not required.)

Instructions regarding War Diaries and Intelligence Summaries are contained in F.S. Regs., Part II. and the Staff Manual respectively. Title pages will be prepared in manuscript.

Place	Date	Hour	Summary of Events and Information	Remarks and references to Appendices
Whitley Camp	17th May 1916		A cold windy day with showers. General Batt. inspection. Morning 23rd Aircraft inspects the Battalion on parade at 10.45 a.m. Similar working party as that of yesterday.	
	9th May 1916		A dull cold windy day with showers of rain. Enemy by 15th period. Enemy shelled HERSIN between 12.30 p.m. and 1 p.m. and again about 4 p.m. No casualties in the Batt.	
	20th May 1916		A bit of of M Thermometer jagged the Batt and field day. House parties HERSIN was again shelled. Battalion moved the NOEUX-LETTE & BOIS dr "BOUVIGNY" remaining at 7.30 p.m. Billets were taken over from the 1st K.R.R. and linked with the 22nd R.F. Battn together with 1st Herrwood Foresters to in Brigade Reserve. the 1st Worcester and 2nd Northampton, being in the trenches - SOUCHEZ Sector. Billets, which were anything but clean, were taken over by 9 p.m.	

WAR DIARY
INTELLIGENCE SUMMARY

Army Form C. 2118.

1st Battalion Worcestershire Regiment

Place	Date	Hour	Summary of Events and Information	Remarks and references to Appendices
	10th May 1916	4 pm	Brigadier Genl Riley having been placed on the sick list, full Colonel Brogan, 1st Worcester Regiment assumed command of the Bde. Capt Wade and his detachment rejoined 1st Battalion from PETIT SERVINS.	
	11th May 1916		A congratulatory parade at 2.30am. 11am and 12pm & 1pm and 1.75 Working party of three officers and 175 other ranks from 7.45 pm.	
	12th May 1916		A dull day with some carrier pigeon and working party to Youtney Bullers were available for the Battn. in the small new store huts.	
	13th May 1916		Heavy rain during the night and most of the day. Arrived and nothing of any moment. C Coy moved 2 to Hopital to BOIS 6 in relief of one Coy, 1st Warwicks Foresters.	

Trench Strength

WAR DIARY
INTELLIGENCE SUMMARY.

Army Form C. 2118.

About 5 (Erase heading not required) 1st Hampshire Regiment

Place	Date	Hour	Summary of Events and Information	Remarks and references to Appendices
	1916		Trench Strength	
In Trenches	14 May			
			Available in trenches — Offrs 14 OR 652	Offrs OR
			In fighting line incl. of Bns — 5	Att'd 181st Coy R.E. — 42
			Regimental Signallers — 18	6 weeks of instruction — 14
			Kitchen Bombs — 21	Att'd 23rd Div. Am. Col — 3
			At Trench H'd Qrs — 4 — 34	Sanitary Section — 4
			Total in Trenches — 18 — 725	A.P.M. Staff — 3
			Regimental Transport — 2 — 61	Gone to UK — 4 — 14
			Att'd R.W. H'd Qrs — 1 — 24	Absent without leave — 2
			In burial party — — 10 — 18	Total employed 15 — 243
			Combatant — 1 — 18	Total strength of Btn. 33 — 968
			2#/1 Trench Mortar (Stokes Gun) — 1 — 13	
			23rd Divn. Signals — 1 — 2	
			69th Bde H'd Qrs — 1	
			23rd Divl. Band — 6	
			Bde Corps H'd Qrs — 8	
			176 Coy R.E. — 42	

Army Form C. 2118.

WAR DIARY
or
INTELLIGENCE SUMMARY.
(Erase heading not required.)

Army Troops ~~Skill 6~~
Calonne sur la Lys — Barrow

Instructions regarding War Diaries and Intelligence Summaries are contained in F. S. Regs., Part II. and the Staff Manual respectively. Title pages will be prepared in manuscript.

Place	Date	Hour	Summary of Events and Information	Remarks and references to Appendices
Hilltop Camp (Souchez)	15th May 1916		A high wind with showers of rain. Enemy quiet in all denominations. The usual working parties. A stormy wet day with a high wind — bursts of rain. Relieved the 1st Worcesters in the trenches (SOUCHEZ) Cheers & the trenches. At 8:30 p.m. Ruby completed up to now hay with there was no great event. Shells fire in the VMY have made little progress, left high Wood L17th Wood — told showers forrest in run left & right high Wood to our right.	
16th May	916		Quiet night. no for walled Battalion was concerned. But the Battn. that relieved Enthias a very fine sunny day. Some shelling with 4.2 and 5.9 inch on French rear in 2 pm. no movement — there a great any ??? Kraft the shelling on both sides. The enemy's largely preparating were active all day.	
17th May 1916			A quiet night. Very high moonlight. The line is in some routine condition Ry Where the Division went has not by barrier	north

T./131. W. W85. 773. 5000. 4/15. Sr. J.C. & S.

Army Form C. 2118.

WAR DIARY
or
INTELLIGENCE SUMMARY.

(Erase heading not required.)

Sheet 4
Essex (?) Regiment

Place	Date	Hour	Summary of Events and Information	Remarks and references to Appendices
	17th May contd		month ago the communication trenches are still unmade and all rations to the Battalion except to Coy are cut off from the sea by day. All the time and energy of the men is taken up carrying rations, water and R.E. stores from the dumps which are ½ a mile away with the loss of 50 yards to the front over the open along a very slippery difficult duck walk. Day fire cloudy and close. Enemy's machine gun fire between 7.30pm and mid-night. Artillery on both sides active. Rx Strad (?) B.1 and machine gun fire between the enemy's perforating — by fire both were still and known. Wind N.W.	
	18th May 1916		A lovely day. Wind N.E. The night was quiet but for machine gun fire and one sniper. The enemy threw 3 trench mortars, one wiring party from the right Coy (D). They threw this away trench amongst them but did no damage. Lieut Shadd was took to staple(?) in charge	

Army Form C. 2118.

WAR DIARY
or
INTELLIGENCE SUMMARY.
(Erase heading not required.)

Shul 5
1st/5th Battn. West Yorkshire Regiment

Instructions regarding War Diaries and Intelligence Summaries are contained in F.S. Regs., Part II. and the Staff Manual respectively. Title pages will be prepared in manuscript.

Place	Date	Hour	Summary of Events and Information	Remarks and references to Appendices
	18th May	cont'd	in charge of the party. The left boy. (D) on my party had one man wounded - gunshot wound in the leg. Some shelling of their trench but very little damage done. 2nd Gordon Regt relieved us on our right. Div relieved 23rd Gordons at 5pm.	
	19th May 1916		A very strenuous night. Enemy machine guns not idly sweeping the Battalion front full from line and supports from front and left seen. Our orders were bombardments with grenades fighting took place in the VIMY Ridge on our right. At 12.30 am the night by (A) reported the enemy cutting his wire opposite he right of the boy. Two officers patrols were sent out one from "D" boy under Lieut. Falby and one from "A" boy under Lieut. Muir Pirrie. The excellent work. They reported Snull - Both Muir Pirrie's and Falby's reports was not correct, in the meantime the Battn "Stand to". Some rifle grenades were fired into "A" Coys front line, our heavy trench mortars retaliating - A lively enemy.	It wounded he had stopped tip 73 the rifle 7 pm he made can from D made can

WAR DIARY
INTELLIGENCE SUMMARY.

Army Form C. 2118.

Of 9th Skill (?) Northumberland Fusiliers (?) Regiment.

Place	Date	Hour	Summary of Events and Information	Remarks and references to Appendices
	19th May 1916		Sunny day. Enemy Arty shelled the trans about 9-30am. There was some shelling again after an French with 4.2" guns. also HELMAR Communication French which was hit. Colonel Stewart and Coy Off/c 10th N.F. watched the time with a view to taking over trenches. Enemy Batty ln/ wrecked the "SUNKEN RD" and the Avo about 10pm. The night was quiet - some fighting on our right - between 9.30 and 10.30 pm. 10th N.F. for the relieved 22nd with on our right.	
	20th May 1916		A lovely day. Wind NE East. Quo aliu' still on down. Shelling but otherwise quiet on our front. Relief in the trenches by 10.N.F. 2 lieut O Hopkins Relief complete by 11pm. Batt in billets at COUPIGNY by 4.30am. (21st May 1916)	Lieut K. Hopkins
	21st May 1916. (Sunday)		A lovely warm day. Church parade for all denominations. Gas "SOS" from 68th Bde reached the Battalion at 4.45pm. Battalion "stood to" until 9.45 pm when normal conditions were resumed. A further SOS was gas from the 10thN.F. was received	

Army Form C. 2118.

WAR DIARY
or
INTELLIGENCE SUMMARY.
(Erase heading not required.)

Shut 10
Staffordshire Regiment

Place	Date	Hour	Summary of Events and Information	Remarks and references to Appendices
	21st May 1916		recvd at 10.30pm and cancelled at 11.15pm. Heavy fight-ing during the afternoon on the VIMY Ridge	
	22nd May 1916		No further alarms during the night - A warm day with the wind @ S.W. - Usual parade at 9am, 11am and 2pm. Some work's men at 5pm - trench board ready tomorrow at halfpur topside. 'Lights out' at 7.45pm - cancelled at 9.30 pm - Known "Alert"	
	23rd May 1916		A fine sunny day - much cooler. closing started 6pm. Battn met Starkers by Coys at FOSSE 9.	
	24th May 1916		Moved parade were held - Bapt Addledean joined the Battalion from England. A fine morning with rain in the afternoon from 2.45pm to 6pm. Usual parades - and fatigue watch the dubb in the morning. Person killed - Pte. H. the Kit - Capt Addledean assumed the duties of senior Major and capt W.H.H resumed the duties of the 1st Hospital	
	25th May 1916		Some heavy rain up to 9.30 am and again at 11.45am. Usual parades - some shelling of Hersin Therouse L.M. and close.	

T.131. Wt. W.708 770. 500 9. 4/15. Sir J.C. & 3.

Army Form C. 2118.

WAR DIARY
or
INTELLIGENCE SUMMARY.
(Erase heading not required.)

[Unit heading, illegible] Regiment

Instructions regarding War Diaries and Intelligence Summaries are contained in F.S. Regs., Part II. and the Staff Manual respectively. Title pages will be prepared in manuscript.

Place	Date	Hour	Summary of Events and Information	Remarks and references to Appendices
	25th May (Sunday)		HERSIN. 9th form parade from our billets at COUPIGNY at about 3pm.	
	26th May 1916		A fine day. Usual parades. Lieut. Burdeter went to FOSSE 2 to report.	
		10	Over the 30 yards range a working party of 2 officers and 180 other ranks paraded at 7.30 pm and returned at 11 pm.	
	27th May 1916		A very fine day. Capt Smith left at 10am & took over temporarily the command of 12th Bt. S. Lanes working party. Tickets to fire evening. In the pm there were the usual games and contests in the water square from 1–3pm. A boy in the range at FOSSE 10 from 2–6pm	
	28th May 1916 (Sunday)		Church parade in the morning to RC and Non-conformists – 6pm C of E voluntary service at 6pm. Paraded at 11am B+C 1/K Hopkins boys in range from 7am to 1pm. Conference of CO's at Bde HQrs at 4.30 pm. A fine day. Wind N.N.E.	
	29th May 1916		A fine day. Parade as usual. 6.0 am Lay company visited BULLY GRENAY and the newer trenches occupied by "6" Battalion in the	

WAR DIARY
or
INTELLIGENCE SUMMARY

Army Form C. 2118.

(Erase heading not required.)

Staff
Kings Own Regiment

Instructions regarding War Diaries and Intelligence Summaries are contained in F.S. Regs., Part II. and the Staff Manual respectively. Title pages will be prepared in manuscript.

Place	Date	Hour	Summary of Events and Information	Remarks and references to Appendices
	29th May 1916		The INGRES sector. Usual working parties. "A" Coy. had a considerable amount of shelling.	
(cont)	30th May 1916		Rain during the night. Rather cloudy day, fine in the afternoon. The Battn Relieving the Batln doing Bttn work in trenches, except the supports. INGRES sector becoming the Battn — Battalion holdings as follows — Battn front line. a. "C" Battalion – Battalion Supports — "D" Coy. in BULLGRENAY. 1 Coy. in platoons and 2 sections of 1 Coy. and 2 sections (Battn. Reserve Cemetery) at CAIRNS t'HR. Remainder of "B" Coy. at METRO CAP du PONT — "A" Coy at MARROCO SOUTH and MECHANICS TRENCH and "A" Coy at MAROCCO SOUTH. P.C.H.	
	31st May 1916		A very fine day. Nearly the whole Battalion on Working parties in trenches or up to the line. Some shelling in the morning, with heavy gunfire to the other side — Quiet day otherwise until about 9.15 p.m. when the enemy sent over some 15 "tear" shells into the tube village, these bursting very little. Movement was Reid Colonel Commdg Kings R.	Stal Kings 42 44 Stal (signed) 25

2 E Essex Regt
Vol 19

WAR DIARY
INTELLIGENCE SUMMARY

Place	Date	Hour	Summary of Events and Information	Remarks and references to Appendices

1st June 1916 — Weather still fine with some clouds about. Men working extremely hard. Carrying parties again employed. Inspection parades one hour at 7 am. 1 injured. Men and Spare some shelling of the village during the morning. About 8 pm a heavy bombardment started on both sides in connection with an attack on MMV Ridge by the 2nd Battn. The firing continued until 2 MN and was very heavy. Enemy fire was heavy at several times.

2nd June 1916 — A fine day with some wind and clouds. Very quiet morning — no shelling. Carrying and working parties as usual. Same.

3rd June 1916 — Fine day. Some shelling. Usual parades and working parties. All tops except the paths "S.O.S." Souchez Kept? II, received at 7.30 pm. cancelled at 8.30 pm

4th June 1916 — Day fine but cloudy with a cold wind & a little rain about 10 pm. Battn. relieved by Worcesters in the trenches becoming "C" Battn. Rev to Sunshine Trench to the right and the Gloucesters to the left. 1st Battn. 1st Divn. to the Butts.

WAR DIARY
or
INTELLIGENCE SUMMARY.

Army Form C. 2118.

Place	Date	Hour	Summary of Events and Information	Remarks and references to Appendices
#tr[...]	[...]/1916 (continued)		Relief commenced at 2pm and was completed by 3.50pm — "A", "B" & "D" Coys in the front line, each with one platoon in support, & four Coys are in reserve. "D" Coy is in reserve support and is in reserve.	
	5.6.1916		A quiet night with a little machine gun fire against "B" & numerous enemy patrols near the Bully Crater front line. Enemy patrols entirely [destroyed?] the parapet to about 2 pm [...] some damage was [...] heavily shelled about 9.30pm. Two men killed & two were shelled about 4pm. A fairly and 2 men killed. No one [...] [...] shelling dug out. Enemy [...] [...] trench. Capt Arrott rejoined the Battn. but enemy withdrew soon from 12th P.S.	
	6th June 1916		Night again quiet with some little machine gun fire & rifle grenades. Very little shelling and trench mortars and rifle [...] [...] and [...] was completely in the morning. Again more officers and men [...] [...]. The night was quiet though [...] Day fine, but cloudy.	

WAR DIARY
or
INTELLIGENCE SUMMARY.

Army Form C. 2118.

Sheet 3

of 1/4 Royal Berkshire Regt.

Place	Date	Hour	Summary of Events and Information	Remarks and references to Appendices
	27th June 1916 continued		There was some machine gun fire against the working parties, & much activity in the rear of the enemy with rifle grenades, but no trench mortars - our retaliation was good. There was hopeless not much shelling - we suspected the reserve Coy ("D") in MAROCCO North, no shells, no casualties. General Shea visited the lines with two of his staff officers. Rum pull about 10pm.	
	28 June 1916.		The night was quiet with the exception of having much machine gun fire which was active again, against our wiring parties. Throughout the day there was much activity on both sides with 1 killed. Rifle grenades and trench mortars. The exp running out forced to the Bully trench, was again damaged by the latter. One inspector only routed the one during the afternoon. The W.O. of the Batten. was killed by the White Guarding Box Rely. in the reply ones are the 1st/Devonshire & Trench. The day was fine but cloudy. Rain fell heavily about 10pm and continued allnight. Fine.	

WAR DIARY
or
INTELLIGENCE SUMMARY

Army Form C. 2118.

Place	Date	Hour	Summary of Events and Information	Remarks and references to Appendices
	7th June 1916		There were very little shelling throughout the 24 hours & quiet night. Fine day. French returns received. Blinded by	
	9th June 1916		The 1st Worcesters Relief complete at 5.15pm. Batt. in billets bivouacs 2 coys at Bully remainder FOSSE 10, by 7pm	150 topas
	10th June 1916		Wet day with heavy showers. Bn under GOC coys "A" "C" coys went the like in Bully, in the afternoon. Ration carrying-party of one then and 85 men for 1st Worcesters Regt, and the officer and 50 men carrying-party for RE stores. In addition 120 other men were employed on various RE digging parties and other fatigues. The Bn is generally being relieved by the ... Bn of the ... Div.	2 hospital
	11th June 1916		More showers. Very showery with low temperature. Voluntary Church services for all denominations took to parade at 10am and 2pm. H coy "B" "C" & coys went to hospital baths at Bully. Similar working and ration parties as	

WAR DIARY

INTELLIGENCE SUMMARY

Army Form C. 2118.

Place	Date	Hour	Summary of Events and Information	Remarks and references to Appendices
	11th June 1916 (cont'd)		rest of yesterday.	
	12th June 1916		A cold rainy day. The Bn. moved from the ANGRES sector. The Bn's billets were taken over by the 20th London Bn. The Battn. marched at 11.30 a.m. to BOIS d'OLHAIN, where they encamped in tents. It was very wet and cold.	
	13th June 1916		A cold and very wet day. Battn. moved off from camp at 7.30 a.m. and reached PERNES at 11.45 a.m. where "A" and "C" Coys were billeted. "B" & "D" Coys billeted at PRESSY, about 1½ miles away. Length of march to PERNES, 13 miles. The drums have played in the march both yesterday and today.	
	14th June 1916.		A cold day with high wind, and driving light rain. Battn. left PERNES at 8.30 a.m. and reached LAIRES, at 12 noon, a distance of 11 miles. In accordance with orders the Battn. will not move tomorrow.	15th June 1916.

Army Form C. 2118.

WAR DIARY
or
INTELLIGENCE SUMMARY.
(Erase heading not required.)

Instructions regarding War Diaries and Intelligence Summaries are contained in F.S. Regs., Part II. and the Staff Manual respectively. Title pages will be prepared in manuscript.

Place	Date	Hour	Summary of Events and Information	Remarks and references to Appendices
	15th June 1916		A cold dull day but no rain. Coy parade at 10.15 am. Hospital and 2 p.m. Bn. Idly visited Bath. Oro. Capt. R.M. Walton reported to Bn.	
	16th June 1916		A cold dull morning but fine afternoon in evening. Coy parade at 9am, 11am and 2pm. Conference at Bn H.Q. Oro at FLÊCHIN. a' + B' Coys were no. 9th Regt Bn Hos.	
	17th June 1916		A cold dull day. Bath paraded at 9 a.m. and returned to hospital. Strike at 5 pm. the day being spent between my nothing manoeuvre ground.	
	18th June 1916		Cold dull morning. Fine afternoon. Parade at 8.45 am. marched to ERNY St JULIEN (manoeuvre area) for church parade at 10 am. leaving until 1pm. returned to billets at 2.15 pm. Conference at 6.0° at Bn H.Q. Oro FLÊCHIN at 2.30 pm.	
	19th June 1916		Cold Dull day. Parade at 8.45 am. for Divisional 12 Hospital field day. The assault of a position. H.Trenches were practised. The Battalion together with the 1st Dorsets Regt, held	

T/134. W3, W738-776. 300,000. 4/15. Sir J.C. & S.

WAR DIARY
or
INTELLIGENCE SUMMARY.

Army Form C. 2118.

Place	Date	Hour	Summary of Events and Information	Remarks and references to Appendices
	19th June 1916 (cont'd)		held our front line to assist nearer the wounded & the wires were passed through. The second and consolidated of the enemy trenches when captured. Relieved by 1.30 pm Capt R.S.M. Watson of the Battalion started on 2nd in command of the trenches of the Bn.	
	20th June 1916		Battalion paraded at 9 pm returning when reinforcements were - further practice in the assault on enemy trenches from trenches run by - Return billets at 4.15 pm & will take morning with a stores train. One evening kind regards back Bn. M.O. to ??? attentions.	
	21st June 1916		A fine day with some sun. Batts paraded at 9 am. such offices in training in the trenches are broken or something up topics carried out. The Brigadier was in the ground & saw the Battalion at work. Returned to billets at 4.30 pm.	
	22nd June 1916		A very fine warm day. Battalion training in the trenches area from 9 am - 12.45 pm. from 6 time & N.C.O.'s	

Army Form C. 2118.

WAR DIARY
or
INTELLIGENCE SUMMARY.
(Erase heading not required.)

Unit 8

Instructions regarding War Diaries and Intelligence Summaries are contained in F. S. Regs., Part II. and the Staff Manual respectively. Title pages will be prepared in manuscript.

Place	Date	Hour	Summary of Events and Information	Remarks and references to Appendices
	22nd June/16.		G.O.C. of the Corps. visit Batt. lines about 6 p.m. (cont) a dull warm day, about rain. Coy parades in billets at 6 p.m.	
	23rd June 1916	10.15 am and 2 p.m	Batt. they preparing for the move tomorrow. Lucendu road.	
		11.50 a.m.	Batt. will entrain at TILLERS at 11.50 a.m.	
	24th June 1916		Transport moved at 3.20 a.m with a fatigue party of 2 off. & 110 other ranks. Batt. fell in & marched off and main & training at TILLERS at 10.50 a.m and entrained. Arrived at LONGUEAU at 6.45 p.m when weather cleared up. when we all clear of the train the troops and transport were all clear of the station by 7.30 p.m. The Batt. then marched to Billets at BREILLY, via AMIENS, arriving at 11.45 p.m. march was twenty one (21) miles. Eleven from Lines & Tillers and ten from Longueau to Breilly. Numbers actually in the train: 28 officers and 943 other ranks.	
	25th June 1916.		Marched at 2.30 p.m. to LONGPRÉ, where the Batt entrained distance	Lists of officers to follow

Army Form C. 2118.

WAR DIARY
or
INTELLIGENCE SUMMARY.
(Erase heading not required.)

Instructions regarding War Diaries and Intelligence Summaries are contained in F. S. Regs., Part II. and the Staff Manual respectively. Title pages will be prepared in manuscript.

Place	Date	Hour	Summary of Events and Information	Remarks and references to Appendices
	25th June 1916		Brigade about 5 miles. Day very hot not clear.	
	26th June 1916.		Coy paraded at 5am and 2pm. Inspection of billets, harness, clothing, equipment etc. Day fine but very cloudy & dull.	
	27th June 1916.		Route March for Baton at 11.15 am. Returned 7.30 pm. and during afternoon which fell heavily & near ST SAY. FUR, AILLY LONGPRE. Alunise & billets 2pm to 6pm. cres of C.O. at BN H.Q. at 5.30 pm.	
	28th June 1916		Coy paraded at 5am, 10.30 am and 2pm. The Bns were to 3 inspected. Alute at RAINNEVILLE and COISY at 9pm. but more were cancelled at 2.30pm. The day was very cloudy with some rain.	
	29th June 1916		A dull cloudy warm day. Baton route march 10.15am to 9pm	
	30th June 1916		A dull cloudy morning. Orders received at 9am that Bn will move during Kelsey to billets to rentences in hope at 6pm. March transport imposed by.	

Army Form C. 2118.

WAR DIARY
— or —
INTELLIGENCE SUMMARY. Sheet 10
(Erase heading not required.)

Place	Date	Hour	Summary of Events and Information	Remarks and references to Appendices
	30th June 1916 (contd)		we learnt of the 6th Bn. who were about to start march for having moved to pauvog train at local entrainment into St Pol Stn, who were sending to the Battalion rations at RAINNEVILLE. Billets were in MOLLIENS-au-BOIS, which were reached at 5.00 pm – the Wycombs, Northunts and Hunts Train rd the billets in the village the afternoon and evening were very fine.	Strenth ab. do= 60. Reinforcements at Marieuma B4

1st July. 1916.

[signature] Lieut Colonel
Commdg [illegible]

E.L. 606

Hd Qrs 24th Inf. Brigade

I attach report of the patrol referred
to in my morning report.
The patrol consisted of the following

2/Lieut E.J. Barrow in charge
2/Lieut E.A. Ellen
No 11500 Sgt Hooker

They carried out the work with the
greatest determination and courage
and although discovered by the
enemy and fired on very early in
the proceedings finished the work
they had set out to do most
thoroughly. A verey light was turned on them
The patrol was to investigate the
ditches at I.16.c.8.4. & I.16. d.4.4. and the
point near I.16.c.1.1. where a
sniper was suspected.

W.S. Hill Lt Col.
Cl. 24/Inf Bde.

REPORT ON A PATROL.

An officer's patrol went out at 6 p.m. from the left of I.16., moving down the right of the LILLE Road. The ditch "A" along the LILLE Road, contains about a foot of water.

Where this ditch meets the ditch "B", there is a large pool and a willow tree, on our side of the junction.

Ditch "B" crosses the LILLE Road underneath a small stone bridge. A single row of chevaux-de-frise (marked xxxxxxxx on map) runs across the road in front of the bridge.

At junction of ditches "B" and "D", there is another large pool, with a willow tree on our side of the junction.

The patrol crossed "B" just to the right of the junction. Whilst endeavouring to find a passage through the German wire alongside "D", the enemy opened fire on the patrol with four or five rifles, at the same time sending up a considerable number of Very lights. Because of this it was only found possible to examine the wire from the outside, and that only after the fire had abated considerably. Although the chevaux-de-frise had been cut to a considerable extent, it still presents a very formidable obstacle.

The patrol then returned to the ditch "B". Between the chevaux-de-frise and the ditch was found a line of cable, attached to stakes. This was thoroughly investigated and found to be used merely as trip wire, and probably had been taken from the standards along the LILLE Road.

The patrol then worked along "B" to the right, still being fired on from the enemy's trenches.

At the junction of "B" and "E" there is a single willow tree, but no pool. Thereabouts, both ditches are 3' wide by 3' deep, and contain about 9" of water.

Ditch "B" extends for a distance of 280 yards, when it widens into a large pool, with a single willow, forming a junction with the ditch "F" which runs along the PAVE. "B" was too wide (about 12') to cross at the point.

The patrol then crossed the PAVE road, and worked up the small ditch on the right of the road, for the purpose of investigating "C".

The junction of "C" and "F" is immediately in front of the German wire, and the ditch goes underneath the wire about 15 yards to the left of the PAVE.

Just after the patrol had completed this investigation, the Germans turned on a searchlight from a point behind the trenches, just to the left of the PAVE. The patrol then proceeded to investigate ditch "G", entering it at the elbow bend (marked E) and working along it for the purpose of capturing a reported sniper at the point P.

At this point a cart track (indicated by dotted line) cuts right across "G". There is a willow tree on each side of the track, on the enemy's side of the ditch.

Although the ground here and for a considerable distance round about, was thoroughly searched, no signs of a sniper post could be discovered. The patrol worked along "G", which varies from 2' 6" to 6' 4" wide, and about 3' deep, and contains about 9" of water. After proceeding as far as the next ditch junction, and discovering nothing of importance, the patrol returned to P, and then moved along the cart track (passing an old plough on the left) and re-entering our trenches about the centre of I.15.a at 8.40 p.m.

Judging from the amount of conversation, coughing, movement, and the volume of rifle fire, it was surmised that the enemy's trenches are held about as strongly as our own.

Continued.

The patrol was unable to move silently, because of the frost on the long grass, which crackled underfoot.

19th Division No. I.70.

56th Infantry Brigade.
57th   ,,   ,,
58th   ,,   ,,
Divisional Artillery.
C. R. E.
5th S.W. Borderers.
****

    Rough plans of certain villages on our front, together with as much information concerning them as it has been possible to compile from air photographs and the statements of prisoners or refugees, are forwarded herewith.
    The villages are -

        POZIERES.
        CONTALMAISON.
        COURCELETTE.
        MARTINPUICH.
        BAZENTIN-LE-PETIT.

    The information, though meagre, is accurate: it is certain that in no cases are their systems of defence round the villages other than the trenches which are shewn on the map and which are for frontier defence only. This, however, does not mean that individual houses have not been put into a state of defence. On this point there is no definite information, but the Germans have certainly improved and strengthened all cellars and in some cases have demolished the superstructures.

    It may be added that the heavy bombardment to which all these villages will be subjected before our troops enter them, may render much of this information quite untrustworthy.

H.Q. 19th Division,
18th June 1916.

                                                Captain,
                                               General Staff.

BAZENTIN LE PETIT.

Most of the houses have been destroyed.   There is said to be stabling for 5 - 600 horses in the village still.

Detail of Buildings.
(1) Chateau. Strongly built old house of brick - 8 to 12 rooms. Small stables and no barns.   Statue in grounds.
(2) Mayors house. Small brick building with small cellar.
(3) Very good brick building (farm) - cellars for 30 - 40 men.
(4) Good brick farm.

Water.
4 wells, marked on map.
Large new pond near the Church.

Information.
(1) No civilians left.
(2) A Regimental H.Q. in N. end of village.
(3) 2 supply dumps.
(4) Many huts.

****

MARTINPUICH.

Village of fair size on undulating ground. About half the houses are built of brick. Those on the 'RUE BASSE' on the N. of the village are the strongest. All of them have good cellars: 2 in particular could easily be made bombproof. They are near the church. In one farm (exact location unknown) there is a big cellar from which opens a gallery leading in the direction of BAPAUME. The village is surrounded by orchards and numbers of hedges.

Detail of Houses, etc.

No.1. The church is strong. The steeple collapsed about 18 months before the War.

No.2. House belonging to a Doctor. One storey, garden in front. Good cellar. Was used as a H.Q. by the Germans in September 1914.

No.3. Large farm by the cemetery. One storey: strong brick house. Large vaulted cellars. Barns overlooking the road.

No.4. Brick house. Barns round the courtyard. Cellars.

Wells.

4 public wells (marked W.1, 2, 3 & 4) good drinking water. One private well. Several rain water cisterns.

Roads.

Were very good. All sunken 200 or 300 yards from the village.

Information.

(1) Usually 550 inhabitants of whom a large proportion remain.
(2) There is an ammunition depot in the village, to which there is a railway from BAPAUME. 2 supply dumps S. of village.
(3) 2 Regimental H.Qrs and 3 supply dumps. 1 Regimental H.Q. probably in house No.4. The other at N.E. end of the village on the main road.

MARTINPUICH

1/5000

1ST PRINTING COY. R.E. 4TH ARMY SECT. (140)

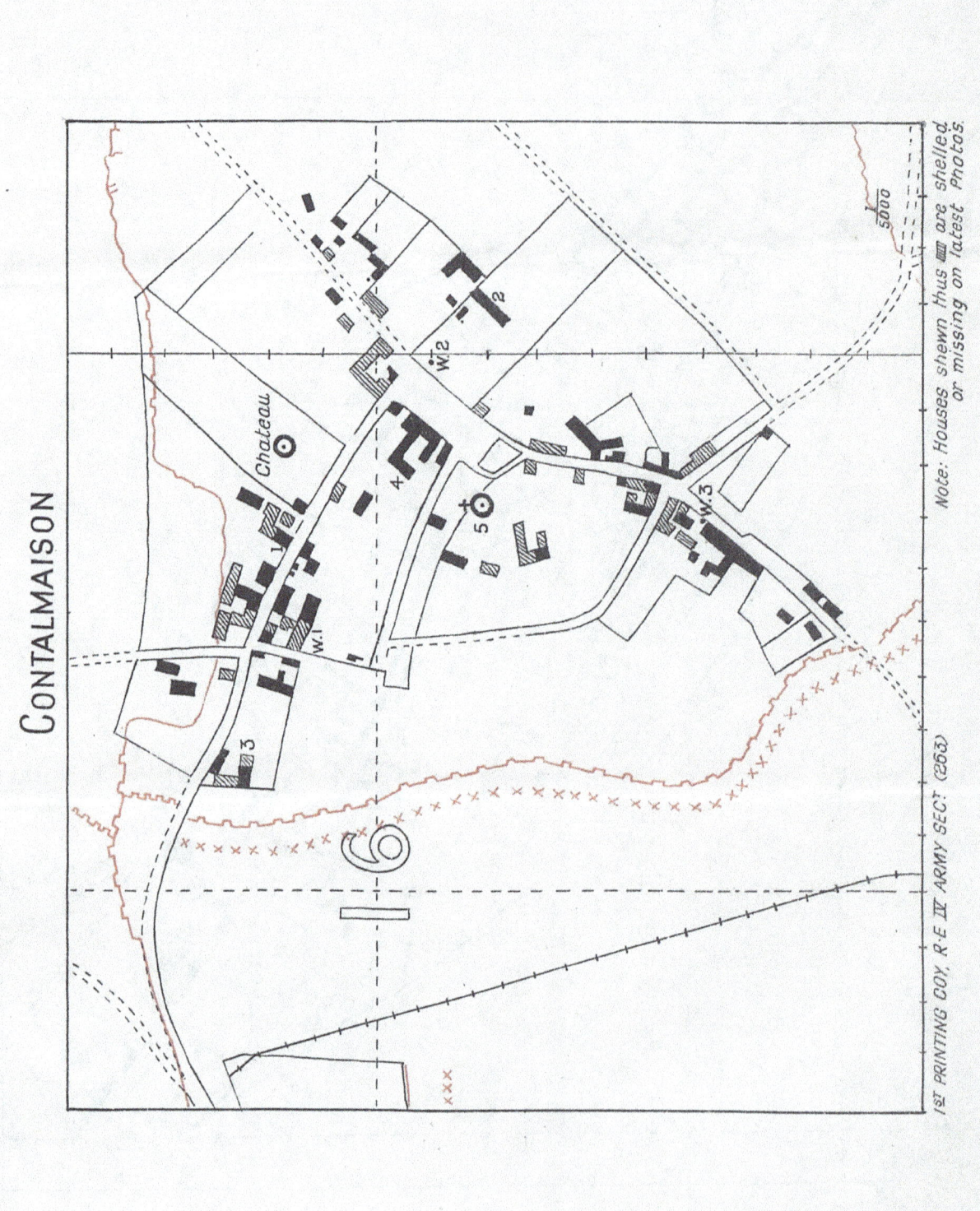

CONTALMAISON.

The village had about 10 well built farms and 3 good private houses - all other buildings are of mud.

Detail of Buildings.

(1) The Chateau is a modern turreted house with 2 stories - rather damaged by shell fire: good vaulted cellars. Building in a park of 7½ acres - surrounded by walls except on N. side where there is a hedge. The house is about 150 m. from the road. A German H.Q. was here in September 1914.
(2) The 'Old Manor' could be made a very strong point. It has small cellars. Distance from road about 200 m.
(3) Last house in LA BOISSELLE road. Good modern house with one storey.
(4) School - in a small lane. Good modern construction with good cellars.
(5) Church - held 200 people. Old and strong in stone-walled churchyard. Tower has been knocked down.
Villa de Contalmaison - outside the village - 1000 yards to the N.E. on road to MARTINPUICH. Very well built farm. No big cellar. Used as observation point.

Wells.

3 public wells about 50 m. deep. 6 private wells, 2 of which are in a cul-de-sac, west of the church. There is a pipe line from the village to the front line which goes back to BAZENTIN. Also a big pond in the village.

Roads.

Were very good - mostly sunken.

Information.

(1) No civilians left.
(2) 4 dumps at S. and S.W. end of the village.

****

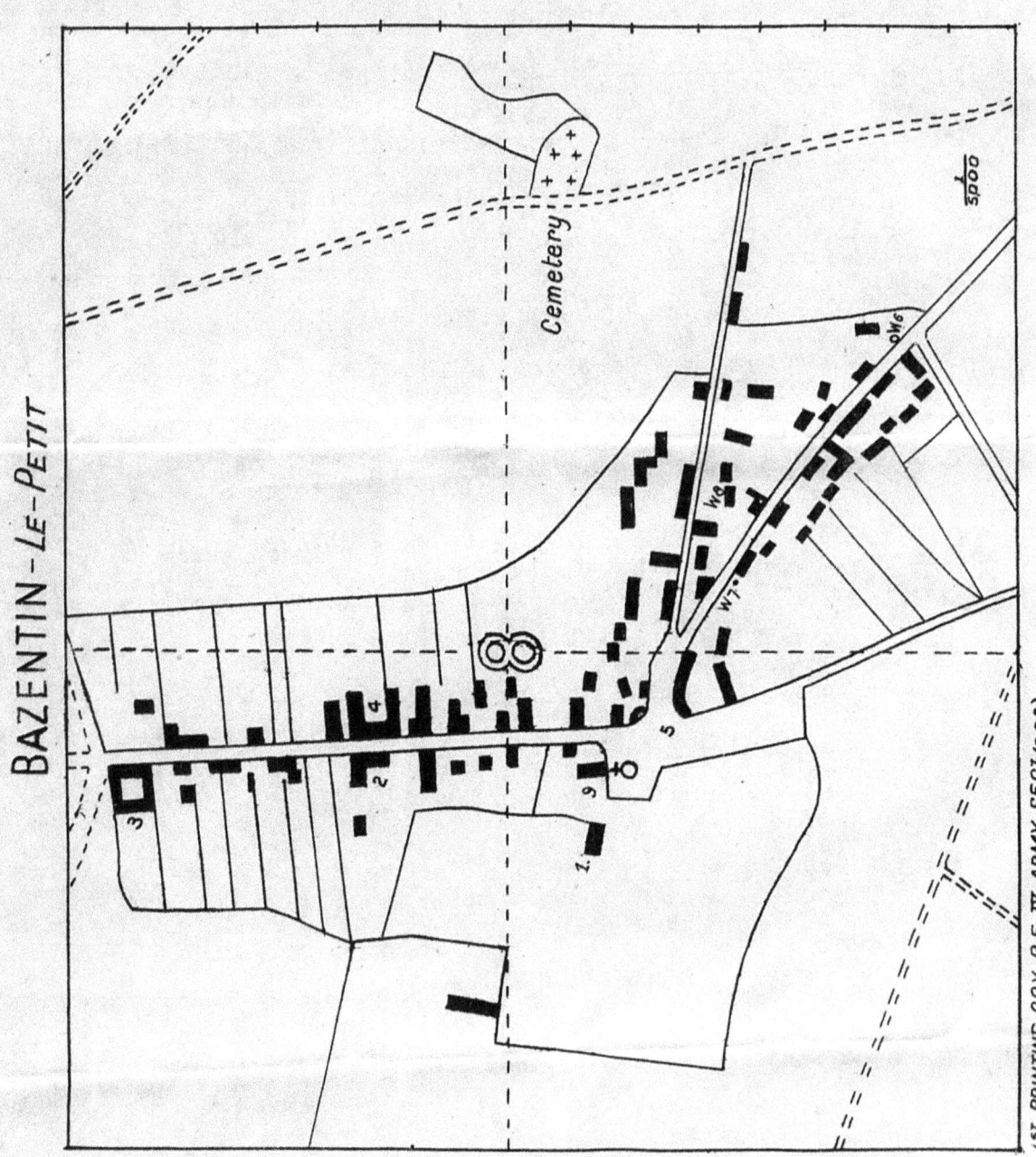

POZIERES (References to attached map).

Village comprises -
(1) A series of modern stone (brick ?) houses along the main BAPAUME road.
(2) A group of houses, N.W. of the main road. Not strong, except those round the square (PLACE DE LEGLISE) which are of stone (brick ?) and have cellars.
(3) Cellars only, S of the main road. All superstructures have been demolished.

Detail of Houses.
No.1. M.FOURNIER - Double storied brick with good cellars - number unknown.
No.2. M.LEPEZ - Estaminet. Mud house: good cellars.
No.3. Estaminet 'RUE VILLAIN'. Double storied brick, 1 or 2 good cellars.
No.4. School and Mairie - Double storied brick, 1 or 2 good cellars.
No.5. Fme.MAGNIER. Single storied brick, 1 or 2 good cellars.
No.6. Double storied brick: good cellars. Mlle BERLANCOURT.
No.7. ,,   ,,   ,,   ,,   ,,   ,,   Sister of above.
No.8. Strong brick: good cellars.
No.9. Double storied brick: cellars.
No.10. Single storied brick: good cellars.

Exact location of following is uncertain -
(a) New house facing BAZENTIN road. Courtyard in front: walls all round: strong cellars. Could be made very strong point.
(b) Farm on the street, near house No.9. One storey, 3 strong cellars. In the courtyard is a dairy with a good vaulted cellar and a vaulted store room above that. The owner considers his house is the strongest in the village, and most likely to be transformed into a fortified post.

Wells.
4 public wells - average depth 35 - 40 m (130 ft) - Marked W.1, W.2, W.3, W.4 on map. Good supply of drinking water. There are 10 wells in the houses on the main BAPAUME road. All houses have rain-water cisterns. In the house opposite to No.6 there is a well in the courtyard which is dry and gives in to a subterranean way towards the church at an unknown depth.

Roads.
Were in excellent state - reloaded yearly. There are pavements 2 m. 50 wide in the main street.

General Information.
(1) The cellars of the houses in the main street could all be, and in some cases, certainly have been joined up. The cellars in the house opposite No.1 are said to be particularly strong.
(2) There are no inhabitants now in the village.
(3) The church is probably used for observation and signalling.
(4) There is a supply dump at N.E. corner of the village on the LE SARS road.
(5) Regimental Command Post said to be in POZIERES mill.

****

COURCELLETTE.

Important village. 99 houses, all well built with small cellars but many have been destroyed.

Buildings.
No detailed information.

There is a Brigade H.Q. in a big chateau close to the W. entrance of the village. This has very large brick barns in the grounds; the outhouse accommodation generally is excellent.

Further up the main street, near the church, is a big brick farm with accommodation for 100 horses.

Near the church there is also a large brick barn belonging to the owner of another chateau - a fine house of brick and stone at the northern end of the village.

There is another brick and stone dwelling-house almost opposite the Brigade H.Q. - possibly sometimes a Regimental H.Q.

Outside the village, to the S. there is a sugar factory - much damaged by fire. In it there is a subterranean smoke conduit 2 m. high and 1.80 wide. Also a very large well which the Germans use for the supply of surrounding villages and the trenches. Water is pumped from it by a gas engine.

Water.
There are 19 wells.
A big pond opposite the church and a watering place for horses.

Information.
(1) About 120 civilians in the village.
(2) Wireless station probably in the factory.
(3) A Regimental H.Q. in a white house with a slate roof on S. side of OVILLERS road. Near it are two big barns of brick.
(4) Regimental rest billets are in the village. According to prisoners every cellar in the village is prepared as a dugout. Digging on the second line is done from here. The line is 20 - 25 minutes march from the village - 6 ft. deep, very strongly wired and with many dugouts.
(5) Supply dumps in S.E. corner of the village.
(6) An R.E. park in the village from which a light railway runs to THIEPVAL R.E. Park. About 1 m. gauge. The railway probably runs back to MARTINPUICH and BAPAUME.
(7) A Battalion H.Q. in the N. of the village.
(8) A Divisional Command Post at the Mill.

www.ingramcontent.com/pod-product-compliance
Lightning Source LLC
Chambersburg PA
CBHW081422300426
44108CB00016BA/2283